SOCIAL MEDIA IN HUMAN RESOURCES MANAGEMENT

ADVANCED SERIES IN MANAGEMENT

Previous Volumes:

SOCIAL MEDIA IN HUMAN RESOURCES MANAGEMENT

EDITED BY

TANYA BONDAROUK

School of Management and Governance, University of Twente, Enschede, The Netherlands

MIGUEL R. OLIVAS-LUJÁN

Clarion University of Pennsylvania, Clarion, PA, USA

United Kingdom – North America – Japan
India – Malaysia – China

Emerald Group Publishing Limited
Howard House, Wagon Lane, Bingley BD16 1WA, UK

First edition 2013

Copyright © 2013 Emerald Group Publishing Limited

Reprints and permission service
Contact: permissions@emeraldinsight.com

British Library Cataloguing in Publication Data
A catalogue record for this book is available from the British Library

ISBN: 978-1-78190-900-3
ISSN: 1877-6361 (Series)

ISOQAR certified
Management System,
awarded to Emerald
for adherence to
Environmental
standard
ISO 14001:2004.

Certificate Number 1985
ISO 14001

INVESTOR IN PEOPLE

To our colleagues … Without their energy and support, we would not have been able to conceptualize this unique collection

Contents

List of Contributors

Roxana Arama	Ursus Breweries, Bucharest, Romania
David A. Askay	California Polytechnic State University, San Luis Obispo, CA, USA
Elena Axinia	Ursus Breweries, Bucharest, Romania
Rita Bissola	Department of Economic Sciences and Business Management, Università Cattolica del Sacro Cuore, Milan, Italy
Anita Blanchard	University of North Carolina at Charlotte, Charlotte, NC, USA
Tanya Bondarouk	School of Management and Governance, University of Twente, Enschede, The Netherlands
Opal Donaldson	The University of Technology — Jamaica, Kingston, Jamaica
Evan W. Duggan	The University of the West Indies — Mona, Kingston, Jamaica
Bernard Fallery	Montpellier Research Management (MRM), University of Montpellier 2, Montpellier, France
Christian Fieseler	Institute for Media and Communications Management, University of St. Gallen, St Gallen, Switzerland
Aurélie Girard	Montpellier Research Management (MRM), University of Montpellier 2, Montpellier, France
Barbara Imperatori	Department of Economic Sciences and Business Management, Università Cattolica del Sacro Cuore, Milan, Italy
Gorazd Justinek	Graduate School of Government and European Studies — Kranj, Kranj, Slovenia
Donald H. Kluemper	Department of Managerial Studies, University of Illinois at Chicago, Chicago, IL, USA

Laxmikant Manroop	Roosevelt University, IL, USA
Miguel R. Olivas-Luján	College of Business Administration, Clarion University of Pennsylvania, Clarion, PA, USA
Emma Parry	Cranfield University School of Management, Cranfield, UK
Giulia Ranzini	Institute for Media and Communications Management, University of St. Gallen, St Gallen, Switzerland
Julia Richardson	School of Human Resource Management, York University, Toronto, Ontario, Canada
Florence Rodhain	Montpellier Research Management (MRM), University of Montpellier 2, Montpellier, France
Huub Ruël	School of Business, Media & Law, Windesheim University of Applied Sciences, Zwolle, The Netherlands
Dino Ruta	SDA Bocconi School of Management, Milan, Italy
Tanja Sedej	International Business School – Ljubljana, Ljubljana, Slovenia
Adriano Solidoro	Milano-Bicocca University, Milan, Italy
Jerome Stewart	University of North Carolina at Charlotte, Charlotte, NC, USA
Ivan Župič	Department of Management and Organization, Faculty of Economics, University of Ljubljana, Slovenia

Social Media and Human Resource Management: It Takes Two to Tango

This volume concludes our two-set edition on social media and management. We again asked the authors to avoid general descriptions of social media, and instead report on the empirical findings or conceptual advancements on the subject. It is, however, our privilege as the editors to outline the main characteristics, definitions, and promised advantages of social media (Olivas-Luján & Bondarouk, 2013). As in other management fields (marketing, entrepreneurship, or supply chain), social media have to some extent replaced traditional media and communication in Human Resource Management (HRM) and forced the HRM business to reconsider its conventional ways of networking, branding, and managing current and potential employees.

This volume specifically focuses on social media in Human Resource Management, where the HRM is broadly viewed as managing employees rather than managing HR functions, and integrating HR activities with each other and within the context of the organizational environment. The unique collection of contributions to this volume discusses ways of how HRM and HR professionals respond to new social media paradigms like sharing of information and experiences within and outside of a firm, tackling collaborative projects, managing identity building and user-generated content. At the same time, research is rightfully asking questions about whether involvement in social media brings new values and competitive advantages to HRM, and what they would be.

With some nuances in the following chapters, we think that the definition from Kaplan and Haenelein (2010, p. 61) is the most suitable one to use, and therefore we view social media as "a group of Internet-based applications that build on the ideological and technological foundations of Web 2.0, and that allow the creation and exchange of User Generated Content."

The usage of social media has matured; the time is past when teenagers were the most dedicated users. Nowadays, "businesses of all types are getting involved in social media in an attempt to reach new audiences and strengthen their ties with existing customers" (Perdue, 2010, p. 3). Facebook statistics declare that among their active users, there are more than 1 million developers and entrepreneurs from more than 180 countries, proving that social media interest is not for entertainment and socializing purposes only. In the United States alone, 86% of the top 100 companies use at least one social media platform (Coon, 2010).

Research about social media or the impact they might have on HRM is rapidly evolving; this particular volume aims at showing the diversity of conceptual understanding of the role of social media in HRM, and revealing empirical confirmation of expectations about this role.

All types of social media (collaborative projects, blogs, content communities, social networking sites, virtual game worlds, or virtual social worlds) are designed for interaction and communication with other users who might have similar interests. Although they seem similar in their overall purpose, each of them is unique and offers different opportunities for HRM. Collaborative projects are designed for knowledge-sharing; the expression "Wikipedia says so" is already commonly heard. Blogs are a form of personal diary accessible to everyone or an alternative for personal websites, which take more time and money. Content communities are strictly designed for sharing media content between users. Social networking sites allow you to connect with partners whom you rigorously select, while virtual game and social worlds offer the possibility of playing/interacting at the same time with people all over the world instead of on your own.

Social media have opened various means of communication that were formerly either impossible or destined for a particular segment of users. What social media bring to the world of HRM is the unique possibility that every single individual or organization can easily participate in any of the types mentioned above. Moreover, it has come to a point where "peer-to-peer communication is proved to be more trustworthy than top-down messages, turning to 'people like us' to get input and advice on products and services," in the opinion of Fichter (2007, p. 57).

Along with the interest in using social media for HRM, there came the interest of using them in behavioral and psychological studies. Following Ervin Goffman's (1959) idea of self-presentation in everyday life, psychological studies suggest that social media allow the individual to self-present in a way that would influence or control the opinion that others might have about them. This matter is the focus of impression management, according to which an individual attempts to control the impression or image someone might have about him (Leary & Kowalski, 1990). The idea of self-presentation is transferred to the organizational environment; if companies decide to use social media, then they could self-present themselves in a way that should create a positive impression for online customers and also a unique image to emphasize their distinctiveness.

As this volume presents, several organizational outcomes can arise from appropriately using social media.

The table offers an overview of the potential advantages of social media for HRM in companies.

Potential advantages of social media	
For individual users	1. Easy access for users
	2. Keep in touch with friends
	3. Social interaction

Potential advantages of social media	
For both individual users and organizations	1. Peer-to-peer communication 2. Strengthening ties with friends/customers 3. Maintain existing contact with friends/customers 4. Free of charge 5. Share knowledge 6. Increase awareness about companies
For organizations	1. Reach new audiences 2. Reach large audiences 3. Transform business 4. Search for job candidates 5. Extensive marketing 6. Timely and direct customer contact 7. Low-cost contact with customers 8. Advantageous for all kind of companies 9. Increase employee engagement 10. Allows formal and informal communication among employees 11. Enhances mutual understanding between companies and employees 12. Offers valuable free feedback 13. Potential for a new product generator 14. Saves time in communication with large audience 15. Saves time and money in communication with subsidiaries located around the world 16. Gain trustworthy and loyal clients 17. Improve customer service department

This volume gives the reader a conceptualization of traditional and novel HRM concepts, a diversity of research methods, and cross-cultural aspects of social media usage for HRM.

Four of the chapters in this volume are dedicated to different aspects of recruitment, from employer and/or employee perspectives. Thus, Chapter 1 by Donald H. Kluemper opens the discussion of the recruitment field and reviews the current state of social networking websites' screening practices. The analysis of the literature and recent social media developments covers such issues as privacy, discrimination, negligent hiring, validity, reliability, generalizability, impression management, and applicant reactions. Rita Bissola and Barbara Imperatori (Chapter 3) continue the discussion into recruitment and explore employee behaviors and expectations of the role of social media when searching for jobs. The results of their in-depth interviews offer recruiters and companies valuable insights into how to design and manage appropriate web-based employer branding and recruitment strategies. Other authors, Aurélie Girard with colleagues (Chapter 5), explore areas of agreement and disagreement regarding the integration of social media in recruitment strategies by means of the Delphi techniques. In Chapter 8, Laxmikant Manroop and Julia Richardson examine the extent to which generation Y (GenY) job seekers use social media to enhance job search behavior. By means of in-depth interviews, they reveal that GenY job seekers are unprepared for the job market despite existing expectations. Many of them are stuck in the traditional ways of looking for a job despite the information that is available to them to exploit modern technologies to enhance their job search experience.

Social media have brought new research agendas to the HRM field like employer branding and internal communication, which is reflected in five chapters in this volume. Chapter 2 by Tanya Bondarouk and her colleagues presents the results of the Delphi study into the future of employer branding through social media. Their research has revealed differences in the opinions of academics and HR professionals on the impact of social media on employer branding. The academics see its general effect as the targeting of an audience for recruitment, marketing/company brand, and ways of communication/HR competencies. The practitioners emphasize the image of the employer, visibility of the company, and organization responsiveness. Tanja Sedej and Gorazd Justinek in Chapter 4 and Emma Parry, Adriano Solidoro in Chapter 6 discuss the role of new social media tools in internal communications. Using different qualitative research methods, these researchers suggest that the use of social media to engage employees will not be successful unless the culture and leadership of the organization already embrace open communication and participation. Chapter 7 (David A. Askay and colleagues) introduces a new concept of entitativity, and examines the affordances of social media to understand how groups are experienced through social media. Specifically, the chapter presents a theoretical model to understand how the affordances of social media promote or suppress entitativity. Giulia Ranzini and Christian Fieseler (Chapter 10) discuss the implications social media have for the self-representation and identity formulation of professionals within organizations. Under the assumption that new, technology-mediated networking possibilities call for a reformulation of the boundaries between the professional and the private, they propose several avenues of investigation. The novel concept of "online personae" is introduced to describe how managers may strive for equilibrium while balancing on- and offline identities with impression management efforts.

Technological and managerial reconfigurations are discussed in the remaining three chapters. Barbara Imperatori and Dino Ruta (Chapter 9) explore if and how online and face-to-face organizational environments can interact, and if and how this interaction could foster managerial practices to sustain personal growth, organizational development, and employee–organization relationships. Technological implications are discussed in Chapter 11 (Opal Donaldson and Evan W. Duggan) and Chapter 12 (Ivan Župič). The authors develop a social information system research model that uses the core constructs intrinsic motivation, extrinsic motivation, and amotivation to explain social networking adoption among tweens, teens, and young adults (Chapter 11), to investigate how social media features enable crowdsourcing, and to gain a rich understanding of the mechanisms that lead from online community design practices to success in crowdsourcing initiatives (Chapter 12).

Concluding Remarks

We believe that the chapters that comprise this volume reveal some of the major conceptual and methodological tensions, paradoxes, and doubts that HRM research and practice currently face with the introduction of social media. Nevertheless, we also see significant support for healthy optimism as it shows the way toward the next phase of social media-enabled HRM research development. The key issues presented in this book lead us to the conclusion that this research is in a transformational stage and is now moving toward crystallizing its theoretical backgrounds and broadening its methodological approaches, as also demonstrated in our previous volume (Olivas-Luján & Bondarouk, 2013).

Tanya Bondarouk
Miguel R. Olivas-Luján
Editors

References

Coon, M. (2010). *Social media marketing: Successful case studies of businesses using Facebook and YouTube with an in depth look into the business use of Twitter*. M.A. thesis, Stanford University, Stanford, CA. Retrieved from http://communication.stanford.edu/coterm/projects/2010/maddy%20coon.pdf. Accessed on June 24, 2012.

Fichter, D. (2007). How social is your website? Top five tips for social media optimization. *Onlinenmag*, pp. 57–60.

Goffman, E. (1959). *The presentation of self in everyday life*. New York, NY: Penguin Books.

Kaplan, A. M., & Haenelein, M. (2010). Users of the world unite! The challenges and opportunities of social media. *Business Horizons, 53*, 59–68.

Leary, M. R., & Kowalski, R. M. (1990). Impression management: A literature review and two-component model. *Psychological Bulletin, 107*(1), 34–47.

Olivas-Luján, M. R., & Bondarouk, T. (2013). *Social media in strategic management* (Vol. 11). Advanced Series in Management. Bingley, UK: Emerald Group Publishing, Ltd.

Perdue, D. J. (2010). *Social media marketing: Gaining a competitive advantage by reaching the masses*. Senior thesis, Liberty University, Lynchburg, VA (pp. 1–39).

Chapter 1

Social Network Screening: Pitfalls, Possibilities, and Parallels in Employment Selection

Donald H. Kluemper

Abstract

Purpose — It is widely established that many hiring managers view social networking websites (SNWs) such as LinkedIn and/or Facebook in the employment selection process, leading to the acceptance or rejection of job applicants. Due to the rapid evolution of social media, scientific study of SNWs has been substantially outpaced by organizational practice. This chapter focuses on a wide range of issues related to SNW screening relevant to research and practice.

Design/methodology/approach — The chapter: (1) reviews the current state of SNW screening practices, (2) describes a wide range of HR issues that should be considered such as privacy, discrimination, negligent hiring, validity, reliability, generalizability, impression management, applicant reactions, and utility, (3) draws connections to related issues already addressed by established employment selection methods to inform SNW screening, (4) discusses pros and cons of potential SNW screening approaches, and (5) provides a framework of best practices that should be incorporated into social network screening policies.

Findings — As an emerging employment selection approach, SNW screening demonstrates potential as a rich source of applicant information, but includes numerous legal and ethical issues. Further, these potential benefits and risks vary widely depending on the approaches used.

Originality/value — Provides HR practitioners with a wide range of information necessary to develop an effective social network screening policy, while making the case for academics to pursue research in this nascent area.

Keywords: Social networking websites; social network screening; employment selection

Social Media in Human Resources Management
Advanced Series in Management, 1–21
ISSN: 1877-6361/doi:10.1108/S1877-6361(2013)0000012005

Due to the rapid evolution of social media, scientific study of social networking websites (SNWs) has been substantially outpaced by organizational practice, yielding a somewhat rare moment in staffing research when practice introduces a new paradigm to research (Roth, Bobko, Van Iddekinge, & Thatcher, 2012a). Recent interest in the topic has emerged across a wide range of research disciplines, such as industrial/ organizational psychology and management (e.g., Kluemper, Rosen, & Mossholder, 2012), law (e.g., Brandenburg, 2008), information technology (e.g., Willey, White, Domagalski, & Ford, 2012), marketing (e.g., Lebrecque, Markos, & Milne, 2011), and psychology (e.g., Back et al., 2010). Although a vast majority of existing research relates specifically to Facebook (Wilson, Gosling, & Graham, 2012), this chapter will focus on the full range of SNWs, such as LinkedIn and Twitter, that have relevance with SNW screening. This chapter will attempt to: (1) briefly describe the current state of SNW screening practices across the globe, (2) describe a wide range of HR issues that should be considered prior to viewing SNWs for selection purposes, (3) draw connections to lessons learned from other employment selection methods that might add value to SNW screening, (4) highlight potential SNW screening approaches, and (5) provide a framework of best practices regarding SNW screening.

The Prevalence of SNW Screening

Various surveys have been conducted in recent years that offer to elucidate current practice regarding SNW screening. Surveys from Career Builder, Reppler, Microsoft, and the Society for Human Resource Management (SHRM) conducted between 2009 and 2011 provide valuable information from which conclusions and trends may be drawn.

CareerBuilder.com conducted a study of 2667 U.S. hiring managers in 2009. Results showed that 45% of employers use SNWs to research job candidates, a jump of 22% from just a year earlier (Forty-five Percent of Employers, 2009). Information technology (63%) and professional and business services (53%) were the most prevalent industries. Of the hiring managers conducting these online searches, 29% used Facebook, 26% used LinkedIn, 21% used MySpace, 11% searched blogs, and 7% used Twitter. Further, 35% of employers reported rejecting candidates for information found. Top reasons given for rejecting applicants include the presence of provocative or inappropriate photos or information, content about drinking or using drugs, bad-mouthing a previous employer, poor communication skills, discriminatory comments, lying about qualifications, and sharing confidential information from a previous employer. Conversely, 18% of employers reported hiring a candidate because of SNW information found. Top reasons given include personality and fit, the profile supported the applicants' job qualifications, applicant creativity, good communication skills, applicant was well-rounded, other SNW users posted good information about the applicant, and that SNW information revealed applicant awards and accolades.

A survey of 300 hiring managers conducted by Reppler.com in 2009 found that 91% of hiring managers use SNWs to screen applicants. The most common SNWs were Facebook (76%), Twitter (53%), and LinkedIn (48%). In this study, 69% of respondents indicated rejecting candidates due to SNW information, while 68% reported hiring a candidate due to the information found on SNWs. The reasons given for rejecting and hiring applicants were similar to those found in the Career Builder survey.

Microsoft facilitated a study in 2010 to examine the role of online information in the hiring process (Cross-Tab Marketing Services, 2010), though it should be noted that screening online information is somewhat broader than screening SNWs. The study included 1345 consumers and 1106 HR professionals, hiring managers, or recruiters. These respondents were equally drawn from the United States, the United Kingdom, Germany, and France. Results show that the percentage of hiring managers who use online information and the percentage of companies with policies requiring such screening is highest in the United States (79% and 75%, respectively) followed by the United Kingdom (47% and 48%, respectively), Germany (59 % and 21%, respectively) and France (23% and 21%, respectively). Further, 70% of U.S. hiring managers have rejected job applicants based on online information, 41% of U.K. hiring managers, 16% of German recruiters, and 14% of French hiring managers. Also, about a third of consumers take no steps to manage their online reputation, but consumers who took steps to manage their reputation were much less concerned about online searches.

More recently, SHRM (2011) surveyed 541 staffing HR professionals. Results indicate that 67% of HR professionals have never used SNWs to screen applicants and do not plan to do so, 4% indicated that they used them previously but will not in the future, 11% never have but plan to (down 7% from 3 years prior), and 18% indicate using SNWs to screen applicants currently (up 5% from 3 years prior). Notably, for-profit organizations are more likely to utilize SNW screening than their nonprofit and governmental counterparts. For example, 44% of privately owned for-profit organizations are reported to use SNWs to screen applicants. The top reason given regarding why these organizations conduct SNW screening is the perceived ability to obtain more information about an applicant than can be gained with a resume and cover letter. Further, the most frequently uses SNWs were LinkedIn (85%), Facebook (78%), far more than MySpace (13%), Twitter (11%), and other SNWs.

Based on these surveys, common themes, trends, and some inconsistencies emerge. A common theme seems to emerge that SNW screening is prevalent (though more-so in the United States than in other countries). Further, the prevalence of SNW screening may depend on the type of job and/or industry of the applicant being evaluated. Trends seem to include a shift from viewing SNWs such as Facebook to more professional websites such as LinkedIn. Also, HR-driven SNW screening policies appear to be on the rise. As far as inconsistencies, it is difficult to determine whether SNW screening is increasing or decreasing. One possibility is that both are true. It seems plausible, from a closer look at the roles of the participants in these surveys, that HR representatives may be less likely to use SNWs for screening purposes (perhaps due to the legal and other risks associated with such use), while non-HR hiring managers may be more likely to use SNWs to screen (perhaps due to the ease of accessing a potential treasure trove of information about the job applicant). These themes, trends, and inconsistencies underscore the need for extensive academic study and debate regarding each of the issues outlined in this chapter.

Issues Related to SNW Screening

As with any selection approach that has been developed within the past century, there are a wide range of issues that collectively provide information regarding the value and risk. These issues generally relate to the extent that the method will benefit the workplace (improved company performance and/or improved worker well-being) and taking into account risks and liabilities associated with the method (e.g., privacy and discrimination). This section addresses a large number of these interrelated issues.

Privacy

The issue of SNW privacy is particularly controversial, as the rapid evolution of technology has presented unique legal and ethical challenges. The fourth Amendment to the U.S. Constitution implies an expectation of privacy. However, it is unclear whether SNW users have a reasonable expectation of privacy that affords legal protection (Brandenburg, 2008). There is disagreement as to what is private and public with SNWs. Applicants may view obtaining such information as an invasion of privacy, while organizations may view SNWs as legitimate public information (Gustafson, 2012). In this vein, just 33% of HR managers are concerned about invading the privacy of applicants via SNWs (SHRM, 2011). Case law has established that websites viewable to the public do not have a reasonable expectation of privacy (e.g., *J. S. v. Bethlehem Area Sch. Dist.*, 2000) though monitoring private Internet chat rooms is illegal (e.g., *Pietrylo v. Hillstone Restaurant Group*, 2008). To add further confusion, expectations of privacy depend in part on the nature of the job, while job applicants have a reduced expectation of privacy from that of current employees (Woska, 2007).

On one hand, employers have a duty to protect stakeholders from injury initiated by employee that the employer knows or should have known may pose a risk to others. Thus, organizations that fail to conduct thorough background investigations may be liable for damages under the tort of negligent hiring (Woska, 2007), particularly for higher level and other sensitive positions. On the other hand, several existing statutes are argued by some to have relevance with SNW screening. The U.S. Fair Credit Reporting Act may apply to companies that search SNWs, particularly information that is intended to be private (Juffras, 2010). The Stored Communications Act may be relevant, as it makes illegal the intentional access of online databases (Brandenburg, 2008), which may include SNWs. The European Union's Data Privacy Directive of 1995 extends to SNWs and requires consent by EU applicants

(Massey, 2009). Further, SNW screening for employment purposes could violate the particular website's terms of use (Willey et al., 2012).

Smith and Kidder (2010) identify multiple ways employers can gain access to SNWs such as Facebook even when pages are set as private, such as "friending" applicants, asking current employees to report on friends, or hiring students who are from the same university as a way of gaining access to applicant profiles. Recent media reports of companies asking applicants for SNW login information (although far more rare than portrayed in the media), as well a tactic termed "over the shoulder" screening (in which applicants are required to log on so that hiring managers can review private online information), has led to applicant anger and frustration, resulting in a wide range of recent legislation and guidance on the issue.

In 2012, Maryland, Delaware, and Illinois passed legislation which generally state that it is unlawful for an employer to request an applicant to provide a password or other related account information or to demand access in any manner to an applicant's profile on a SNW. Similar legislation has been proposed in California, Massachusetts, Michigan, New Jersey, and Germany. Further, in March of 2012, U.S. Senators Richard Blumenthal and Charles Schumer called on the EEOC and the Department of Justice to provide guidance as to whether the practice of obtaining applicant passwords for invasive SNW screening is legal under federal law.

Discrimination

The SHRM survey (2011) indicates that 66% of HR managers are concerned about legal risks associated with SNW screening; issues about protected characteristics such as age, race, gender, religious affiliation, etc. Further, many recent academic papers identify issues relating to discrimination (Brown & Vaughn, 2011; Davison, Maraist, Hamilton, & Bing, 2012; Gustafson, 2012; Kluemper & Rosen, 2009; Kluemper et al., 2012; Roth, Bobko, Van Iddekinge, & Thatcher, 2012b; Slovensky & Ross, 2012; Smith & Kidder, 2010; Willey et al., 2012). There are two basic forms that discrimination can occur in the selection contest: disparate treatment (when an applicant is treated differently based on a protected class status) and adverse impact (a facially neutral employment practice that has the result of disproportionately affecting an underrepresented group). SNW screening creates a greater possibility of disparate treatment than many other selection methods due to protected class status information prevalent on SNWs, such as religion or certain disabilities not found in a resume or in-person interview (Davison et al., 2012). Disparate impact may occur, for example, with older and socioeconomically disadvantaged groups, such as Spanish-dominant Hispanics, who have less access to SNWs (Davison et al., 2012).

The primary U.S. Federal laws relating to SNW discrimination on the basis of race, color, religion, sex, gender, nation of origin, disability, and age are Title VII of the Civil Right Act, the Americans with Disabilities Act, and the Age Discrimination in Employment Act. For example, Title VII dictates that preemployment inquiries are not lawful if they disproportionately screen out applicants based on protected class status not justified through business necessity/job relatedness (Woska, 2007). Beyond U.S. Federal law, most states have established legal protection for sexual orientation as well as other characteristics. Further, though legal protections differ by country, many countries provide similar or expanded legal protection from employment discrimination (Myors et al., 2008).

Students self-reported the following on SNW profiles: sexual orientation, relationship status, birth date, religious beliefs, and political affiliation (Karl, Peluchette, & Schlaegel, 2010). Further, gender and race impact which SNWs a user is likely to adopt (Pike, 2011) while older individuals are less likely to have SNW profiles (Smith & Kidder, 2010). Those older SNW users are likely to post information in different ways and may not be as comfortable when posting personal information (Epstein, 2008). This may be a particularly salient issue, given that the applicant and hiring managers are often of different generations (Smith & Kidder, 2010). Also, robust information available on SNWs may lead to similarity bias with the individual doing the hiring (Smith & Kidder, 2010).

Roth and colleagues (2012b) found no articles that reported empirical data on the adverse impact potential when using social network screening. The manuscript provides convincing evidence that a lower representation of minorities and older individuals in regard to Internet access and unstructured SNW assessments may bias the rater; potentially leading to adverse impact. These authors urge research in this area. Due to the prevalence of SNW screening and the likelihood that discrimination occurs in SNW screening context, it is likely that SNW-related discrimination cases will arise (Gustafson, 2012).

Negligent Hiring

Organizations should conduct reasonable background checks when screening applicants because failure to do so incurs legal liability for employers. In particular, organizations involved in public safety may find themselves defending a lawsuit when employees engage in illegal behavior and it is discovered that information about prior illegal behavior was available at the time of hire (Levashina & Campion, 2009). As such, failing to screen SNWs may itself incur legal liability, particularly for companies in certain industries (Slovensky & Ross, 2012). Thus, if an employer identifies (or should have identified) negative SNW information about a job applicant but still hires the individual, the employer could be sued for negligent hiring if the employee later harms a coworker or customer (Davison et al., 2012).

Validity

There are several forms of validity, each relevant to SNW screening. First, in the context of SNWs, screeners may be casually scanning profiles, thus not attempting to measure anything in particular. If they are attempting to measure a particular set of constructs, the question becomes whether this operationalization actually measures what it claims to. Does the operationalization of a construct actually measures what it purports to measure (construct validity)? If so, does the measure comprehensively cover all aspects of this construct (content validity)? Does this measure correlate with other measures that it is theoretically predicted to correlate with (convergent validity) or other measures of the same construct (concurrent validity)? Does this measure appear to measure what it claims to be measuring (face validity)? Though each of these forms of validity are important, in the context of SNW screening, a critical form of validity is criterion-related or predictive validity, such that there is a correlation between what is assessed via SNWs and relevant outcomes. Job-relatedness has been identified as an important aspect of SNW screening (Smith & Kidder, 2010). Criterion-related validity establishes that a selection test is job related (i.e., the construct being measured related to a core function of the job in question). In the context of employment selection, the most relevant outcome is task performance, such that the SNW evaluation is able to identify and weed out individuals that would otherwise yield lower levels of performance on the job (or identify and hire individuals that will result in higher levels of job performance). Finally incremental validity (whether a new test adds predictive value beyond existing methods) needs to be evaluated in relation to application blanks, biodata, self-report personality tests, etc. (Roth et al., 2012a).

To further stress the importance of criterion-related validity, any selection test that fails to provide criterion-related validity serves little purpose in an employment selection system. This should be the first and most important hurdle for SNW screening. If SNWs cannot be shown to establish criterion-related validity, particularly given the legal issues, these assessments serve little purpose. With that said, several established selection methods (e.g., interviews, cognitive ability tests, personality tests) have been studied across hundreds if not thousands of academic studies attempting to demonstrate and improve criterion-related validity. SNW screening is in its infancy and practice has outstripped research in this area. There are two implications of this. First, academics need to study this phenomenon in order to learn whether SNW screening has criterion-related validity and/or design ways to improve criterion-related validity. Second, practitioners should be aware that little evidence exists regarding this important issue. This should serve as a warning that current SNW screening approaches may not yield valid and legally defensible results, despite being intuitively appealing to those currently engaging in SNW screening.

This is not to say that the potential for criterion-related validity does not exist. Although 45% of HR managers believe that information about job candidates taken from SNWs may not be relevant to job performance (SHRM, 2011), SNWs may reveal unique job-relevant applicant information, such as education, work history, and professional membership (Davison et al., 2012). Though no evidence yet exists, it stands to reason that the presence of information about, for example, drug use, discriminatory comments, or misrepresentations of qualifications (Forty-five Percent of Employers, 2009) might identify individuals with low levels of job performance or other negative organizational outcomes. In this vein, the criterion-related validity of SNWs should also be assessed in relation to other variables beyond task performance, such as organizational citizenship behavior, workplace deviance, lateness, absentee-ism, turnover (Roth et al., 2012a). Further, there are various issues which may harm the validity of a selection method, such as a lack of reliability, low generalizability, and applicant impression management. These potential threats to validity are particularly relevant to SNW screening.

Reliability

Reliability represents various ways to demonstrate that a measure is consistent and is a necessary but not sufficient condition for validity. In other words, reliably assessing a construct does not mean the approach is valid, but failing to establish consistency of measurement, by definition, indicates that the selection method lacks validity. Three types of reliability are germane to SNW screening; test–retest reliability (consistent from one test administration to the next), inter-rater reliability (the degree to which test scores are consistent when measurements are taken by different evaluators), and internal consistency reliability (the consistency of results across independent pieces of information within an assessment).

SNW information can be inaccurate (Smith & Kidder, 2010), such as information that is false (Davison et al., 2012) or widely exaggerated, perhaps even posted by others without the users' knowledge or consent. In addition, there is a possibility of mistaken identities, differences in information across multiple accounts, and the creation of imitation accounts (Slovensky & Ross, 2012), creating further inconsistencies. The variability in the type and amount of information available on SNWs prevents a completely standardized approach to collecting profile information (Brown & Vaughn, 2011) and require evaluators to deal with incomplete information (Roth et al., 2012a). In this vein, 48% of HR managers are concerned about the inability to verify information from an applicant's SNW, while 34% are concerned that not all job candidates have information on SNWs (SHRM, 2011).

Changes in one's behavior across phases in one's life (Slovensky & Ross, 2012) potentially lead to inconsistent SNW screening results over time, potentially harming test–retest reliability. Incomplete information and inconsistencies across SNW profiles may lead to differences in evaluative judgments from independent raters, a potential problem for inter-rater reliability. Finally, information (or entire SNW profiles) that may be present for one job applicant may not be present for others, thereby creating a challenge to the generation of internal consistency reliability. Thus, problems associated with reliability when screening SNWs must be taken into consideration.

Generalizability

The concept of generalizability implies that what may be valid in one context may not be in another. One aspect of SNW screening that relates to generalizability is that there are numerous SNWs with divergent purposes, user demographics, ability to restrict access, volume and type of information provided, etc. For example, there are numerous differences between Facebook and LinkedIn regarding a wide range of issues. Facebook (when compared to LinkedIn) has more users, generally has more information, is typically geared toward "friends" (rather than professional "connections"), has a greater ability to restrict access, is the focus of legislation, etc. LinkedIn, on the other hand, is more like an expanded resume and is used for the explicit purpose of connecting professionally, including that of recruitment and selection. Therefore, on just about any issue discussed in this chapter, issues regarding Facebook or MySpace may not be germane to LinkedIn or Twitter, and vice versa.

Another aspect of generalizability relates to the relevance of SNW screening of various occupations. For example, SNW screening may be more prevalent with IT, professional, and business service positions (Forty-five Percent of Employers, 2009). As such, SNW screening may be more widespread, and/or more widely accepted by applicants in certain industries such as military suppliers, banking, child care, and private security firms (Slovensky & Ross, 2012). Further, it stands to reason that certain aspects of SNW information may be more relevant to some jobs than others. For instance, it may be more job-relevant to screen out gang members as prison guards, discriminatory police officers, drug users in industrial manufacturing, and those who share confidential information about employers in high security jobs. Thus, the extensiveness of related approaches such as background checks should reflect the severity of the risk posed to individuals affected once that applicant is hired (Woska, 2007). In this connection, all professions are not equivalent with regard to privacy rights. For example, according to the Department of Labor, the Employee Polygraph Protection Act of 1988 applies to most private employers, but does not cover federal, state, local government agencies, and private employers related to national security. It stands to reason that select occupations (e.g., national security) may be more likely (perhaps even legally compelled) to conduct more invasive SNW screening, such as "friending" and "over the shoulder" screening. It should also be noted that these practices will likely evoke lawsuits due to privacy concerns. Legislation and case law will continue to emerge on this issue. For this reason (among others), organizations lacking a strong justification to engage in such invasive practices should avoid them.

Finally, the little we now know about SNW screening is largely based on findings from young college students in the United States. Although this may be the most relevant context in which to begin study (e.g., Facebook began primarily with U.S. college students), a more generalizable range of characteristics needs to be considered.

Impression Management

As noted by the Vice President of HR at CareerBuilder.com Rosemary Haefner, "Social networking is a great way to make connections with potential job opportunities and promote your personal brand across the Internet. Make sure you are using this resource to your advantage by conveying a professional image and underscoring your qualifications" (Forty-five Percent of Employers, 2009). However, little is known about the prevalence of impression management/faking/personal branding on SNWs. It has been suggested that SNW users engage in self-presentation to influence the impressions of others (Karl et al., 2010) and some content can be manipulated by users to present themselves in a more favorable manner (Kluemper et al., 2012). Users can clean up SNWs to remove embarrassing or offensive content (Davison et al., 2012), even hiring firms to help manage their SNW information (Shiller, 2010). Further, Pike (2011) found that the more value a user places on self-presentation via SNWs, the more suitable the candidate will be perceived by a hiring manager. Further, Bohnert and Ross (2010) conducted a laboratory study using 148 student evaluations of hypothetical job candidates and concluded that individuals with positive SNW profiles that were more family oriented or professional were seen as more suitable for employment than those with party-oriented SNW profiles. Thus, developing a favorable online presence may have a positive impact on hiring decisions.

Although SNW users may attempt to impress others, these distortions may depend on the intended viewer (Davison, Maraist, & Bing, 2011) such that users may be creating them for specific audiences or blurring personal, family, and professional aspects (Pike, 2011). SNW users engage in impression management, but are often misdirected or insufficient in their efforts. In particular, SNW users find impression management difficult, particularly during life changes or when attempting to manage multiple audiences (Lebrecque et al., 2011). Further, it has been suggested that information might be more accurate on certain SNWs because one's connections can contradict inaccurate information (Davison et al., 2011) yielding potentially less censored SNW information (Davison et al., 2012). Kluemper and Rosen (2009) argue that SNWs may be less susceptible to socially desirable responding than other selection methods such as personality tests. Kluemper et al. (2012) argue that faking SNW information runs counter to the fundamental purpose of SNWs (i.e., Facebook) and that some information may be difficult to fake via social media, such as information posted to a user's website by others, number of friends, and the content of photos. Thus, some hiring managers may focus on SNW information written by "friends" of the applicant, as such information may be seen as less subject to impression management attempts (Slovensky & Ross, 2012). In support of this perspective, Back and colleagues (2010) found that ratings of SNW user Big Five personality was far more closely aligned with actual personality rather than ideal-self ratings of personality, indicating that SNWs accurately represent user personality traits. Further, there is a strong correlation between a SNW users' online and offline identity, but a weak relationship between an applicants' SNW identity and self-presentation on a resume (Pike, 2011).

Thus, it appears that at least some form of impression management via SNWs is possible and may have a favorable impact on hiring decisions. However, manipulating some aspects of a profile may be difficult or even impossible and that SNW users may choose not to alter their profiles for a range of reasons described above. As impression management may harm validity, it is important to better understand the characteristics of those who choose to engage in SNW impression management, the extent that it is done, and in what contexts.

Some users may utilize personal branding, such that personal profiles may be designed with the intention of networking for job opportunities. This is likely the case for SNWs such as LinkedIn, and may be increasingly true for SNWs such as Facebook. In this vein, the applicant may prefer that their SNW profile is evaluated, believing that this may provide some advantage in the job search process. It is clear that the nature of the content of SNWs such as Facebook has changed dramatically in recent years. For example, the nature of the information posted in the first few years of Facebook was generally geared toward college peers. However, that online behavior changed when the nature of college student network connections changed to include parents and coworkers. It is difficult to predict how these independent SNW platforms and intended audiences will change over time. In the SNW screening context, this relates to the issue of applicant reactions when potential employers access such information.

Applicant Reactions

Applicants, aware that SNW information has been used by a hiring manager, may develop perceptions of informational, distributive, and procedural injustice possibly resulting in a reduction of applicant attraction to the organization (Slovensky & Ross, 2012). Applicants have been shown to have more favorable views of certain selection approaches (e.g., job interviews, job knowledge tests, and work sample tests) than others (e.g., cognitive ability tests, personality tests, and college transcripts) (Reeve & Schultz, 2004), such that applicants who view the hiring process as intrusive or lacking validity may be more likely to perceive the process as unfair and potentially file a lawsuit (Wallace, Page, & Lippstreu, 2006).

Applicants might perceive that they have more of a right to SNW privacy than the law provides, leading qualified applicants to remove themselves from consideration from a job. Further, these negative applicant reactions may be contagious, affecting firm reputation via others in the users' social network (Davison et al., 2012). Black, Johnson, Takach, and Stone (2012) have developed a theoretical model regarding applicant reactions to SNW screening. The authors provide theoretical rational and hypotheses regarding potential negative applicant reactions to social network screening due to informational, procedural, socio-cultural, and individual factors. These factors are posited to result in negative organizational consequences such as fewer job acceptances, applicants' propensity to sue, and damage to company reputation.

Empirical research regarding applicant reactions to SNW screening has begun to emerge. Gustafson (2012) found that undergraduate students view Facebook screening as unfair, but that these negative perceptions were reduced when applicants were asked permission to access the SNW. Siebert, Downes, and Christopher (2012) conducted a laboratory study of 204 undergraduate students. Results indicate that the use of social network screening did not impact organizational attractiveness or intentions to pursue employment, even though social network screening did negatively impact applicant attitudes toward the selection procedure. However, more invasive social network screening procedures (i.e., searching publicly available information vs. requiring the acceptance of a friend request from the hiring manager) had negative effects on applicant reactions. Sanchez, Roberts, Freeman, and Clayton (2012) conducted a laboratory study of 156 undergraduate students. Results revealed no negative effects of SNW screening on five applicant reaction variables: perceptions of SNW checks, organizational attractiveness, job pursuit intentions, procedural justice, and informational justice. Further, participants' perceptions to SNW checks were, counter intuitively, positively related to the applicant reaction constructs. The authors explain these findings by arguing that college-age applicants generally expect and value that employers check SNW profiles. Thus, little is known about applicant reactions to SNW screening. A wider range of empirical study is needed to better understand the issue.

Utility

SNWs are used because they are quick and cheap (Davison et al., 2012; Slovensky & Ross, 2012). More specifically, only 17% of HR managers believe it takes too much time and effort to screen SNWs in relation to the information gained, while 63% of those HR managers that use SNW screening indicated that this approach takes little time and effort in relation to the information gained via SNW screening (SHRM, 2011). Further, it is incumbent on human resource departments to obtain as much information as possible about an applicant to avoid negligent hiring (Woska, 2007). However, these quick and inexpensive approaches to SNW screening are likely unreliable, relatively invalid, and legally problematic. Well developed and validated SNW screening approaches (to be discussed later) are likely to incur significantly more time and resources than generally exists in current practice. As such, the cost to benefit ratio of SNW screening needs to be assessed more thoroughly.

Parallels in Employment Selection

The wide range of issues discussed above poses serious questions for SNW screening. Many of these issues, however, are issues common to various established selection methods. Thus, much knowledge has been gained through other selection approaches that provide a foundation useful for an improved understanding of SNW screening. One such issue is that of personal (nonwork) information when hiring. While applicants may not perceive this information as relevant, many established selection methods, such as criminal records checks, credit checks, sex offender registry checks, etc., tap exclusively into personal information. Other established selection methods may tap into a mix of work and nonwork information, such as background checks, biodata, interviews, personality tests, personal references, etc. A key factor, as with these other established methods, is whether and for which occupations this information establishes criterion-related validity. This perspective does not imply that all personal information is job related. Further, some non-job related information has the potential to discriminate against protected class applicants. A selection approach with no (or little) criterion-related validity which leads to discrimination has no benefit but substantial potential for negative repercussions. Again, this highlights the importance of criterion-related validity when conducting SNW screening. If, for example, criterion-related validity can be established and the SNW screening procedure causes adverse impact, there is simultaneously a benefit and a risk.

The widely studied use of cognitive ability in employment selection serves to inform this issue regarding SNW screening. It is widely established that cognitive ability tests both can demonstrate substantial criterion-related validity with job performance (Hunter & Hunter, 1984) and differ based on racial and/or ethnic groups, thus leading to adverse impact (Berry, Clark, & McClure, 2011). In fact, the *Griggs v Duke Power Co.* case (1971), in which Duke Power inappropriately used a cognitive ability test for selection purposes, was instrumental in establishing the concept of adverse impact. In the majority decision, Chief Justice Burger wrote that "The facts of this case demonstrate the inadequacy of broad and general testing devices." This quote would seem to generally apply to the current state of SNW screening. It should also be noted, however, that cognitive ability testing remains widely used and is legally defensible if used appropriately; an important parallel for SNW screening. In this vein, the Uniform Guidelines on Employee Selection Procedures (1978) states that evidence of both validity and utility of a selection procedure should support a selection method, particularly when that method has greater adverse impact than other methods that could be used.

The vast literature on employment interviews may serve to inform practice regarding how to improve the validity of SNW screening. Job interviews have much in common with social network screening such that both include the subjective evaluation of a large volume of information (Roth et al., 2012b). Virtually all studies over the past 100 years have concluded that adding structure to job interviews improves reliability and validity (Campion, Palmer, & Campion, 1997) while reducing racial differences associated with adverse impact (Roth et al., 2012b). Although not all aspects of adding structure in the interview context apply to SNW screening, several approaches can be used to benchmark against. Six of these, as outlined by Campion and colleagues (1997) with interviews, may have relevance for SNW screening.

1. Structured interviews generally begin with a job analysis. Similarly, SNW screening could focus on measurable characteristics which have the greatest likelihood to result in a prediction of job performance for specific jobs (Davison et al., 2012).
2. Structured interviews ask the same questions of all applicants, so as to compare apples to apples. For SNW screening, it is even more of a challenge to compare information consistently, due to differences across profiles and platforms. However, the criteria being evaluated can be clearly documented. Roth and colleagues (2012b) call for the use of structure when conducting SNW screening by developing a list of characteristics being assessed.

3. The use of well-constructed rating scales is also a hallmark of structured interviews. Although little is known about how practitioners perform SNW evaluations, it is likely that these assessments are quite subjective, with no formal ratings whatsoever. As with the interview literature, adding objectivity to SNW ratings via standardized rating scales is likely to add reliability and validity, such as the use of behaviorally anchored rating scales (Roth et al., 2012a, 2012b).
4. Just as multiple interviewers have been shown to improve the reliability and validity of interviews, SNW screening may benefit from multiple evaluators (Roth et al., 2012a, 2012b).
5. Structured interview approaches advocate for the use of the same interviewer. This approach reduces the idiosyncratic bias that occurs when there is a lack of interviewer consistency across interviews. Similarly, this approach may add consistency to SNW screening.
6. Finally, interview training has been shown to improve the value of interviews. As such, training SNW evaluators about the aspects of structure described above as well as the legal issues associated with SNW screening may improve validity while minimizing legal risk (Roth et al., 2012a, 2012b).

Another relevant area of study is personality testing. Personality is defined as that which permits a prediction of what a person will do in a given situation (Cattell, 1965). In the work context, personality traits have been shown via multiple meta-analytic studies to predict organizational outcomes such as task performance, citizenship behavior, workplace deviance, interview performance, burnout, work accidents, team performance, leadership, absenteeism, job satisfaction, commitment, training performance, and so on (see Ones, Dilchert, Viswesvaran, & Judge, 2007). These results depend on the trait in question and on the job, demonstrating moderate criterion-related validity of up to .30. However, personality testing has been criticized for its susceptibility to social desirability/faking in high stakes situations such as selection testing, potentially harming the criterion-related validity of personality test scores (Bing, Kluemper, Davison, Taylor, & Novicevic, 2011). Drawing from the field of psychology, personality has been shown to be accurately assessed in various contexts such as through the assessment of photographs (Robbins, Gosling, & Donahue, 1997), attire (Burroughs, Drew, & Hallman, 1991), offices and bedrooms (Gosling, Ko, Mannarelli, & Morris, 2002), e-mail (Gill, Oberlander, & Austin, 2006), word use (Fast & Funder, 2008), resumes (Cole, Feild, & Giles, 2003; Cole, Feild, & Stafford, 2005), and on personal websites (Vazire & Gosling, 2004). In the organization literature, a recent meta-analysis revealed that observer rated personality traits generally have higher validity coefficients than do self-reports (Oh, Wang, & Mount, 2011). A relevant theoretical perspective regarding the evaluation of personality via SNWs (Kluemper et al., 2012) incorporates the Realistic Accuracy Model (RAM), behavioral residue, and identity claims. RAM (Funder, 1995) posits that rating accuracy is enhanced with an array of observable cues that are available to the observer. These observable cues are represented as physical traces of activities conducted in the environment (behavioral residue) and behaviors individuals engage in to reinforce their personal preferences or to display their identities to others (identity claims) (Gosling et al., 2002). Despite the inconsistent nature of the information available on SNWs, high-volume but low-intensity cues may manifest themselves across a wide range of observable behaviors available via SNWs, making possible the accurate assessment of personality traits.

Approaches to SNW Screening

Assessing personality via SNWs is likely one of the primary uses by hiring managers (Davison et al., 2012; Pike, 2011). This is not surprising, as undergraduate students higher in conscientiousness, agreeableness, and emotional stability are shown to be less likely to report posting problematic content on SNW profiles (Karl et al., 2010). Kluemper and Rosen (2009) conducted a study using 63 undergraduate students, who conducted ratings of the Big Five personality traits, intelligence, and grade point average, each for six Facebook profiles. Results indicate that each of these characteristics can be reliably assessed via SNW profiles. Further, more intelligent and emotionally stable raters were shown to be more accurate when evaluating SNW profiles than their less intelligent and neurotic counterparts.

Kluemper et al. (2012) provide evidence from two studies that Facebook can be used by trained evaluators to reliably assess various personality traits, traits shown in existing literature to predict academic and job success and to be legally defensible for selection purposes. Study 1 included 274 Facebook users. Results conclude that Facebook-rated personality (1) correlates with traditional self-reported personality, (2) demonstrates internal consistency and inter-rater reliability for personality and hireability, (3) correlates with evaluator preferences to hire the Facebook user, and (4) correlates with supervisor ratings of job performance for a subsample of 56 Facebook users who were employed six months later. Study 2 included 244 college students. Results conclude that Facebook-rated personality (1) correlates with traditional self-reported personality tests, (2) demonstrates internal consistency and inter-rater reliability, (3) is stronger than self-reported personality and IQ in predicting academic success, and (4) provides incremental prediction of academic performance beyond what was obtained from self-rated personality and intelligence tests combined. Taken together, these studies provide initial evidence that information available on Facebook can be used to identify individuals who are more successful in college and on the job.

Roth et al. (2012a) highlight issues with the Kluemper et al. (2012) manuscript. Issues include a small sample size for job performance ($N = 56$; though the full sample size across the two studies exceeded $N = 500$), the evaluators were not recruiters (though one was a former HR employee, now a PhD, and two were seniors in management who had undergone rater training after completing a senior level employment selection course), the subjects had cross-job variation, and that the magnitudes of the validity coefficients fell in the moderate range and thus are not as high as some established selection methods (though an uncorrected correlation of .31 found for agreeableness is higher than most selection instruments, it is not higher than the most robust selection instruments, such as an uncorrected correlation of .33 for cognitive ability tests; Berry et al., 2011). Though the personality testing approach via SNWs shows some promise regarding reliability and validity, these limitations should give pause to practitioners seeking to use this approach, given the absence of additional research evidence.

A related approach is that of biographical data. Biodata identifies questions about life and work experiences and is based on the premise that past behaviors, opinions, values, beliefs, and attitudes will predict future behavior. Biodata has been shown to have moderate criterion-related validity and is generally legally defensible (Mumford, Costanza, Connelly, & Johnson, 1996). As such, it has been suggested that SNW screening has strong similarities to (Davison et al., 2012) and would benefit from an approach based on the biodata literature (Slovensky & Ross, 2012).

It has also been suggested that SNWs might be able to assess particular aspects of knowledge, skills, abilities, and other characteristics (KSAOs) beyond personality traits. Possible KSAOs that might be assessed via SNWs include fluency in a particular language, technical proficiencies, creative outlets, teamwork skills (Smith & Kidder, 2010), network ability, creativity (Davison et al., 2012), communication, interpersonal, leadership, persuasion, and negotiation skills (Roth et al., 2012a). Written communication, including grammar, spelling, and composition may be assessed, though informal writing may not represent the applicant's workplace communication style (Davison et al., 2012). However, some KSAO information obtained via SNWs is likely to be largely redundant with information obtained via established screening techniques (Davison et al., 2012). For example, typical poor grammar and misspellings may not provide value beyond other selection methods, such as writing samples (Davison et al., 2012). More work is needed in this area to identify whether these KSAOs can be accurately assessed via SNW screening and whether criterion-related validity can be established.

It is widely acknowledged that hiring managers may try to measure person-organization fit via SNW screening (Davison et al., 2012; Roth et al., 2012a; Slovensky & Ross, 2012). However, this approach likely tends to be more subjective than other approaches discussed here, so demonstrating criterion-related validity in the SNW context presents a challenge, particularly considering the legal issues associated with SNW screening. An approach to P/O fit would need to be highly structured, such as formally assessing fit characteristics like innovation, team orientation, achievement orientation, etc. at the organizational level, then assessing them via SNW profiles.

Probably the most common current approach to SNW screening is to view profiles for potential disqualifying information. This approach resembles a type of back-ground check. While it seems feasible that applicants with SNW information pertaining to drug use, discriminatory comments, misrepresented qualifications, or shared confidential information about a current employer (Forty-five Percent of Employers, 2009) might provide a strong basis to reject an applicant, particularly when considering the potential for deviant workplace behaviors. In this vein, a primary concern of some organizations may be related to public relations, such that potential employees have a clean online presence not likely to harm the organization if public access information is viewed by company stakeholders. However, other information used to disqualify candidates might be more idiosyncratic and subjective. For example, drinking is legal in the United States, for individuals at least 21 years of age. Drinking socially does not necessarily equate to drinking on the job (which is likely against company policy). Some SNW screeners, particularly when there are no specific established criteria with which to assess, may use this information to eliminate a candidate from contention. Other screeners may consider the photo appropriate in a social context or even view the applicant more favorably due to an impression that the applicant gets along well with others or has a wider range of network connections. Eliminating candidates based on "gut feel" is less likely to be valid and more likely to involve disparate treatment or adverse impact. With any of these potential SNW screening approaches, there are several best practices that should improve validity and/or decrease legal risks.

Best Practices

Hiring managers and HR departments are using SNWs with limited policy guidance and have been recommended to adopt a social screening policy (Davison et al., 2012; Willey et al., 2012). The SHRM survey (2011) indicates that 56% of organizations have no formal policy with regard to SNW screening, 17% report an informal policy prohibiting SNW screening, 12% report an informal policy allowing for SNW screening, 8% have a formal policy allowing for SNW screening, and 7% have a formal policy prohibiting SNW screening. If the organization decides not to conduct SNW screening, this decision should be documented through a formal social screening policy. If an organization chooses to engage in SNW screening, the organization should address a wide range of relevant issues after appropriately weighing the benefits against the risks (Davison et al., 2012; Slovensky & Ross, 2012), then incorporate these best practices into a social screening policy.

1. Require informed consent: Have applicants sign a written consent form prior to conducting SNW screening (Slovensky & Ross, 2012), perhaps including SNW screening in the same disclosure typically used to obtain related information, such as references and credit checks. The Fair Credit Reporting Act requires applicant consent prior to conducting certain background checks. Thus, if employers use SNWs as a background check, candidates may be legally entitled to have this information disclosed to them (Smith & Kidder, 2010).
2. Verify the accuracy of information: Social screening policies should incorporate a procedure to verify that an applicant's SNW is indeed their own (Davison et al., 2012).
3. Discourage covert tactics: If an organization has adequately weighted the pros and cons of invasive SNW screening practices and had made a decision to utilize invasive procedures, these procedures should be part of a formal policy rather than allowing or encouraging engaging in practices such as "friending" or "over the shoulder" screening. Note that these practices are illegal in some states,

likely less legally defensible than accessing open public information, and are likely to result in negative applicant reactions. Thus, these practices are ill advised for most jobs, with the possible exception of those related to national security, law enforcement, etc.

4. Conduct SNW screening toward the end of the hiring process: The Reppler.com (2009) and SHRM (2011) studies found that SNW screening occurs at different stages in the hiring process. Some SNW screening protocols may do so very early in the selection process, prior to an interview to allow the applicant to address issues raised, or after a conditional job offer has been given. While there are pros and cons to various approaches, in general, adverse impact is reduced if an assessment is conducted later in the selection process (Sackett & Roth, 1996).

5. Conduct a job analysis: Base procedures on job analysis (Davison et al., 2012), or in the case of person-organization fit, base procedures on an organizational analysis.

6. Develop standardized instruments: Standardized rubrics should be developed (Davison et al., 2012; Roth et al., 2012b) based on the job analysis, consistently used by screeners (Kluemper et al., 2012), and added to personnel files.

7. Use multiple screeners: Multiple screeners will likely improve reliability and validity of SNW screening (Kluemper & Rosen, 2009; Kluemper et al., 2012; Roth et al., 2012b).

8. Use the same screeners: Consistency is likely to improve when using the same evaluators for all applicants (Kluemper et al., 2012).

9. Outsource or Insource: In this vein, job-relevant information could be conducted by independent evaluators within HR, then passed to hiring managers. As such, these hiring managers would have no knowledge of job-irrelevant information (Davison et al., 2012) such as disability status and sexual orientation. In addition, some firms minimize legal liability by hiring a third party to view SNW profiles, thereby relaying only job-relevant information to the employer (Slovensky & Ross, 2012).

10. Establish criterion-related validity: Conduct criterion-related validity studies (Kluemper et al., 2012) and adverse impact analyses in accordance with the EEOCs Uniform Employee Selection Guidelines.

11. Train raters: Due to concerns about potential discrimination, inaccuracy, inconsistency, and violations of applicant privacy, SNW evaluators need to be trained regarding these and other issues (Slovensky & Ross, 2012).

This chapter endeavored to elucidate the current state of research and practice regarding SNW screening. In doing so, a large number of issues were outlined regarding this practice, such as privacy, discrimination, negligent hiring, validity, reliability, generalizability, impression management, applicant reactions, and utility. As various established selection methods have addressed these issues in past research, relevant approaches were discussed regarding personality testing, structured inter-views, cognitive ability tests, and various approaches dealing with personal information. These approaches yield a number of best practices that should be incorporated into organizational social screening policies. In general, this review should result in caution on the part of practitioners attempting to utilize SNW screening. At the same time, several avenues for academic research are highlighted and sorely needed this nascent area.

References

Back, M. D., Stopfer, J. M., Vazire, S., Gaddis, S., Schuukle, S. C., Egloff, B., & Gosling, S. D. (2010). Facebook profiles reflect actual personality, not self-idealization. *Psychological Science, 21*, 372–374.

Berry, C. M., Clark, M. A., & McClure, T. K. (2011). Racial/ethnic differences in the criterion-related validity of cognitive ability tests: A qualitative and quantitative review. *Journal of Applied Psychology, 5*, 881–906.

Bing, M. N., Kluemper, D. H., Davison, H. K., Taylor, S., & Novicevic, M. (2011). Overclaiming as a measure of faking. *Organizational Behavior and Human Decision Processes, 116*, 148–162.

Black, S. L., Johnson, A. F., Takach, S. E., & Stone, D. L. (2012). Factors affecting applicant's reactions to the collection of data in social network websites. Presented at the Academy of Management Annual Conference, Philadelphia, PA.

Bohnert, D., & Ross, W. H. (2010). The influence of social networking websites on the evaluation of job candidates. *Cyberpsychology, Behavior, and Social Networking, 13*, 341–347.

Brandenburg, C. (2008). The newest way to screen job applicants: A social networking nightmare. *Federal Communications Law Journal, 60*, 598–614.

Brown, V. R., & Vaughn, E. D. (2011). The writing on the (Facebook) wall: The use of social networking sites in hiring decisions. *Journal of Business and Psychology, 26*, 219–225.

Burroughs, J. W., Drew, D. R., & Hallman, W. K. (1991). Predicting personality from personal possessions: A self-presentational analysis. *Journal of Social Behavior and Personality, 6*, 147–163.

Campion, M. A., Palmer, D. K., & Campion, J. E. (1997). A review of structure in the selection interview. *Personnel Psychology, 50*, 655–702.

Cattell, R. B. (1965). *The scientific analysis of personality*. London: Penguin.

Cole, M. S., Feild, H. S., & Giles, W. F. (2003). Using recruiter assessments of applicants' resume content to predict applicant mental ability and Big Five personality dimensions. *International Journal of Selection and Assessment, 11*, 78–88.

Cole, M. S., Feild, H. S., & Stafford, J. O. (2005). Validity of resume reviewers' inferences concerning applicant personality based on resume evaluation. *International Journal of Selection and Assessment, 13*, 321–324.

Cross-Tab Marketing Services. (2010). *Online reputation in a connected world*. Retrieved from download.microsoft.com/download/C/D/2/CD233E13-A600-482F-9C97-545BB4AE93B1/DPD_O. Accessed on September 26, 2012.

Davison, H. K., Maraist, C., & Bing, M. N. (2011). Friend or foe? The promise and pitfalls of using social networking sites for HR decisions. *Journal of Business and Psychology, 26*, 153–159.

Davison, H. K., Maraist, C. C., Hamilton, R. H., & Bing, M. N. (2012). To screen or not to screen? Using the internet for selection decisions. *Employee Responsibility and Rights Journal, 24*, 1–21.

Epstein, D. (2008). Have I been Googled? Character and fitness in the age of Google, Facebook, and YouTube. *The Georgetown Journal of Legal Ethics, 21*, 715–727.

Equal Employment Opportunity Commission, Civil Service Commission, Department of Labor, & Department of Justice. (1978). Uniform guidelines on employee selection procedures. *Federal Register, 43*(166), 38290–38315.

Fast, L. A., & Funder, D. C. (2008). Personality as manifest in word use: Correlations with self-report, acquaintance report, and behavior. *Journal of Personality and Social Psychology, 94,* 334–346.

Forty-five Percent of Employers. (2009). *Forty-five percent of employers use social networking sites to research job candidates, CareerBuilder survey finds: Career expert provides dos and don'ts for job seekers on social networking.* CareerBuilder.com Press Releases. Retrieved from http://www.careerbuilder.com/share/aboutus/pressreleasesdetail.aspx?id=pr519&sd=8/19/2009&ed=12/31/2009

Funder, D. C. (1995). On the accuracy of personality judgment: A realistic approach. *Psychological review, 4,* 652–670.

Gill, A. J., Oberlander, J., & Austin, E. (2006). Rating e-mail personality at zero acquaintance. *Personality and Individual Differences, 40,* 479–507.

Gosling, S. D., Ko, S. J., Mannarelli, T., & Morris, M. E. (2002). A room with a cue: Personality judgments based on offices and bedrooms. *Journal of Personality and Social Psychology, 82,* 379–398.

Griggs v. Duke Power Co., 91 S. Ct. 849 (1971).

Gustafson, D.A. (2012). *Perceived fairness in the use of Facebook in the selection process.* Unpublished master's thesis. University of Texas at Arlington.

Hunter, J. E., & Hunter, R. F. (1984). Validity and utility of alternative predictors of job performance. *Psychological Bulletin, 96,* 72–98.

J. S. v. Bethlehem Area Sch. Dist., 757 A.2d 412. (Pa. Commw. Ct. 2000).

Juffras, D. (2010). Using the Internet to conduct background checks on applicants for employment. *University of North Carolina School of Government Public Employment Law Bulletin Number, 38,* 1–22.

Karl, K., Peluchette, J., & Schlaegel, C. (2010). Who's posting Facebook faux pas? A cross-cultural examination of personality differences. *International Journal of Selection and Assessment, 18,* 174–186.

Kluemper, D. H., & Rosen, P. (2009). Future employment selection methods: Evaluating social networking websites. *Journal of Managerial Psychology, 24,* 567–580.

Kluemper, D. H., Rosen, P., & Mossholder, K. (2012). Social networking websites, personality ratings, and the organizational context: More than meets the eye? *Journal of Applied Social Psychology, 42,* 1143–1172.

Lebrecque, L. I., Markos, E., & Milne, G. R. (2011). Online personal branding: Processes, challenges, and implications. *Journal of Interactive Marketing, 25,* 37–50.

Levashina, J., & Campion, M. (2009). Expected practices in background checking: Review of the human resource management literature. *Employee Responsibilities & Rights Journal, 21,* 231–249.

Massey, R. (2009). Privacy and social networks: A European opinion. *Journal of Internet Law, 13,* 1–17.

Mumford, M. D., Costanza, D. P., Connelly, M. S., & Johnson, J. F. (1996). Item generation procedures and background data scales. Implications for construct and criterion-related validity. *Personnel Psychology, 49,* 360–398.

Myors, B., Lievens, F., Schollaert, E., Cronshaw, S. F., Mladinic, A., Aguinis, H., ... Sackett, P. R. (2008). International perspectives on the legal environment for selection. *Industrial and Organizational Psychology: Perspectives on Science and Practice, 1,* 206–246.

Oh, I. S., Wang, G., & Mount, M. K. (2011). Validity of observer ratings of the Five-Factor model of personality traits: A meta-analysis. *Journal of Applied Psychology, 96*, 762–773.

Ones, D. S., Dilchert, S., Viswesvaran, C., & Judge, T. A. (2007). In support of personality assessment in organizational settings. *Personnel Psychology, 60*, 995–1027.

Pietrylo v. Hillstone Restaurant Group. (2008). WL 6085437 (D.N.J. 2008).

Pike, J. C. (2011). *The impact of boundary-blurring social networking websites: Self-presentation, impression formation, and publicness.* Unpublished doctoral dissertation. University of Pittsburg.

Reeve, C. L., & Schultz, L. (2004). Job-seeker reactions to selection process information in job ads. *International Journal of Selection and Assessment, 12*, 343–355.

Robbins, R. W., Gosling, S. D., & Donahue, E. M. (1997). Are personality judgments based on physical appearance consensual and accurate? In J. Bermudez, B. de Raad, J. de Vries, A. M. Perez-Garcia, A. Sanchez-Elvira & G. L. van Heck (Eds.), *Personality psychology in Europe* (pp. 70–75). Tilburg, The Netherlands: Tilburg University Press.

Roth, P. L., Bobko, P., Van Iddekinge, C. H., & Thatcher, J. B. (2012a, August). Using social media information for staffing decisions: Some uncharted territory in validity research. Paper presented at the Academy of Management Annual Conference, Boston, MA.

Roth, P. L., Bobko, P., Van Iddekinge, C. H., & Thatcher, J. B. (2012b, August). Social media and employee selection: Literature-based expectations of adverse impact. Paper presented at the Academy of Management Annual Conference, Boston, MA.

Sackett, P. R., & Roth, L. (1996). Multi-stage selection strategies: A Monte Carlo investigation of effects on performance and minority hiring. *Personnel Psychology, 49*, 549–572.

Sanchez, R. J., Roberts, K., Freeman, M., & Clayton, A. C. (2012, August). Do they care? Applicant reactions to on-line social networking presence checks. Paper presented at the Academy of Management Annual Conference, Boston, MA.

Shiller, K. (2010). Getting a grip on reputation. *Information Today, 27*, 1–44.

SHRM. (2011). *SHRM survey findings: The use of social networking websites and online search engines in screening job candidates.* Retrieved from http://www.shrm.org/research/survey findings/articles/pages/theuseofsocialnetworkingwebsitesandonlinesearchenginesinscreening jobcandidates.aspx

Siebert, S., Downes, P. E. & Chrostopher, J. (2012, August). Applicant reactions to online background checks: Welcome to a brave new world. Paper presented at the Academy of Management Annual Conference, Boston, MA.

Slovensky, R., & Ross, W. H. (2012). Should human resource managers use social media to screen job applicants? Managerial and legal issues in the USA. *Info, 14*, 55–69.

Smith, W. P., & Kidder, D. L. (2010). You've been tagged! (Then again, maybe not): Employers and Facebook. . *Business Horizons, 53*, 491–499.

Vazire, S., & Gosling, S. D. (2004). E-perceptions: Personality impressions based on personal websites. *Journal of Personality and Social Psychology, 87*, 123–132.

Wallace, J. C., Page, E. E., & Lippstreu, M. (2006). Applicant reactions to pre-employment application blanks: A legal and procedural justice perspective. *Journal of Business and Psychology, 20*, 467–488.

Wilson, R. E., Gosling, S. D., & Graham, L. T. (2012). A review of Facebook research in the social sciences. *Perspectives on Psychological Science, 7*, 203–220.

Willey, L., White, B. J., Domagalski, T., & Ford, J. C. (2012). Candidate-screening, information technology and the law: Social media considerations. *Issues in Information Systems, 13*, 300–309.

Woska, W. J. (2007). Legal issues for HR professionals: Reference checking/background investigations. *Public Personnel Management, 36*, 79–89.

Chapter 2

What Is the Future of Employer Branding through Social Media? Results of the Delphi Study into the Perceptions of HR Professionals and Academics

Tanya Bondarouk, Huub Ruël, Elena Axinia and Roxana Arama

Abstract

Purpose — HR professionals have identified the power of information sharing for employer branding that could be obtained through the rapid growth of social media usage. The growing interest in and power of social media seem to be important for companies that want to make themselves known as interesting employers and to recruit prospective employees, using techniques that are more common to job seekers and recruiters. This study aims to explore the immediate future of employer branding through social media, as envisioned by academics and HR practitioners.

Design/methodology/approach — To look into the future of employer branding, we use the Delphi technique for forecasting, planning, issue identification, and framework development (Bobeva & Day, 2002). Two groups of respondents participated in this three-part study: 11 academics and 20 HR professionals. They were selected because of their research into the integration of HRM and IT from the e-HRM Global mailing list. The panelists participated in the research via electronic communication. The data were collected in three rounds from November 2010 to April 2011.

Findings — Research has revealed differences in the opinions of academics and HR professionals on the impact of social media on employer branding. The academics see its general effect as the targeting of audience for recruitment, marketing/company

Social Media in Human Resources Management
Advanced Series in Management, 23–57
Copyright © 2013 by Emerald Group Publishing Limited
ISSN: 1877-6361/doi:10.1108/S1877-6361(2013)0000012006

brand, and ways of communication/HR competencies. The practitioners see the image of the employer, visibility of the company, and organization responsiveness. The study presents other findings within the boundaries of employer branding value proposition, internal and external marketing, and the role of HR professionals. According to the academics, HR professionals in the future will need to possess knowledge about marketing and communication studies and web-based applications/ develop new skills. They think that social media will impact the image of HR in organizations. On the other hand, HR professionals think that the future of their activities will depend on their awareness of recruitment trends, HR innovative thinking, and HR networking skills. Although the object of their activity will remain recruitment, HR professionals will have to be continuously updated on what is new in the social media in terms of recruitment.

Originality/value — This study presents the results of the Delphi technique, which is itself considered an original research method and not widely accepted in the tough "publish or perish" world. The value of the research is its forecast about the future developments of employer branding through social media, as envisioned by academics and HR practitioners.

Keywords: Employer branding; social media; Delphi study; HR professionals; organizational attractiveness

> *On social media, visibility and presence are very volatile …*
>
> *You are what Google says you're …*
>
> *There are no secrets anymore, no 'damage' control, no ways to censor any event that takes place …*
>
> From experts' answers

Introduction

HR professionals have identified the power of information sharing for employer branding that could be obtained through the rapid growth of social media usage. Companies have Facebook profiles to announce job openings, use LinkedIn to search for qualified personnel, and advertise new jobs on blogs, Twitter, or YouTube. Creating an image of a desirable and unique employer through social media has been a focus of attention in the last few years, producing a new "hot" HRM topic: employer branding. According to a survey conducted by OSCAR GbmH (a European student management consultancy based in Cologne) and presented on March 2010, 53% of companies already use social media for recruiting and employer branding, while 2/3 of the internet population regularly visits social media sites. The growing interest in and power of social media seem to be important for companies that want to make themselves known as interesting employers and to recruit prospective employees, using techniques that are more common to job seekers and recruiters.

Employer branding "cuts across many traditional HR specialists and becomes an umbrella program that provides structure to previously separate policies and practices" (Edwards, 2010, p. 5). The attractiveness of employer branding, enhanced through the social media, is rooted in the great opportunities for HR professionals to get involved in activities beyond their traditional tasks. As with many new media technologies, employer branding seems so promising once it is initiated through the social media. Thus, recruiting is expected to become more interesting and efficient by tweeting a job opening; head hunting could be better facilitated by the vast number of LinkedIn profiles; employees could enhance their organizational image by blogging about how it is to work in that company; and/or the number of good applicants could increase.

Such expectations are not new. Management studies have known several examples of "hypes" provoked by the use of information and/or media technologies: e-HRM, e-recruitment, shared service centers, learning organization, to name but a few. We are witnessing great expectations, but little research has tried to seriously tackle the future of such "hypes." Therefore, we have decided to challenge the social media-enabled employer branding by looking into its future.

To look into the future of employer branding, we use the Delphi technique as it is known for "forecasting, planning, issue identification/prioritization, or for framework/strategies development" (Bobeva & Day, 2002, p. 104). Studies have been conducted with the use of the Delphi method to forecast globalization, international business and trade, the future of knowledge management, management in general (Swartz, 2010), and the future impact of enterprise resource planning systems on supply chain management. Findings by Rowe and Wright (1999) suggest that Delphi groups outperform both statistical groups and standard interactive groups, while Landeta (2006) confirms, based on a literature review, that the Delphi method "is a valid instrument for forecasting and supporting decision-making."

The focus of our study is academics and HR practitioners, who are considered experts given their knowledge and research experience in HRM and employer branding. Therefore, our study aims to explore the future of employer branding through social media, as envisioned by academics and HR practitioners.

Employer Branding Defined

The search process started with the word "branding" and resulted in 3800 hits on Scopus and 794,000 on Google Scholar. The next addition was the word "employer branding," resulting in 32 hits on Scopus and 32,900 on Google Scholar. In order to make a selection of the most cited articles that debate the employer branding issue, the following selection process was added:

- For Scopus, only articles in English were selected which had the exact word combination in the title from business, management, accounting, economics, econometrics and finance subject areas, resulting in 8 articles.

- For Google Scholar, only articles in English were selected which had the exact word combination in the title from business, administration, finance and economics subject areas, resulting in 54 articles.

The four researchers involved in the process of selecting the necessary articles decided to classify the articles on "employer branding" according to the number of citations of each one. This reduced the total to 21 articles (from 66 citations to 1 citation per article). After examining their abstracts, 10 articles for employer branding were commonly agreed upon. The 10 final articles were chosen according to the information provided by the abstract, taking the following aspects into consideration: conceptualization of employer branding, dimensions of employer branding, and outcomes of employer branding. In addition to these 10 articles taken from Google Scholar and Scopus, 4 more articles were found during the theoretical research.

Corporate brand personality has become interesting. While Google produced about 3000 hits in 2004 for "employer branding" (Backhaus & Tikoo, 2004), the number had increased to more than 6,450,000 in 2012. Companies spend considerable sums of money on creating an identity inside and outside themselves, which they hope will add value to their organization. Along with human capital, brands have become a firm's most valuable asset (Backhaus & Tikoo, 2004). "There is an increasing realization that corporate brands serve as a powerful navigational tool to a variety of stakeholders for a miscellany of purposes including employment or consumer buying behavior" (Balmer & Gray, 2003, p. 972). Thus, corporate branding refers to the general strategy of branding within a company which also includes employer branding; personnel play a crucially important role in transmitting the brand's values, and this makes them the heart of the corporate branding process (Balmer & Gray, 2003, p. 979). But employer branding is more than the personnel within a company, it is an entire process designed for the image of the company as an employer, the employees, and future prospective candidates.

The concept originated in the 1990s and started being widely used in the management world. It underwent various definitions during the years and development of the academic material. Reichenberg (2009) discusses employer branding as involving the development and communication of the culture of an organization as an employer, defining and delivering the employment experience. According to him, the basic principle is that all employees are consumers who must be recruited and retained. A definition given in 1996 by Amber and Barrow and taken over by Backhaus and Tikoo (2004, p. 502) refers to the rewards of employer branding, calling it "the package of functional, economic and psychological benefits provided by employment and identified with the employing company." Following Backhaus and Tikoo (2004, p. 501), employer branding is defined as "a targeted long-term strategy to manage the awareness and perceptions of employees, potential employees and related stakeholders with regards to a *particular* firm." The conclusion reached in their study defined employer branding "as the process of building identifiable and unique employer identity, and the employer brand as a concept of the firm that differentiates it from its competitors."

In this study we consider both definitions, but suggest the following combination: *Employer branding is viewed as a long-term strategy of any given company, aimed at both building a unique and desirable employer identity and managing the perceptions of prospective and current employees, in order to gain competitive advantage.*

Employer branding is a significant part of the HR function, supporting a more strategic focus (Bach, 2007, p. 268) in the search to identify workers who would best fit that organization's culture, values, and vision. "A stronger employer brand therefore fosters a positive image, identity, reputation and encourages employees to identify with the organization." Thus, HR specialists are in charge of creating a compelling and unique environment that would convince the job seeker that their organization is the best place to work. This fact brings out the concept of employer attractiveness, which refers to the "envisioned benefits that a potential employee sees in working for a specific organization" (Brethon, Ewing, & Hah, 2005, p. 151).

Employer branding is believed to attract better candidates, as it helps them picture themselves as being a part of the corporation. By using employer branding, companies show how they differ from their competitors and why the best applicants should choose to work for them. "Employees as well as customers like to be associated with distinctive organizations. One role of employer branding should be then to distinguish the employer in the minds of the employees" (Davies, 2008, p. 670). Furthermore, it creates loyalty, satisfaction, and emotional attachment for the already existing employees. Employees become loyal as long as their opinions are heard, and they are less likely to quit their job unless they deal with stressful situations at work, job dissatisfaction, or lack of commitment to the employer (Davies, 2008, p. 670). One purpose of employer branding is to increase the degree of satisfaction among employees. Employees who are satisfied also create better relationships with customers (Davies, 2008, p. 670). A powerful employer branding campaign ultimately results in the emotional attachment of the employees toward the company. They view their job and company based on their affective evaluation rather than objective rational criteria. "As the success of branding is concerned with promoting and emotional response from the target, the employer branding should promote an effective response from the employee" (Davies, 2008, p. 671).

Employer branding can be seen as a threefold process, according to Backhaus and Tikoo (2004):

- *Value proposition*: information on the organization's culture, management style, qualities of the current employees, current employees' image, etc. — an image of what the company can offer to its employee.
- *External marketing*: presenting the value proposition to recruiting companies, placement counselor, to reach and attract the target population. Creating a unique image allows possible candidates to picture themselves working for the company, increasing the degree of commitment. Distinctiveness of the brand allows the firm to acquire distinctive human capital.
- *Internal marketing*: involves respecting the promises made to the employees before recruiting them and so it becomes a part of the organization's culture. It

is meant to build a workforce that is difficult to imitate and committed to the organizational goals, but also to achieve an unique culture and increase employee retention.

Lievens, Van Hoye, and Anseel (2007) concluded that the identity perceived by outsiders is usually ranked higher than the actual identity known to the current employees. The study was conducted in the Belgian army, on a sample of 179 employees, suggesting that the applicants might have a more optimistic view of the army than the employees themselves (Lievens et al., 2007, p. 11).

Employer Branding and Social Media

With the social media, it is "easy to access an ever growing source of people, brands have begun to realize the potential to reach these people through social networks" (Coon, 2010, p. 2). How to make the best use of social media; how to promote a company as the best employer; what if a job seeker receives negative information or feels the company does not offer enough information about the job openings? These are questions that marketing, HR professionals, public relations, and advertising practitioners are trying to answer. Studies have shown that "social media are replacing traditional media in the eyes of the consumer by informing their views on brands, purchases and services offered" (Fichter, 2007, p. 57). The outcomes and benefits of the diffusion of information through social media could be of major interest for companies willing to establish a strong employer branding reputation. Organizations could lose a qualified and fit potential candidate for their vacancies. Indeed, not all companies are comfortable about "a world where the consumers can speak so freely with each other and businesses have increasingly less control over the information available about them on the cyberspace" (Kaplan & Haenelein, 2010). Companies might notice that the struggle to recruit and retain competent employees takes place in a world where technological advances and global competition are driving widespread changes in employment patterns.

It seems that organizations understand that social media may offer the possibility of promoting themselves at less cost, gaining competitive advantage and improving the quality of their service. Although employer branding, in general, has been on the minds of researchers in the past years, it is important to address the future of employer branding strategies since "there is no telling what the future will hold for business, but social media will only continue to grow" (Coon, 2010).

For the purpose of this volume, we have decided to skip a general overview of social media types in this chapter, as the editorial introduction addresses this issue. Instead, we offer a match between the characteristics of each type of social media and employer branding, based on our theoretical considerations listed above (Figure 1). We consider how different types of social media — social network sites, blogs, collaborative projects, content communities, virtual game worlds — can contribute to employer branding.

For example, Social Network Sites could enhance *value proposition* through their ability to provide organizational profiles, peer-to-peer communication, knowledge sharing, creating a trustworthy and loyal image; enhance *external marketing* by creating a profile that represents the company, filtering information for specific target groups, reaching new and large audiences, searching for job candidates, timely and direct customer contact; and also enhance *Internal Marketing* through formal and informal communication with the employees, instant messaging, and strengthening ties with and between employees.

In addition to our Figure 1, solely based on the literature review, we put forward three propositions on how organizations can use social media when engaging in employer branding activities without insisting that the use of social media is either beneficial or harmful.

Proposition 1. Social media and employer value proposition.

To create value and the image of a desirable employer, and strengthen the organizational culture-value proposition, companies might use blogs, Twitter, and/or Facebook instant messages to keep current and future employees continuously informed. Wikipedia could also provide information about the uniqueness of a company since the content is generated by users all over the world. The responsibility of HR managers is to make sure that what they promise and propose as an employer is valid and long-lasting.

Proposition 2. Social media and external marketing.

It should be possible to recruit a target population and create a unique and distinctive image of an employer through all the social media channels. Since blogging is the elemental form of social media, companies and managers could easily benefit from keeping their blogs alive. Bloggers exchange information continuously and spread the word around faster than any other media channel. Facebook, Twitter, and LinkedIn could offer a new perspective of recruiting for HR practitioners since all the personal and professional information of users is available online. Posting original and creative videos on YouTube could allow the creation of a unique and desirable organization and also promote job openings for ideal candidates. Virtual games and worlds allow companies to create their own space where they can promote themselves as a company but also as a desirable and open-minded employer.

Proposition 3. Social media and internal marketing.

To respect the promises made while recruiting and building a workforce difficult to imitate, companies could actively use social networks and blogs. Having an account on either Facebook or Twitter allows the organizations to promote themselves daily using tweets or instant messages or suggest topics of discussion.

The most important aspect of social media is that companies have to promote only what they already have. The advertised image of the company has to match the

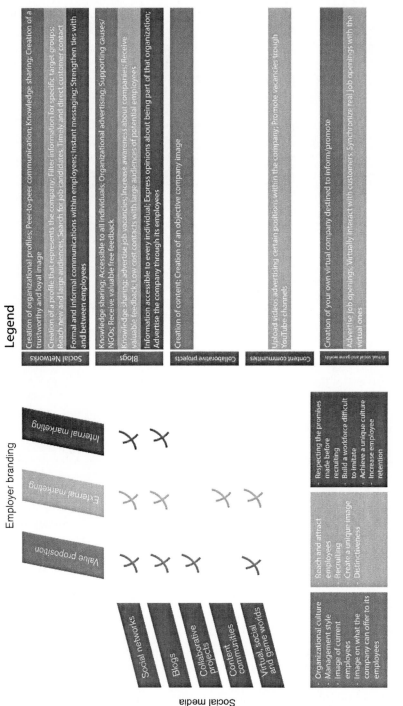

Figure 1: Social media-based employer branding.

reality. Social media might be a fast way of communicating and spreading your values and intentions as an employer, but if the information is not true and turns out to be fake advertising, then the negative publicity will probably spread even faster.

Methodology: The Delphi Method

Researchers at the Rand Corporation began to develop the Delphi method at the end of 1960s, to use individual estimations to predict short-term future trends (Dalkey, 1969). The Rand Corporation conducted studies and built the Delphi method from the simplistic version — formulate group judgments — to how it is used nowadays. One of the experiments to prove the method's validity took place at UCLA (University of California, Los Angeles), where senior students were asked general but difficult questions. They were encouraged to make an educated guess based on their background knowledge. Some of them received additional feedback relating their answers to the group's answers. The results showed that the participants' range of responses got progressively narrower and that the group response became more accurate (Dalkey, 1969).

The method has been used now for many years, and various definitions have appeared. For instance, Hasson, Keeney, and McKenna (2000, p. 1008) defined it as "a group facilitation technique, which is an iterative multistage process, designed to transform opinion into group consensus." Landeta (2006) stated that "the Delphi method was conceived as a group technique whose aim was to obtain the most reliable consensus of opinion of a group of experts by means of a series of intensive questionnaires with controlled opinion feedback. (...) It is a method of structuring communication between groups of people who can provide valuable contributions in order to resolve a complex problem" (Landeta, 2006, p. 468).

According to Landeta (2006), the main characteristics of the Delphi method are:

- Repetitiveness — participants should be questioned at least twice on the same items
- Anonymity — answers are kept anonymous and considered as part of the entire group
- Controlled feedback — the communication between experts is externally controlled
- Group statistical response — all the answers can be found in the final answers.

As the literature argues, "in all subject domains Delphi has been primarily employed for forecasting, planning, issue identification/prioritization, or for framework/strategies development (...)Whatever the perceived reasons for its choice, the method offers reliability and generalizability of outcomes, ensured through iteration of rounds for data collection and analysis, guided by the principles of democratic participation and anonymity" (Bobeva & Day, 2002, p. 104). The argumentation underlying the statement focuses on the valuable solutions that are offered to problems through the reduction of undesirable psychological influences, like dominant behaviors, and selective feedback providing valuable information and more extensive consideration thanks to the repetition (Landeta, 2006). Okoli and Pawlowski (2004,

p. 16) emphasized a very important advantage of the method in the way that it "avoids direct confrontation of the experts," strengthening the independence and originality of the answers.

We borrowed the definition of the Delphi method from Landeta (2006) and viewed it as "the method conceived for forecasting, planning, issue identification/prioritization, and/or for framework/strategies development (Bobeva & Day, 2002) through obtaining the most reliable consensus of opinion of a group of anonymous experts by means of a series of intensive questionnaires with controlled opinion feedback" (Landeta, 2006).

The literature review presented three considerations regarding the Delphi method. First, in terms of purpose, Delphi studies have been developed to identify and prioritize various factors (Okoli & Pawlowski, 2004). The method is valid and accurate for both long- and short-range forecasts (Landeta, 2006). Forecasting studies have been massively developed in Japan, Austria, India, and Korea. There is also an institute specialized in forecasting — Institute for Prospective Forecasting Studies — that mainly uses the Delphi method (Landeta, 2006, p. 469). Second, in terms of procedure, by using the Delphi method, the panelists are free of social pressure and the risk of personality influence; individual dominance is completely reduced, enhancing independent thinking and helping them to take time and gradually formulate assumptions. The participants do not meet each other and remain anonymous. The method allows researchers to select the necessary information to be shared among all participants, who are experts in their field. It is based on iterative rounds of questions (open and/or structured), along with feedback from the previous session. Skulmoski and Hartman (2007, p. 11) suggested that the number of rounds depends on the purpose of the study, but mostly a two- or three-iteration Delphi is enough. In each round participants are allowed to modify their answers and to argue about their decision. This exercise is repeated until consensus is reached, and in the end a final summary is sent to all participants. Third, in terms of reliability, "while the Delphi method is flexible and superficially simple, the researcher needs to take into account many design considerations in order to use the method" (Skulmoski & Hartman, 2007, p. 9). Starting with the panelists, questionnaire, data gathering, achieved consensus, and findings, each stage has to be rigorously explained and organized, so that the study can be considered accurate and proficient. This method has received criticism centered mainly on its "sloppy execution" and accuracy (Rowe & Wright, 1999, p. 367).

The research on employer branding and social media captures the uncertainty and unpredictability of the platforms being developed. We do not know if social media will grow or vanish, nor if employer branding will shift from traditional media to Web 2.0 applications, following the trend. There are numbers indicating the growth and usage of social media for employer branding activities, but still no information about what the future will bring for HR representatives. The experience and information that experts have would allow us to analyze the data received both qualitatively and quantitatively, in order to generate consensus regarding the future of employer branding through social media. Controlled feedback would enable us to narrow down the most important ideas of the experts and obtain reliable and general information.

Data Collection and Analysis

The experts considered for this study were academics and HR practitioners. They were selected based on their research into the integration of HRM and IT, from the e-HRM Global mailing list. Eleven academics and 20 practitioners agreed to participate in the study. The group of academics represented experts who were researching and teaching courses in the fields of Management, HRM, Leadership, Work and Organizational Studies, Social Networks, Online Recruiting, International Business, and Knowledge Transfer. The selected HR professionals were recruitment managers with expertise in staffing and recruiting, HRM directors in public and private organizations, and/or HR consultants. The participants were sent an e-mail in which they were kindly asked to confirm their willingness to participate. We chose to use e-mail because the panelists are international, and sending questionnaires by mail would have taken too long; we opted for a quick turnover to keep enthusiasm alive and participation high.

The data were collected in the period from November 2010 to April 2011, in three rounds.

First round of the Delphi study. After receiving the confirmation from the participants, we sent another e-mail containing all the information necessary for this study: its purpose, methodology, and six first-round questions to be answered in two weeks' time (Table 1).

After two weeks, we received three answers from the academics and five from the practitioners. We sent a reminder to the remaining respondents about how important their answers were to proceed to the second round. After the reminder, another five answers were received. During this entire process, permanent contact was established with the experts, to inform them about the work in progress and thanking those who had already replied. By January 2011, after a third reminder, it was concluded that the research would go ahead with the 10 academics and 15 practitioners who had responded by that time.

Table 1: Round 1 — initial questions.

1.	What are the consequences of using employer branding through social media?
2.	Which developments of social media will positively and/or negatively influence employer branding in the coming 5 years?
3.	What implications will social media have for the employer branding proposition in the coming 5 years?
4.	What implications will social media have for internal marketing in the coming 5 years?
5.	What implications will social media have for external marketing in the coming 5 years?
6.	What implications will these developments have for the role of the HR professionals?

The next step was to analyze the answers and to cluster the responses to prepare for the second round. The four researchers independently separated each response into items that could be clustered into various categories. A total number of 225 items (48 clusters) were created by academics, and 172 (53 clusters) by practitioners. After all the work was done separately, the researchers discussed each of their interpretations. We also calculated the inter-coder reliability.

For this round, the inter-coder reliability was used to make the clusters clearer by classifying the same data separately and discussing the agreements and disagreements. The inter-coder reliability was calculated as: ICR = number of agreements/(total number of agreements+disagreements). The ICR was calculated for each question, among the four researchers. Thus, the first question had an ICR of 81%/80% reliability for academics and practitioners, respectively, question 2 had an ICR of 78%/80%, question 3 had an ICR of 92%/73%, question 4 had an ICR of 78%/85%, question 5 had an ICR of 78%/86%, and question 6 had an ICR of 82%/84%.

As a result of the discussions, we decided to combine the first question (*What are the consequences of using employer branding through social media*) with the second one (*Which developments of social media will positively and/or negatively influence employer branding in the coming 5 years*) because most of the answers were similar, or the respondents had difficulty separating the meaning of these two questions.

After the analysis of the first round, the clusters were titled according to the main idea of the items comprising them. We also decided that using words such as "better," "increased," or "higher risk" could somehow influence the experts' opinion, and therefore we kept to neutral phrases for the second round. Since the overall purpose was to reach consensus and under no circumstances to point out the positive or negative side of social media, it was decided that the final clusters/categories should be impartial so that the experts would decide for themselves.

Second round of the Delphi study.   In the second stage, the experts received the feedback containing the clusters for each of the five questions. The first e-mail for this round was sent in February 2011. On February 23, a reminder was sent to the participants who had not replied. The panelists were asked to state on a scale from 1 to 5 the extent to which they agreed with each statement. All of the statements were based on the clusters taken from the first round. At this step, the panelists could extensively influence the next round. Since all the qualitative texts were coded into quantitative data, we established a scale to be used for the second round. We invited participants to express their attitudes toward each statement by choosing among a number of grades on the r-grade Likert scale. For this round, we used a 5-point Likert scale, where 5 represented the strongest agreement. The purpose of using the scale was to create consensus with respect to the relevant factors. The questionnaire for the second round comprising five statements was sent to all respondents. In this round, 10 academics and 12 practitioners sent their questionnaires back.

For the following round, the researchers aimed at creating a top five for each proposition from all the items previously sent. A three-step process was followed. The first step was to calculate the frequency of the "Good" answers, which were considered the ones scoring 4 and 5. For each question only the items with a high frequency of good answers were selected. More than five items remained. The next step was to check if there were any similarities between items and to see if they correlate. If so, then they were considered one item, and the number was reduced. If a total of five items per question was not reached, the next step was to select from the remaining items only the ones with a mean of 4 or above, or where necessary the ones with the highest mean, if the number of items was below five when using only the items with a mean of 4 or above.

Third round of the Delphi study.   There was a consensus about the final questionnaire comprising five categories for each question, asking the experts to rank the propositions from the most important (1) to the least important (5), and it was sent out at the end of March 2011.

All of the answers were received by the end of April 2011. It seemed more appropriate for this study to show the statistical data and explain the answers for each proposition and each category. If a situation arose in which the categories of the same proposition were ranked the same, the mean distinguished between them. Since 1 was most important and 5 least important, the smallest mean indicated a distribution of answers toward 1. Thus, based on the frequencies of the answers, the mode, and the mean, the most important clusters were discussed.

Findings: Round 1

General consequences of using social media for employer branding.   The first-round responses formed the basis of the entire study; with the initial qualitative data received from the experts, it was possible to formulate the second- and third-round questionnaires. All the answers were elaborated and well justified, showing not only an interest from the expert's side but also an understanding of the terms implied by employer branding or internal/external marketing.

After grouping the first two questions into a single one, various categories were identified that would be influenced by social media, in the panelists' view. The experts suggested that by introducing social media within the companies, major changes would develop, including new policies, competencies and/or management positions. The distribution of answers did not imply either positive or negative sides of using social media, but reflected both advantages and disadvantages that may occur in the future. According to the responses, numerous positive implications can be identified, but most of the time, this depends on the approach the company decides to take for their employer branding.

The panelists suggested that social media would open a new way of communication for companies, one that is different and innovative in comparison to the traditional means of communication, "*forcing them to rethink the way they communicate.*" "*This way you reach a mass of people with various communication tools,*" "*you have a better way to easily disseminate information about your brand,*" and "*increase the company's communication channels.*" Closely related to this new way of communication were the costs involved. The experts suggested that by using social media to interact, "*it can enable organizations to share information with a wider audience at a lower cost than* with traditional methods of employer branding," resulting in a "higher cost efficiency of communication employer branding."

Respondents thought that, as a consequence of new ways of communications, companies will eventually become "more transparent." Internet users, applicants, employees, and employers would provide information about themselves on an open platform available to every individual. If companies want to use social media to benefit from this, then they "must interact more directly with potential applicants, partners and employees, by giving more and more information and being transparent about their activity and work conditions." For the employees and applicants, there will be "more actions to better know the employer" since "the messages that are communicated through social media are highly visible to a vast array of individuals." Interactivity with customers would be direct, and it could have a positive implication for companies: "employers will have to use social media in order to be positively perceived by a large segment of the applicant population (especially recent university graduates)." One respondent pointed out that how companies share their information online is important, as is the message they transmit: "If companies use social media to really interact with people and not to manipulate opinions, it can only be positive." This interaction can also have an impact on the relationship between employer and employees, because employer branding through social media "will help the creation of a strong emotional bond between the employers and the applicants/employees." To produce positive consequences, "organizations should strive to make this connection to create an undeniable sense of belonging among their potential and current employees."

One of the most frequently mentioned aspects related to employer branding activities was targeting of the audience for recruitment. In the respondents' views, social media would allow companies to access and send information to "a wider audience" than before, and "it can enable organizations to engage with a larger cohort of potential employees through the mass dissemination of messages." By using social media, organizations could also "identify and recruit appropriate talent who identifies with the employer branding."

The findings also revealed that "new competencies are needed to manage these media." If companies use social media for employer branding, then it will be necessary to "employ social media experts," which is not a well-established function within organizations. In addition, "employees must know how to efficiently represent the employment brand when using social media." Along with these new competencies, it would also be necessary to develop specific organizational policies, since employees and also HR professionals need to be informed about how to use social media. "Positive social media policies to help and encourage employees to use it will come up," and "different practices toward diverse employees" should be put in order.

Experts also noted the disadvantages of using social media, as negative information, once released, can be spread very easily. One of the most important aspects is that companies must share messages that are real and reflect the true employer branding values; otherwise the audience will respond in a negative way, and the information can be spread widely "much faster than with traditional media":

> If companies fail to deliver the set of benefits they suggest through their employer branding, individuals will have the potential to express mass negative feelings.

If done in a manner that ends up as being perceived as Machiavellian or manipulative, the strategy may backfire and tarnish the company's reputation.

"Facebook will be the most powerful platform for negative complaints regarding organizations." In the same manner, companies need to pay a lot of attention to the amount of information that is shared, and also to the extent to which they allow their employees to be involved. Experts suggested that companies will try to control employees, so that only the information that they desire is sent to social media users. If the control is used for existing employees, *"it could be perceived as an intrusion into the employee's private life,"* but also the control could manifest as *"how potential employees see the employer."*

Social media, according to the experts, could also have an impact on the company's brand, and by *"using it for employer branding, it shows that organizations are innovative in doing PR, recruiting and communications." "Organizations can use social media to enhance the visibility of their organization to current and future stakeholders"* and to *"make themselves known on the labor market."*

Value proposition and social media.   The experts considered that social media can impact, positively or negatively, the creation of the value proposition and the realistic employer branding. Due to the associated transparency, constructing the employer branding proposition could be either difficult or improved. First, the answers suggested that because of the loss of control of the information, it would be harder to construct and promote a real value proposition due to *"unbalanced branding proposition (large differences between proposition and reality)," "difficulty in matching the external speech and the internal reality," "less control over their own branding propositions,"* and *"a possible gap between proposition and reality."* The experts explained that as companies were transparent and open to the market, employees and job applicants could directly see what kind of employer branding proposition was being promoted.

Second, the answers also suggested that *"organizations that do not use social media would probably have a harder time building a positive brand."* Since social media are accessible to everyone, companies should listen and understand what employees and candidates prefer, and create a positive value proposition that will result in a competitive advantage. Consequently, *"companies will have the opportunity to improve, adapt their employer branding proposition by taking into account the needs and issues expressed by applicants and employees," "emergent communication about employer branding will make it more realistic and up to date,"* and *"the creation of opportunities for organizations to engage with current and potential employees, so that it positively share its policies and practices."* Moreover, this also suggests engagement with both employees and applicants, which is another issue addressed by the experts.

There is also the opportunity to promote the HRM strategies. With social media, *"the idea is to integrate the different initiatives and think about a consistent employer branding strategy"* and *"to create tactics that contribute toward generating a positive employer branding proposition, their measurement and follow-up."* Also, strategically constructing the value proposition provides the opportunity to target a specific audience; since communication is done *"in a way which is familiar and particularly appreciated by young people," "it will enable an organization to communicate its branding and value proposition to a specific target."*

Internal marketing and social media.   At this stage, internal marketing was explained briefly to the respondents as all activities aimed at identifying and attracting employees and the creation of a unique image that will allow candidates to picture themselves within the company. The tendency was to imply that social media can have positive implications for the internal marketing, but with some disadvantages if not used accordingly. Mainly, it was found that *"organizations will benefit from including effective social media into their overall recruiting process," "announcing jobs on Twitter could enhance visibility of the job posting," "it will valorize better the employer branding proposition, HR actions, work conditions, and the expertise and competencies of the current employees"* and also enhance, improve, and positively create a favorable internal marketing. A real example given by an expert also encouraged the idea that using social media could benefit the organization by providing realistic job previews:

> In the recruitment blogs of Microsoft, current employees write about their typical day at work. Thus, potential applicants get a real glimpse of the jobs in Microsoft and can self-select if they want to work for the company.

In contrast, even if social media could improve or ease the recruitment process, it could be *"more challenging to assess recruiting practices"* since the *"information flow is less centralized"* and a possible *"loss of control where the job posting will go."*

The experts obviously considered it important for companies to be honest and real when approaching employer branding activities through social media: it is crucial to *"strike a balance between being honest and real and creating a favorable impression"* and *"to have consistency of the web internal marketing with the real work conditions,"* otherwise the risk is *"to lose credibility and damage the company's reputation."* In addition, although the experts suggested that allowing employees to get involved in social marketing activities would benefit the internal marketing and organizational image, *"it's unlikely that many organizations will give employees free rein to interact like this,"* thus controlling the employees' behavior. If companies use social media for internal marketing, then the HR professionals need to be retrained and possess more skills than before; they will have to be *"highly professional"* in order to *"to communicate a positive image about your organization"* and *"learn where and when their potential customers and employees are online."* Thus, *"marketing and communication skills will become more valued talents in an organization."*

Findings: Round 2

The analysis of the second round developed differently. In all cases the data were analyzed qualitatively and quantitatively due to the high number of items that had to be reduced. For example, from a number of 17 items for the first statement (Table 3), the researchers analyzed the data to reach the top 5. Statistical analysis of the distribution charts was used to filter the categories that received "good" answers ($M = 4$–5). In the second round the respondents received only a few items for each question, and they were asked to grade each item on a scale from 1 to 5 based on the importance each item presented for them. The overview of the five questions and answer categories are presented in Table 2.

In the second round the number of propositions per question had to be reduced to the top 5. Thus, propositions within question 1 (the general impact of social media) had to be reduced from 17/17 (academics/practitioners) to 5; question 2 (employer branding value proposition) from 12/9 to 5; question 3 (internal market) from 11/10 to 5; question 4 (external market) from 12/8 to 5; and question 5 (the role of HR professionals) from 10/9 to 5. We did this on the basis of three issues that we approached interdependently: we checked for the inter-item correlations (factor analysis), we analyzed and discussed descriptive statistics and distributions, and we discussed and estimated the potential consensus for the propositions.

Findings: Round 3

In this round participants were asked to rank five propositions per question, with 1 = greatest importance, 5 = least importance. Table 3 shows 25 propositions (top 5 from the second round × 5 questions) that were sent to the respondents, and their ranking.

General impact of social media on employer branding. According to the results, the most important categories differed as ranked by the academics and practitioners. The academics saw the general effect of social media on employer branding as targeting of audience for recruitment, marketing/company brand, and ways of communication/ HR competencies. The practitioners stressed image of the employer, visibility of the company, and organization responsiveness.

"Targeting of audience for recruitment" was considered most important by the majority of academics. They suggested that social media "*will largely influence the way applicants are recruited as we see more of Gen Y in the workforce, hence organizations may find that social media methods of recruitment are very critical,*" "*will involve in particular young employees and contribute a lot to the transparency of the labor market, allowing both the parties to access more information,*" and that companies "*must adapt their communication by using social media to target potential applicants.*"

> Using social media for recruiting is clearly growing and has, in my opinion, the most potential to impact actual employer branding. I don't see marketing and customer relations as having so much impact on the company's brand as an employer.

"Marketing/Company brand" was composed of two clusters from round 1; it seemed very important to the academics, since the majority of rankings were 1 and 2. According to them, social media "*seem to be used more for communicating with customers than to attract employees*" and "*the proliferation currently and in the future is focused upon marketing and company branding rather than being another form of HR technology or e-HRM.*"

Table 2: Perceived important impacts of social media on employer branding and HR professionals.

Academics		Practitioners
In general, in the coming 5 years, social media will influence …		
Cost implications	1	Visibility of the company
Transparency	2	Employees' involvement and empowerment
Targeting of audience for recruitment	3	Image of the employer
Interactivity	4	Organization's policies
Ways of communication	5	Company communication and information sharing
HR competencies	6	Organization's responsiveness
Organization's reputation	7	Recruitment process
Marketing	8	Customer service
Relationships between employer and employees	9	Consumers' role
Employee involvement	10	Competitive advantage
Organizational policies	11	Budget
Control issues	12	Control of employees' behavior
Risk management	13	Quality of employer branding
Company brand	14	Overall impact on the organization
Employee mobility	15	Market expansion
Reaching employees with mobile devices	16	Competition
Control over employee behavior	17	Technological developments
In the coming 5 years, social media will influence Value Branding Proposition …		
Realistic value proposition	1	Management of communication
Balance between proposition and reality	2	Time investment in employer branding
Engagement with both employees and applicants	3	Direct financial investments
Building the value preposition	4	Organization's strategy
Employee involvement in EB activities	5	HRM activities
F2F activities	6	Organization privacy
Control issues	7	Organization image
Transparency	8	Organization security
Equity between employers and applicants	9	Relationships employer–employee
Opportunities for promoting the organization	10	
HRM strategy	11	
Targeting of specific audience	12	

Table 2. Continued.

Academics		Practitioners
In the coming 5 years, social media will influence Internal Market ...		
Recruitment	1	Communication within organizations
Control over employee behavior	2	Work–private life boundary
Openness about working in that company	3	Strategy alignment
Organization's image	4	Organization image
Organizational boundaries	5	Knowledge sharing within organizations
Legal implications	6	Management flexibility
Marketing strategies	7	Employee commitment
Decentralization	8	HR skills
HR skills	9	Marketing
Employee involvement in organizational performance	10	Quality of internal market
Organizational performance	11	
In the coming 5 years, social media will influence External Market ...		
Employee involvement	1	Recruitment strategy
Competition	2	Management strategy
Organizational policies	3	E-devices knowledge
Internal vs. external information	4	Knowledge sharing
Employee's training	5	Marketing
Organization's modernization	6	Organization's privacy
Organizational resources	7	Organization's visibility
Organizational barriers	8	External possibilities
Reputation	9	
Flexibility	10	
Talent management	11	
Transparency	12	
In the coming 5 years, social media will influence the role of HR professionals		
Need for knowledge of web-based applications	1	HR professionals' collaboration with marketing
Need to develop specific skills	2	HR professionals' knowledge of business processes
Need of knowledge in Marketing and Communication Studies	3	HR professionals' networking skills

Table 2. Continued.

Academics		Practitioners
Need for knowledge of social structures in organizations	4	HR professionals' knowledge of IT and e-applications
HR policies	5	HR professionals' interactive role
Strategic role	6	HR professionals' knowledge of marketing
Development of new roles	7	HR professionals' informative role
Segmentation considering HR practices	8	HR professionals' innovative thinking
Need for knowledge and understanding of legal implications	9	HR professionals' awareness of recruitment trends
Image of HR in organization	10	

> The difference in social media is that it can be used by many functions of the organization, and the consequences extend further than HR.

Another correlation resulting from the second round among academics was "Ways of Communication/HR competencies." Only one respondent ranked this category as his number one choice, the rest gave it 2 or 3. Moreover, as the last quote from the previous category suggests, new ways of communication with employees are paramount; social media will influence how HR will communicate with applicants and employees, requiring them to be competent in doing so.

A clarification of his most important choice was given by the following respondent:

> The ways HR people, employees and future potential employees communicate get enriched by various social media means. HR staff will need to get new competencies (information systems, internet research, and marketing skills) to properly use and understand the value and implications of social media as communicating, recruiting and marketing tool. The job boundaries between HR, Strategy, Marketing and Operations staff may overlap and require a clear strategic orientation and role descriptions to know what one's job will entail in the future and what is part of another department's duties.

"Organization's reputation" and "Interactivity with customers" are considered least important by the academics. While the last category has a mode of 5 and a mean of 3.5, one respondent did rank it number 1, and suggested that in the future, social media will influence what it has already started to influence, interactivity with customers: "*When I was ranking the categories, I was thinking of social media like e.g. Facebook, MySpace and Ping, and not professional communities of interest. I gave 1 to the interactivity with customers, as that is what companies already do and will even continue building up their presence.*"

Out of the 12 HR practitioners, 4 thought that "Image of the employer" was the most important and 4 more scored it as second. HR practitioners thought that

Table 3: Diverse impacts of social media on employer branding and roles of HR professionals, ranked by consensus among academics and HR professionals.

Academics		Practitioners
In general, in the coming 5 years, social media will influence ...		
Targeting of audience for recruitment	1	Image of the employer
Marketing/Company brand[a]	2	Visibility of the company
Ways of communication/HR competencies[a]	3	Organization responsiveness/Impact on the organization[a]
Organization's reputation	4	Customer role
Interactivity with costumers	5	Recruitment process
In the coming 5 years, social media will influence Value Branding Proposition ...		
Engagement with both employees and applicants	1	Organization image
Opportunities for promoting the organization	2	Communication management
Targeting of special audiences	3	Organization privacy/Organization security[a]
Employee involvement in employer branding activities	4	HRM activities
HRM strategies	5	Time investment
In the coming 5 years, social media will influence Internal Market ...		
Organization's image/Marketing strategies[a]	1	Work–private life boundary
Openness about working at that company	2	Communication in organization/ Knowledge sharing in organization[a]
Internal recruitment	3	Marketing
Organizational boundaries	4	Employees' commitment
Legal implications	5	Organization image
In the coming 5 years, social media will influence External Market ...		
Reputation	1	Organization visibility
Talent management	2	Recruitment strategy
Transparency of organizations	3	Marketing
Competition	4	External possibilities
Employee involvement	5	E-device knowledge

Table 3. Continued.

Academics		Practitioners
In the coming 5 years, social media will influence the role of HR professionals ...		
Need of knowledge in Marketing and Communication studies	1	HR awareness of recruitment trends
Need for web-based applications knowledge/Need to develop new skills[a]	2	HR innovative thinking
Image of HR in organizations	3	HR networking skills
Need to understand legal implications	4	HR informative role
HR policies	5	HR collaboration with marketing

[a]Similarities were identified based on first-round responses and SPSS correlations, thus considered as one category with the common meaning.

communication will be enhanced and will happen faster and easier due to social media. Fewer limits will exist between companies and competitors, candidates, and clients. Customers will have a big impact on exchanging opinions and ultimately on the company's image. Recruitment will also be done online: "*The image of the employer will be in my opinion the one most affected by social media in the upcoming five years since there will be a wider forum to share, discuss and venture meanings about employers.*" The implications will soon be noticed by the employers. In the long run social media will be used for recruiting, and those companies that adopt it and use it properly will gain a competitive advantage:

> This directly affects the organization and especially in the short term, this will be noticeable to employers, and this can also be affected. Please note that in the long term I expect that the recruitment process will be affected the most by social media, however this will take some time before companies recognize the potential competitive advantage the social media can offer to assist them with their recruitment process. I especially expect the middle-big companies (international/national company) to be sceptical about the synergy effects of E-devices and social media.

With a mode of 1, but a mean of 3, "Visibility of the company" was considered another important category that is influenced by social media. Furthermore, brand awareness will become the primary goal of companies. Companies can use social media to attract a valuable workforce and avoid spending time on recruiting inexperienced candidates. If social media become visible, they can enhance the quality of the candidates: "*You probably cannot take the risk of being overlooked by young professionals who are looking for a (new) job because the company was not using the social media technologies to represent itself on the market.*"

"Organization responsiveness" was also considered to be significantly influenced by social media. Five of the HR practitioners placed it in first and second place. The main argumentation was that the mandatory dialogue will take place through social media and will be very quick, but at the same time it demands a constant monitoring and swift reaction.

> The companies will have to cope with a relation that consists of an immediate dialogue that demands a constant monitoring and swift reaction.

Some HR practitioners believed that "Customer role" can be extremely relevant for a social media impact on employer branding. By using social media, companies will go fully online with no privacy. Impressions of happy or angry customers of a company can have significant consequences. Valuable feedback will be obtained from customers, and potential customers' trust in peer-to-peer communication will increase dramatically. Companies should use social media for their own good and encourage online communication: "*Whether the company wants it or not, the customer can and will provide feedback. This will influence other (potential) customers. In my view this is why organizations must join the social media conversation.*" Nevertheless, five HR practitioners graded it 4 and 5, establishing its mode at 5. "Recruitment process" had a mode of 4, due to six HR practitioners who believed it to be one of the least important categories. There was one answer arguing for a no. 1 score: "*There is so much info and there are so many social media that those groups that are most interested will search and participate most with social media and hence will be influenced the most.*"

Impact of social media on value branding proposition.   When it comes to the influence of social media on the employer branding value proposition, the most important categories for academics seemed to be Engagement with both employees and applicants, Opportunities for promoting the organization, and Targeting for specific audience.

> Social media is about involving and engaging employees and applicants, they will also be much more strongly involved in proposing employer brand value.

> Organizations all over the world are moving towards a strong presence in the social media world as employees and applicants spend a predominant time on social media networks. In an effort to stay engaged with both employees and applicants, organizations will be socially active.

One academic explained that he selected this particular category as the most important one because it can be a general term for the other three categories: "*I selected engagement as the most important because it is a broader category than can include some of the others (e.g., employee involvement in employer branding activities would be part of an engagement strategy).*"

Opportunities for promoting the organization came second in this category for the academics. An interesting explanation came from one respondent which not only explained why he made his decision but also suggested the potential dangers of social media for value proposition creation:

> I assume that communication, promotion and marketing an organization's brand is key to social media and the opportunities will increase further. Yet engagement between employees and potential applicants needs to be considered with a critical lens — what HR people may like and

find innovative may be annoying for an organization's customers and applicants. HR staff should not get the idea to spy and over-do social media campaigns yet employer branding without social media may belong to the past web 1.0 generation. Interactivity will increase but also the dangers to it and strategy planning to manage a positive image.

There was a pattern in the academics' responses. Some categories were similar in content and purpose but for different propositions; it seemed that those who chose to consider social media as a platform for promotion and marketing responded similarly, choosing their number one category per proposition in a manner related to their previous response:

> Following on from my thoughts as stated above, the opportunities presented to the organization through social media are in relation to marketing and branding. As part of the proliferation of information, organizations will be able to promote their organization, operations and products and services. Through social media avenues like Facebook, they will be able to disseminate lots and lots of information.

> Again, I am choosing my number 1 rank based upon the assumption or observation that social media is not used as much for intra-organizational purposes but for interacting with external stakeholders.

> I have given 1 again to a more marketing-related category. I think that if companies have to choose they would first and foremost pursue marketing objectives, and only then focus on activities like involving employees through social media.

Second-round findings discussed "Targeting for specific audience" because it was present for more than one proposition. This suggests it could be of some importance for the academics. Although it was mostly ranked as 1 for the previous category, it was somewhere in the middle for value proposition. Nevertheless, it is an important category since it was ranked 2 and 3.

Employee involvement in employer branding activities closely follows Targeting for specific audience, while HRM strategies is a category ranked as 4 and 5 by the majority of academics. Only one respondent considered it difficult to rank the categories, because in his view, "*social media will influence in some way HRM strategies in general (recruitment, HR policies, competence management etc.).*"

According to the results of the 12 HR practitioners, most of them had the same idea about the most and the least important categories of employer branding value proposition. The top three preferences of practitioners were organization image, communication management, and organization privacy/organization security.

More than half of the HR practitioners believed that "organization image" would be affected by the usage of employer branding through social media. Seven respondents graded this category as 1 and another two as 2. HR practitioners think that "B*y using social media as a company you can quickly and easily bring out the image you want into the outside world. Even if you do not use them, that will send out a message by itself* ..."

> Nothing is hidden any more. If you are not a good employer, everybody will know in a few seconds. What you express to your customers must be aligned with what you give to your employees. When you provide your customers with the most customer-friendly tools to order your products, you must provide your employees the same standard. External = internal & vice versa.

The distance between the first and the second items is considerable. If the majority supported the first one, only five answers placed "communication management" among the first two important categories. According to the HR practitioners, communication within companies has to be smooth, so the external messages are connected to the internal vision, and the speed of the external dialogues can be really fast.

The third most important category of employer branding value proposition, "organization privacy/organization security," was considered important because *"social media themselves become important for growing numbers of employees for diverse reasons. Many organizations block employees from the use of social media (and downloading the associated programs). This is for reasons of security/privacy. This means a gap between certain propositions as being a modern employer and real life."*

Although there was a big difference between the most important category of employer branding value proposition, HR practitioners agreed which ones were the least important. Therefore, for the item HRM activities, even if it had a modal score of 4 like organization privacy, the mean was calculated as 3.58, unlike organization privacy which had a mean of 2.91. Also, no answer placed this item as being the most important, the grades starting from 2.

Time investment in employer branding was considered the least important, with a modal score of 5. In complete contrast to the most important item (organization image), the Time investment scored 7 grades of 5.

Impact of social media on internal market. Regarding the influence of social media on the Internal Market, academics chose organization's image/marketing strategies, Openness about working at that company, and Internal recruitment as the most important aspects.

Academic respondents made a reference when ranking organization's image/ marketing strategies to their number one choice for value proposition, Opportunities for promoting the company, suggesting that both aspects are related, and social media will mainly influence them.

> Through social media, organizations will be able to disseminate information about many facets of the organization and its operations both externally and internally. Organizations will use social media to inform and educate internal stakeholders who will then be able to better represent the organization and its operations. This dissemination of information is believed to have a number of positive implications for the organization.

> As for the internal labor market, I believe that social media will contribute to the employees' idea that transparency and open communication are valuable for the company, thus sustaining meritocratic career paths.

> Various social media applications eventually impact an organization's image. Organizations may not be fully aware of positive/negative digital communication.

The "Internal recruitment" category is the middle one, mostly ranked 2 and 3, despite one academic who suggested that social media will mainly influence internal recruitment *"by easily identifying experts, competencies within the company (ex. some companies are developing their own social network)."*

"Organizational boundaries" was another category on the mind of only one respondent who argued that "*with social media, organization boundaries are becoming blurred in general — this should have an impact on the internal labor market. I see several of these concepts as very much related to the idea of organizational boundaries.*" As for "legal implications," with a mean of 4.5 and a mode of 5, it seems obvious that academics predicted that social media will not have any important impact on this aspect of internal marketing.

The most important aspects of Employer Branding Internal Market for the HR practitioners were Work–private life boundary, Communication in organization/ Knowledge sharing in organization, and marketing.

"Work–private life boundary" represented the most important category of the internal market, chosen by seven of the HR practitioners, because "*the social media are used in both professional and private matters, therefore the boundary will fade away. Social media are used so much to stay connected to 'friends,' but also to build up a professional network. The boundaries between these different kinds of networks will gradually diminish.*"

> The organizational exposure via social media will increase the most in the upcoming five years, since the gross of employees tends to use social media to share their e.g. working activities, organizational news, and upcoming vacancies with the forum of social media. Additionally, their private posting could be associated with the company's image by the forum's audience. E.g. pictures of drunken people at a lawyer's Friday afternoon drink on the forum, could tarnish their professional image. Therefore, companies will have to keep a close watch on the postings of their employees to see if these postings don't conflict with their working activities.

Built as one big cluster from the connection of "Communication in organization and Knowledge sharing on organization," it was considered to be second in importance by the HR practitioners, with a modal score of 2 and a mean of 2.33.

> social media will give us the means to share knowledge and expertise, and shall enable us to communicate directly with each other. Boundaries between departments can disappear.

HR practitioners, who placed this item in first place, also presented strong arguments from their own experience.

> Internal knowledge does not through go the line, but through social media it gets faster and more effective and you can communicate both internally (eg Yammer) and externally. We are currently using Yammer internally and it works very well in terms of knowledge.

The third aspect, *marketing*, with a modal score of 2 like *Communication in organization/Knowledge sharing on organization* but a mean of 2.83, was chosen by the HR practitioners as being relevant for the impact that social media will have on employer branding.

The two remaining clusters were considered as being the least important ones for this study. *Employee commitment* as well as *organization image* were not the first choice for any of the HR practitioners. Moreover, *Employee commitment* did not even get any grades of 2, being considered totally irrelevant.

Impact of social media on external market. In the view of academics, social media will mostly impact the following categories of external marketing: Reputation, talent management and transparency of organizations. Respondents gave explanations for these most important categories:

> External Market will be mostly influenced by the opportunities and risks to an organization's reputation. New opportunities for talent management will emerge, and innovative companies may benefit from 'first mover' advantages. Increasing transparency of organizations will require new jobs to be created to manage an organization's online image (blogs, forums, Facebook, company profiles, etc.).

> Information disseminated through the various mechanisms of social media will have implications for an organization's reputation. The information shared has the potential to be both positive and negative, but either way, an array of stakeholders will have access to more real-time information about an organization, its operations as well as the conduct and opinions of their internal and external stakeholders.

> Talent management will become more of a challenge in many ways due to social media. While it allows new opportunities for talent management, it also becomes more difficult in part because of effects on competition (increasing) and reputation (harder to control).

Social media for external marketing will impact talent management "*by establishing long-term relationships with a talent pool, even before the beginning of the recruitment process.*"

Although only one respondent ranked this category as number 1, transparency in organizations was mentioned more than once in other responses, suggesting that in the future, academics do believe social media will have on impact on it, but not as much as for the other categories:

> I think social media can contribute to give a more realistic image of the organization and let the potential employees have an idea of the organizational culture and kind of work environment. What is critical for candidates is to understand what is reality and what is just image, but social media should be of help also in this case, because of the opportunity of finding people who had a direct experience in that organization.

For practitioners, the top three most important aspects of External Market were organization visibility, recruitment strategy, and marketing.

In terms of internal marketing, the choices HR professionals made differed to some extent. For example, seven respondents thought that the extent to which an organization is visible on the external market is of great importance, arguing that "*People go and look for organizations or subjects that are associated with an organization on internet. If you are not visible, you can forget it! This applies to recruitment (which becomes important over the years due to a graying population, baby-boomers, etc.) but also for marketing success.*"

Having a modal score of 2 and a mean of 2.58, the "recruitment strategy" proved to be important for the future of employer branding through social media. "*Social media (and more broadly internet) brings changes in the time people spend on different types of media and the ways they look for jobs. To reach potential employees, traditional recruitment strategies must be reconsidered.*"

Similar to the internal marketing, the marketing aspect was in the top three relevant categories of employer branding. Half of the HR practitioners placed it in the first two places and half placed it at third and fourth. No 5 scores were given, leading to a modal score of 3 and a mean of 2.58.

HR practitioners believed that *"marketing will definitely change. Social media will strengthen the concept of fans and followers."*

With respect to the "e-device knowledge," two HR practitioners believed that it will be highly impacted by social media:

> The knowledge about the synergy effects of E-devices on the competitive advantage is still very scarce among companies, i.e. companies do not yet fully embody E-devices within their company strategy. The upcoming social media provides more opportunities for E-device suppliers to strengthen the synergy effects of E-devices and integrate this more obviously in the marketing of the short-term and long-term advantages of E-devices. Thereby companies could be tempted to invest more in E-device technologies.

Impact of social media on the roles of HR professionals.   According to the academics, HR professionals will be influenced by social media as they will need in the future to possess Knowledge in Marketing and Communication Studies and Knowledge for Web-based applications/develop new skills. Overall, academics thought that social media will impact the Image of HR in organizations.

> In order to best represent their organization and its operations, HR professionals will need to be aware of the organization's marketing strategy, business strategy and how both of these align with the organization's HR strategy. If organizations are to use social media in a way that is beneficial for them, then HR will need to understand and recognize these opportunities rather than be concerned with controlling the use of the technologies. This may require a change in mindset for more traditional HR professionals.

> HR professionals will have to learn how to use social media as a tool to properly package and diffuse their solutions — this could correlate strongly with the success of their interventions.

> HR professionals have already begun using the word communication, and the focus on communication is increasing. In some companies I have studied, HR departments have already begun recruiting employees with degrees from communication-related studies.

> I feel HR staff first need to become aware of the changing role requirements and evaluate various social media tools to communicate with current and future employees. Larger organizations may give the social media/communicating/promotion role to separate departments and not the HR function, while smaller organizations may embed more responsibilities such as developing web-based knowledge, marketing skills and legal knowledge of online communication into the HR role. The boundaries between marketing, HR and IS jobs need to get re-designed.

> There probably will be national differences as some cultures are more jealous of their privacy than others. As we know, there are already strong differences in the way that personal data can be shared with others between Europe, the USA and many other nations. This suggests that, in some countries, the need to understand legal implications and develop appropriate HR policy will be higher than in others. Regardless, I believe that the need to "stay on top" of new skills and ongoing technological developments will be of great importance for HR pros.

The Image of HR professionals in organizations was ranked as 2 and 3. The image created by a company was among the preferences of academics for other propositions, so it seemed natural for them to suggest that the HR image will also be impacted by social media:

> I think social media give the HR Department the opportunity to communicate more directly with both potential employees and the internal labor market, thus letting people have direct perceptions of its initiatives and actions.

Although the legal implications category was chosen for both the role of HR and Internal Marketing, and despite one particular academic's firm point of view, it seemed that for both cases the respondents suggested that social media will have a higher impact on other aspects of employer branding.

According to the HR professionals, the future of their activity will change a lot due to the usage of employer branding through social media. As shown in the table above, the HR awareness of recruitment trends, HR innovative thinking, and HR networking skills are aspects that will mainly suffer. Although the aim of their activity will still remain recruitment, HR professionals will have to be continuously updated on what is new in matters of recruitment.

> The market of social media and reaching people is changing in such a fast manner, you need to be constantly up to date with the latest trends. Otherwise, you cannot distinguish yourself from other organizations and you lack visibility. Or even, using other methods makes you invisible.

With a modal score equal to HR awareness on recruitment trends, the HR innovative thinking had a mean of 2.83, which made it second in importance for HR practitioners.

> To make sure the skills to use social media are truly embedded in an organization, HR needs to think innovatively and coach the entire organization. Social media is not something that can be managed by just a web-care team or a department. Every individual can play a role in (re)presenting the organization. Some people will already be good at it, others need some more support.

> Social media are already used commonly by companies to advertise for vacancies or to market their image. The key advantage HR professionals can provide with regard to social marketing is to use their innovative way of thinking to take competitive advantage of social media which isn't apparent at the moment for those companies. I expect that the embodying of e-devices will free up time for HR professionals (e.g. administrative HR activities can be done in a less time-consuming way), thereby the HR professionals can focus on creating and delivering competitive advantage via social media & HR in the company strategy. The role for innovative thinking is thereby expedient in order to create such a competitive advantage.

HR must be more commercial and focus more on networking skills. These skills will soon be necessary for the proper people at the right time and at the right price to recruit and earn your loyalty. HR plays a key role.

HR collaboration with marketing was considered the least important for the changes social media might bring. It had a modal score of 3 and a mean of 3.16. HR informative role had a modal score of 5 and a mean of 3.41, but was still considered as being the most important aspect by two HR professionals.

Discussion

When Information Technologies entered the lives of HR professionals, it heralded a fundamental change for the employees stuck behind their piles of documents and papers. They were promised that an IT specialist would help them understand and facilitate the usage of IT programs for HR purposes and that this would be the new way of managing HR matters. It was a matter of transition that would eventually settle into a state of equilibrium. This study, like many others that tackle social media, is here to prove that this change within the HR department is bigger than was anticipated.

When it comes to the role of HR professionals and the impact social media might have on it, our respondents agreed that in the future we will see more HR pros with Marketing and Communication Studies and that more knowledge regarding web-based applications is needed. Why is this important? It indicates that social media usage might determine the competences of HR professionals in the future. Currently, they are required to skillfully master the HR delivery and be competent in using various technological programs aimed at facilitating their work. Now more than ever, if social media is becoming a part of their strategy, they will need to learn/know the principles and tricks of using them and communicating in a professional demeanor. This raises questions for future research on the role of HR professionals within a company. Is it important and cost efficient for them to engage in employer branding activities through social media that require technical, marketing, and communications knowledge? Or should these activities be passed to marketing or PR specialists, who have this knowledge but lack the HRM understanding? Or should there be a new position within the HR department, such as community manager or social media manager, as some respondents suggested? Also interesting and related to the topic of branding and change is the conclusion of a recent study on social media, *"when so much is changing, can we still claim we are practicing brand management? Or, is it time for a new paradigm to take hold?"* (Fournier & Avery, 2011, p. 206).

As regards Marketing Studies, it seems fair that respondents consider it relevant to possess marketing knowledge since they also feel that social media will have an impact on the company brand and on the marketing of the organization as an employer. According to the panelists, social media will provide the opportunity to create a company brand with a unique employer branding strategy through large-scale organizational image marketing. If so, HR professionals might need to know the principles of marketing and branding and apply them for HRM. Marketing and Communication Studies are required so that they can learn how to represent the company online. In addition, using social media for employer branding will also have an impact on the image of the HR department in the organization.

An important aspect of change will affect the way the HR department communicates with the employees and applicants. Social media are already showing that new ways of communication are being chosen by many organizations to interact with their customers, and who knows if in the future employees will eventually end up being contacted with mobile devices. But this new means of communication might mostly influence recruitment, by allowing companies to target the right audience.

Both first-round and third-round respondents mentioned Generation Y, suggesting that since young applicants and graduates are mostly on the web, they will be the first to whom companies will appeal through social media. A study published in April 2011 on SHRM Online warns that "*Employers in the U.S. looking to recruit members of Generation Y for their workforces might want to consider their organizations' social media strategies and incentives, according to survey findings from 8,088 university students from the Class of 2011.*" Labrecque, Markos, and Milne (2011) developed a study on personal online branding which eventually supported the idea "*that people both explicitly and implicitly brand themselves using the content they place online. Professional information displayed in the profile, in terms of education and work experiences, is important, as are pictorial accounts of their social life and the public conversations posted.*" In any case, this draws attention to the authenticity of the information posted on social media platforms. With traditional HR practices, only the resume or cover letter was available to gain an impression of that person. Nowadays, everyone can see an individual's profile on an SNS, even an HR professional looking at a resume that might seem interesting. The chances are that he/she might be impressed by the resume but dislike the pictures, comments, or interests of that person or be impressed by the image intentionality created by the applicant. Either way, there is an influence that could benefit or harm an applicant.

But Generation Y is not the only one that can be targeted for recruitment; it is just the one most present on the web. Targeting for recruitment could also mean focusing on a specific professional or technological audience of interest for a certain company. One respondent pointed out at the beginning of the study that "*some potential employees, who do not use social media as much as younger generations, are unwillingly discriminated against.*" Some questions should be raised about the older generations and how they can be part of the employer branding strategies through social media. "*If we do not properly cope with the rapidly changing socioeconomic activities with social computing, we will face the type of serious digital divide in our society that we have never experienced before, and the problems of that digital divide will be larger than we have ever suffered*" (Jansen, Sobel, & Cook, 2010).

While constructing the theoretical framework of this study, a possible match was developed between the six social media types and employer branding (Figure 1). For each category of employer branding: value proposition, external marketing, and internal marketing, there were suitable types of social media that could be used to enhance some of their characteristics. Although what we proposed resonates with the panelists' opinions, there are some differences as regards value proposition and external marketing.

According to the academics, social media for value proposition will influence the engagement with employees and applicants and provide opportunities to promote the company as an employer. Engagement will be influenced because the availability of information and openness to any comment or opinion will encourage, if companies chose to do so, engaging in conversations, chats, micro blogging, or instant messaging with interested applicants or current employees. It seems that along with social media, there is a new trend in online users, their willingness to participate. "*These individuals seek greater engagement with their preferred brands, and involvement — with or without the company's approval — in creating brand personalities*" (Parent, Plangger, & Bal, 2011, p. 219).

Similarly, this particular study proposes that companies, when creating their value proposition, could make use of different social media platforms for peer-to-peer communication, knowledge sharing, creation of a trustworthy image, organizational advertising, creation of an objective company image, and creation of a virtual company to promote it. Next in importance for the academics was targeting of the audience for recruitment, a category that came up twice in different propositions; it is then clear that in the future social media will impact this characteristic of employer branding, as also discussed above.

Academics predicted that social media will influence employer branding by providing the opportunity to target the audience and by allowing companies to communicate the branding and value proposition to a specific target, while this study only took into consideration targeting a specific group through external marketing.

We have discussed marketing strategies and creation of a desirable brand or image, but it is important to understand how they are connected to a company's reputation. With social media everything is connected and all the information is open and available, that is why academics consider that "*social media will have an enormous effect on reputation*" and "*external marketing will be mostly influenced by the opportunities and risks to an organization's reputation.*" Why? Because a company's reputation as an employer has probably the highest impact on its image, branding, and marketing; "*it is the currency in which Web 2.0 brands deal regularly*" (Fournier & Avery, 2011, p. 203). This is why respondents were suggesting that "*if companies fail to deliver the set of benefits they suggest through their employer branding, individuals will have the potential to express mass negative feelings.*" These negative feelings may harm their reputation, and promoting the employer branding strategy through social media will be extremely difficult because the negative information is available to everyone for a long period of time. This brings up another important aspect for the academics, transparency of organizations. A recent study on branding and social media took this into account, considering it the age of transparency where the "*availability of and convenient access to information is one of the more empowering and revolutionary forces of the Internet. Previously the venue of trained journalists, now anyone with a casual interest can decipher the story behind the story and figure out when a company is misrepresenting the truth*" (Fournier & Avery, 2011, p. 198). It is important for organizations and HR professionals to promote the truth and the real image within the company when using social media, because everyone has the freedom to express their opinion at an unimaginable speed and to share that opinion with others.

Talent management will also be influenced by the social media. There are two possibilities, either talented applicants are attracted and selected according to the external marketing strategy or, as one respondent pointed out, "*it will become more of a challenge in many ways due to social media. While it allows new opportunities for talent management, it also becomes more difficult in part because of effects on competition (increasing) and reputation (harder to control).*"

We established that targeting a specific audience for recruiting will be influenced by social media in the future. What will also impact employer branding, specifically Internal Marketing, is the organization's image and marketing strategies when deciding to use social media. If companies choose to use social media for internal marketing, they have to be aware that the most important thing they have to keep in mind is the strategy they plan and the image they want to promote to their employees. This is why respondents eventually decided that HR professionals would need to have knowledge of marketing, because they will have to create and communicate these strategies to the employees. Moreover, internal marketing through social media would allow more openness to the outside world about how it is to work at that company, using the help of their employees, if permitted.

According to the match assumed by the researchers between social media and internal marketing, companies can strategically market their image and be open about their working environment by formally and informally communicating with the employees, allowing them to express their opinions of how it is to work there and by advertising the company through their employees, all on different social media platforms.

Perhaps the most noticeable difference lies in the prediction of social media's influence on the role of HR professionals. Academics say we will see a greater Marketing/Communication background, technological competencies, and image created for the HR department. On the other hand, practitioners think that in the future the social media will impact their HR awareness on recruitment trends, HR innovative thinking and HR networking. In their view, HR professionals will have to be continuously updated on what is new in the matters of recruitment, "*use their innovative way of thinking to take competitive advantage of social media*" and "*must be more commercial, and focus more on networking skills. These skills will soon be necessary for the proper people at the right time and at the right price to recruit and earn your loyalty. HR plays a key role.*"

All in all, there is not just one answer to the research question, "What is the future of employer branding through social media?" We cannot say it will be bright, dark, better, or worse. Social media will definitely be used for employer branding activities, and it will have an important impact on its creation of strategy. In the minds of our respondents, knowledge of marketing will be required to build proper strategies aimed at enhancing and promoting the organizational image as an employer, reputation, company brand, talent management, internal recruitment, and targeting a specific audience for recruitment. Information will be more transparent, and companies will be more open to the audiences about how it is to work at that company. HR competences will change; they will need to have knowledge of web-based applications and marketing/communication studies, all reflecting a better image of the HR department. So before any company chooses social media for their employer branding, they should first discover whether they are willing to accept these changes.

Conclusions

To determine what will be the future of employer branding through social media in the next 5 years was a difficult task even for a group of experts already dealing with this issue. Round one was full of qualitative information that needed to be compressed in a way that would allow all the experts to have an idea of each other's opinions. The Delphi method was chosen based on its characteristics such as forecasting orientation, controlled feedback, iterative and reflective communications with respondents, and the consensus goal reached.

This study tackled a subject that has not been discussed before in the literature, and it opens the door to new research and understanding of how social media will work for employer branding. We propose continuing the research with a higher number of respondents and using different characteristics of employer branding, either internal or external marketing or the roles of HR professionals. This study explicitly shows that there is a future with social media for employer branding, and it is up to others to go into more depth.

Acknowledgment

The authors are thankful to Lieke van der Steen for the design support in preparing this manuscript.

References

Bach, S. (2007). *Personnel management in transition in managing human resources in context* (pp. 3–45). Blackwell Publishing.

Backhaus, K., & Tikoo, S. (2004). Conceptualizing and researching employer branding. *Career Development International, 9*(5), 501–517.

Balmer, J. M. T., & Gray, E. R. (2003). Corporate brands. What are they? What of them? *European Journal of Marketing, 37*(7–8), 972–997.

Bobeva, M., & Day, J. (2002). *A generic toolkit for the successful management of Delphi studies business school.* Bournemouth University, UK: Institute of Business and Law.

Brethon, P., Ewing, M., & Hah, L. L. (2005). Captivating company: Dimensions of attractiveness in employer branding. *International Journal of Advertising, 24*, 151–173.

Coon, M. (2010). *Social media marketing: Successful case studies of businesses using Facebook and YouTube with an in depth look into the business use of Twitter.* Communication Stanford MA project. Retrieved from http://communication.stanford.edu/coterm/projects/2010/maddy%20coon.pdf

Dalkey, N. C. (1969). *The Delphi method: An experimental study of group opinion.* Rand Santa Monica, CA: The Rand Corporation.

Davies, G. (2008). Employer branding and its influence on managers. *European Journal of Marketing, 42*(5–6), 667–681.

Edwards, M. R. (2010). An integrative review of employer branding and OB theory. *Personnel Review, 39*(1), 5–23.

Fichter, D. (2007). How social is your website? Top five tips for social media optimization. *Onlinenmag*, pp. 57–60.

Fournier, S., & Avery, J. (2011). The uninvited brand. *Business Horizons, 54*, 193–207.

Hasson, F., Keeney, S., & McKenna, H. (2000). Research guidelines for the Delphi survey technique. *Journal of Advanced Nursing, 32*(4), 1008–1015.

Jansen, B. J., Sobel, K., & Cook G. (2010). Gen X and Y's attitudes on using social media platforms for opinion sharing. *CHI 2010*, ACM, New York, NY (pp. 3853–3858).

Kaplan, A. M., & Haenelein, M. (2010). Users of the world unite! The challenges and opportunities of social media. *Business Horizons, 53*, 59–68.

Labrecque, L., Markos, E., & Milne, G. (2011). Online personal branding: Processes, challenges and implications. *Journal of Interactive Marketing, 25*, 37–50.

Landeta, J. (2006). Current validity of the Delphi method in social sciences. *Technological Forecasting & Social Change, 73*, 467–482.

Lievens, F., Van Hoye, G., & Anseel, F. (2007). Organizational identity and employer image: Towards a unifying framework. *British Journal of Management, 18*, 45–59.

Okoli, C., & Pawlowski, S. D. (2004). Delphi method as a research tool: An example, design considerations and applications. *Information & Management, 42*(1), 15–29.

Parent, M., Plangger, K., & Bal, A. (2011). The new WTP: Willingness to participate. *Business Horizons, 54*, 219–229.

Reichenberg, N. (2009). Branding the government as an employer of choice. Retrieved from http://unpan1.un.org/intradoc/groups/public/documents/UN/UNPAN021819.pdf. Accessed on November 10, 2010.

Rowe, G., & Wright, G. (1999). The Delphi technique as a forecasting tool: Issues and analysis. *International Journal of Forecasting, 15*, 353–375.

Skulmoski, G. J., & Hartman, F. T. (2007). The Delphi method for graduate research. *Journal of Information Technology Education, 6*, 1–21.

Swartz, J. (2010). Social media's effects on marketing. *USA Today*, August.

Chapter 3

Recruiting Gen Yers through Social Media: Insights from the Italian Labor Market [☆]

Rita Bissola and Barbara Imperatori

Abstract

Purpose — The aim of this chapter is to explore employee behaviors and expectations of the role of social media when searching for jobs, to offer recruiters and companies valuable insights to design and manage appropriate web-based employer branding and recruitment strategies.

Methodology — The research strategy is based on semi-structured in-depth interviews involving 34 central informants: talented Gen Yers and social media recruitment experts and mangers. The project focuses on the Italian context, an exemplary country with the highest social media penetration rate.

Findings — The results demonstrate the "bounded" popularity of social media as a recruitment tool among Gen Yers who implement up to five active and passive behaviors, albeit not all widespread, according to varying patterns and using different social media for different purposes: *receiving, seeking, sharing, leading*, and *experiencing*. Gen Yers, with aims that vary in line with various staffing phases, collect and share rumors and voices from both internal and controlled organizational sources but also, and above all, from external and organizational sources that companies do not control directly.

Practical implications — Social media seem to offer appealing and valuable opportunities to attract and engage talented young individuals, sustaining the *quality, quantity*, and *fairness* of employment relationships. Conversely, they also involve some organizational risks and costs. The chapter offers some managerial cautions and

---

[☆] Authors contributed equally and are listed in alphabetical order.

Social Media in Human Resources Management
Advanced Series in Management, 59–81
Copyright © 2013 by Emerald Group Publishing Limited
All rights of reproduction in any form reserved
ISSN: 1877-6361/doi:10.1108/S1877-6361(2013)0000012007

advocates a radical change in the prevalent HRM mindset for the improved management of transparency that social media solutions entail.

Originality/value — Results contribute in understanding *how* social media can better sustain employer branding and recruitment activities, especially considering the needs and expectations of talented young employees and professionals in the Italian context. Italy is an emblematic context, where the social media potential appears to be extremely interesting, considering its high rate of social media penetration.

Keywords: Y generation; e-HRM practices; person-organization fit; Web 2.0 recruitment; employer branding; talent management

Introduction

Employer branding and recruitment activities, particularly concerning young employees and highly qualified and competent applicants on an international scale, have in the last decade essentially switched to the Internet. The Internet allows reaching a potentially global audience, thus enabling attracting competent individuals and to better manage the shortfall of talent (Ployhart, 2006). Firms are aware of this success and many are already using social networks for marketing purposes, such as advertising and communication, virtual product sales, and marketing research (Bradley & McDonald, 2011).

More recently, organizations are also considering virtual social worlds in terms of the opportunities they offer in the HRM domain (Kaplan & Haenlein, 2010). The huge success of social media is currently challenging organizations, requiring them to rethink their HRM practices and, specifically, their staffing activities in view of the ideological and technological revolution that social media has brought about especially with regard to participant connectivity, user-generation content, information sharing, and collaboration (Martin, Reddington, & Kneafsey, 2009).

Despite the social relevance of this phenomenon, empirical evidence on the possible outcomes of using social media for employer communication and recruitment purposes is still limited and controversial. The scarce academic literature on the topic mainly examines success and failure case studies and provides managerial suggestions predominantly on *what* the possibilities and the potential risks related to social media use are, but not on *how* to design and implement effective solutions to manage the emerging and new social media challenges.

Based on the P-O fit framework, which enables us to adopt a relational perspective, and considering the limited literature on Web 2.0 recruiting practices, this study aims to make a step forward in understanding how social media can better sustain employer branding and recruitment activities, especially considering the needs and expectations of talented prospective employees and professionals. Our aim is to understand the needs and expectations of the different parties involved in employment relationships as well as the state of the art and development perspective of social media in terms of employer branding and recruitment strategies, with particular attention to the Italian context.

Italy is an emblematic context, where the social media potential appears to be extremely high, also considering that this country has the highest rate of social media penetration, with 86% of Internet users accessing social networks. Moreover, social media are most popular in Italy, Brazil, Spain, and France, thus confirming that the Latin culture appears to be more familiar with the new way of communicating (State of the Media: The Social Media Report, Nielsen, 2011).

The chapter is organized as follows. In the first part, we present our research framework combining the Person-Environment fit literature, Generational Theory approach, and the social media context. In the second part, in accordance with our exploratory aim, we propose a study involving 34 key informants within the recruitment and social media context to capture trends, alignments, and misalignments between applicant behaviors and recruiter practices in relation to social media solutions. The results enable us, in the third part of the chapter, to discuss both theoretical and managerial implications. Conclusions and future research steps complete the chapter.

Attracting Talent in the 21st Century

P-O Fit and Staffing Challenges

Our study frames Gen Y preferences and behaviors during recruitment and staffing processes in the Person-Environment (P-E) fit literature (Ployhart, 2006). In fact, P-E fit theory states that the complementarity between individual features (e.g., needs, values, or competences) and environmental characteristics (e.g., job supply, job requirements, or organizational values) is an important predictor of attitudes and behaviors such as satisfaction, commitment, engagement, and turnover (Krisof-Brown, Zimmerman, & Johnson, 2005). P-E fit is a type of umbrella framework traditionally pertaining to the stress domain that aggregates perspectives on either the fit between employee values and the environmental offer to fulfill these values (S-V fit) or the fit between environmental demands and employee abilities (D-A fit) (Edwards, 1996). Among the topics that form part of the P-E fit concept, Person-Job fit (P-J fit) and Person-Organization fit (P-O fit) are specifically relevant in recruitment and selection research, since these promote applicant self-screening, should increase applicant attraction to the organization and the intention to remain in the selection process. In this case, P-J fit should be considered in terms of expectations (Bunderson, 2001).

Another important issue in the fit domain is that the strategy to assess fit can be both subjective, by directly asking people to report their perceived fit, and objective, when researchers indirectly assess fit through the explicit comparison of separately rated Person and Job or Organization characteristics (Krisof-Brown et al., 2005). With reference to our study, the subjective perspective of P-O and P-J fit is particularly relevant since our main aim is to understand the functionalities and characteristics of recruitment and selection practices developed in a Web 2.0 environment that attract, and are appreciated by, Gen Yers. This is appropriate to investigate since literature has demonstrated that P-O and P-J fit predicts the positive outcomes of the employee–organization relationship such as performance, strain, withdrawal behaviors, tenure, and intention to quit (Dineen, Ash, & Noe, 2002; Krisof-Brown et al., 2005; Ployhart, 2006).

In particular, in the context of web-based recruitment, Dineen et al. (2002) found that both feedback level and objective P-O positively relate to attraction. Subjective P-O fit fully mediates these relationships. In addition, self-esteem and agreement with P-O fit feedback moderate both the relationship between objective P-O fit and attraction on one hand, and the level of P-O fit feedback and attraction on the other. Similarly, Hu, Su, and Chen (2007) found that people with high subjective P-O fit receiving high P-O fit feedback reported higher attraction. Moreover, an interaction effect was found between P-O fit feedback and consistency between this information and the subjective P-O fit. Both these results were obtained through an experiment that considered the real-time interactive feedback of websites. These therefore emerge as particularly relevant in further avenues of investigation, such as expanding the research domain to the staffing phase and considering data collected on the job market.

Based on the P-J and P-O fit framework, our research is of an exploratory nature in the budding but uncharted field of "recruitment and staffing in the Web 2.0 era" and aims to investigate the habits and expectations of Y Gen employees with reference to Web 2.0 functionalities. The evidence is then compared with the ideas and considerations of other relevant actors in this domain, that is, Web 2.0 specialists and recruiters on the firm side. This study is also consistent with the call for a more rigorous theoretical foundation of empirical studies in the field of web recruitment and staffing (Hu et al., 2007).

The New Employees: Gen Yers at Work

According to Generational Theory (Strauss & Howe, 1991), Generation Y designates a cohort of people born between 1982 and 2003 (Strauss, Howe, & Markiewicz, 2006). There are various studies describing Gen Yers from different perspectives: from a wider sociological point of view (Howe & Strauss, 2000; Wilson & Gerber, 2008) to more work-related and managerial approaches (Alsop, 2008; Dries, Pepermans, & De Kerpel, 2008; Twenge & Campbell, 2008; Wong, Gardiner, Lang, & Coulon, 2008).

Wilson and Gerber (2008) identify seven Gen Yer distinguishing traits. They are "special" in terms of their parents' care; "sheltered," namely, wrapped in cotton wool; "confident," namely, optimistic about their future prospects; "team-oriented," that is, skilled in their collaborative efforts; "achieving," particularly in respect of their careers, without involvement in idealistic activities; "pressured," especially by their workaholic parents; and finally, "conventional," namely strongly attached to parents and family even if born in a divorce culture.

Alsop (2008), from a managerial perspective, describes Gen Yers as having a strong sense of entitlement. Their work expectations include high pay, flexible working hours, fast-track careers, and work–life balance. They multitask and have low power distance attitudes.

While baby boomers make decisions based on data and facts, postmodern youths are more likely to make decisions based on the influence of their own peers. Rather than making independent decisions based on core values, they live in a culture encouraging them to embrace community values, and to reach consensus. Y Gens seek more than just friendships, they want community: to be understood, accepted, respected, and included (Wong et al., 2008).

Proserpio and Gioia (2007), focusing more on the technological side, describe them as the Virtual Generation, familiar with virtual technologies and hence characterized by virtual cognitive, learning, and communication styles, requiring aligned pedagogical teaching and means of interaction: nonlinear, virtual, autonomous, networked, and conceiving learning as fun.

From a generational perspective, although they differ from the previous Generation X, there are still numerous gray areas concerning their work expectations and careers drivers (Dries et al., 2008). How to design effective organizational systems to manage them is still an enigma (D'Amato & Herzfeldt, 2008; Erickson, Alsop, Nicholson, & Miller, 2009; Howe & Strauss, 2000).

New HR Practices: Employer-Brand Image and Staffing Strategy through Social Media

Social media — or Web 2.0 applications — are collaborative online solutions that enable participation, connectivity, user-generated content, sharing of thoughts, views, information, and personal details among a community of users; they encourage people to share ideas, promoting discussion, and fostering a greater sense of community (Baumann, 2006; Beer & Burrows, 2007). Web 2.0 could be seen as triggering new possibilities to change the emphasis from browsing and consuming to participating and contributing and allows users to contribute to discussions, to watch and listen to streaming video and audio, provide feedback, and participate in conversations (Beer & Burrows, 2007; Dearstyne, 2007).

Social media include a variety of technologies and online environments, such as social networking sites, wikis, blogs, podcasts, online virtual worlds. They influence a wide range of user behaviors in almost all life activities and contexts, such as interpersonal communications processes and social ties, consumer actions, entertainment, as well as work-related behaviors (Kaplan & Haenlein, 2010; Kietzmann, Hermkens, McCarthy, & Silvestre, 2011).

In terms of the work context, social media are challenging the role of HR departments, enabling new e-HRM practices and suggesting new HR professional competencies and profiles (Bradley & McDonald, 2011; Martin et al., 2009; Ruel, Bondarouk, & Looise, 2004). They can be considered as new opportunities to sustain and develop employee attraction and brand perception, offering the possibility to personalize labor relationships, giving authentic voice to employees and signaling company investments in the employee–organization relationship (Bissola & Imperatori, 2009; Dearstyne, 2007; Tapscott & Williams, 2007).

Social media are challenging the way companies recruit and how applicants search for jobs (Henderson & Bowley, 2010). Thanks to Web 2.0 applications, job seekers have greater access to more jobs and information while recruiters have greater access to more candidates while maintaining constant connectivity and communication (Wandel, 2008).

There is preliminary evidence that the use of Web 2.0 can create a variety of recruitment and employer branding opportunities as well as positive outcomes from an HRM perspective.

Social media enable HR professionals to communicate and share organizational images in a "live" and continuous way via advertising and promotional activities to build a positive reputation within the labor market (Scott & Lane, 2000). They offer companies the opportunity to show their "human side" as well as insights into their daily activities that no other medium can provide as easily (Richards, 2007).

Moreover, Web 2.0 enables organizations to open a two-way dialogue by providing applicants with the opportunity to ask questions, express viewpoints, and to better understand organizational processes (Bruning, Dials, & Shirka, 2008). Web 2.0 applications could help companies to build and reinforce personalized and individualized relationships with applicants during the recruitment process (Williams & Verhoeven, 2008), providing opportunities for two-way engagement, personal responses to individual needs, and opportunities to develop relationships between employers and candidates (Gallagher & O'Leary, 2007).

Social media are also useful to reach passive job seekers, using their networks, and enlarging the scope of the organization's recruitment campaign (Furness, 2008; Gallagher & O'Leary, 2007). They can help recruiters to better match jobs to people and to support employer branding (Martin et al., 2009).

Finally, social media could also be a cost-efficient way to search for candidates, enabling employers to collect a greater amount of low-cost information.

However, although the use of Web 2.0 can benefit the staffing process, it also presents challenges and risks. There are, for instance, legal concerns about the use of social networking sites for staffing purpose, since they can potentially disclose marital status, sexuality, and age and thus engender privacy issues and discrimination (Mead, 2008).

Furthermore, Web 2.0 is undoubtedly a rich source of institutional information but also allows collecting noninstitutional information on employers, recruiters, and career opportunities; employers may feel the need to control their own web presence to a greater extent and as a consequence start observing and monitoring the activities of employees who have set up networks around work and employment matters, thereby raising issues of practicality and ethics (Richards, 2007).

These contributions highlight that despite the social relevance of social media and their intrinsic relational and interaction value, the phenomena is still relatively new. Empirical results and evidence on the possible role of social media in employer branding and recruitment processes are still scarce and controversial. It would seem that there are positive opportunities especially considering high technologically sensitive Y Gen employees, but also risks and costs related to monitoring web activities, to developing innovative HR competences and designing new dedicated roles. While companies are facing these dilemmas, HR professionals are exploring new solutions, although no consolidated practices exist.

A significant part of the uncertainty relates to the still unclear behaviors of users when considering social media for employment and work activities. The aim of this chapter is to explore the employee perspective on the role of social media when searching for a job, to help recruiters, and to better design and manage an appropriate web-based employer branding and recruitment strategy, also comparing the employee perspective with the experiences of HR managers and job market professionals.

Method

In accordance with the exploratory nature of our study, the research strategy is based on semi-structured in-depth interviews involving all central informants in the phenomena under study. The research focus mainly concerns young talented individuals and their behaviors and expectations in relation to social media when involved in recruitment processes.

The project aims to analyze the Italian context, which has the highest social media penetration (Nielsen, 2011). As previously stated, the countries where social media are most popular are respectively Italy, Brazil, Spain, and France, thus confirming that the Latin culture is more familiar with the new way of communicating.

The study used a convenience sample of 34 interviewees, among them 26 Y Gens with excellent educational curricula (see Table 1), 5 recruitment experts (3 internal company recruiters and 2 head hunters, all with a strong professional background in the Italian labor market), and 3 social media industry managers (2 from sales and 1 from a service development department).

Our main focus is on understanding how young employees use social media when looking for a new job and when involved in the selection process: what type of activities do they undertake when they are looking for job opportunities? What type of activities do they undertake when they are involved in selection processes? Do they use different social networks for different purposes? What are they looking for in each social network? What do they expect to find in social media with reference to firms and job opportunities? What do they expect companies to do in social networks? What type of information are they interested in?

Table 1: Research sample: Y Gen applicants.

Male	62%
Average age	26.3 years
Professional tenure	≤2 years: 7; >2 and ≤5 years: 10; >5 years: 9
Education	Graduates: 71%; undergraduates: 29%
Background	Technical-scientific: 52%; humanistic: 48%

With the aim of comparing the strategies of young job applicants with those of recruiters, we also interviewed staffing specialists asking them to describe their social media strategies, as well as their opinions on the future development of employer branding and recruitment activities through social media.

Finally, to initially identify the trends of the activities and use of social media, we collected the opinions of some professionals who work for key social networks in Italy or who support companies in defining and implementing their social media strategy. They told us about the opportunities offered to companies in relation to the job market and to future developments in terms of new services and functionalities.

The data analysis employed common grounded theory building methods (Glaser & Strauss, 1967; Miles & Huberman, 1994). All interviews followed a common structure in accordance with the research aims. We adopted an open-ended format in order to collect both factual data and personal impressions. All the interviews were recorded and transcribed. Each researcher independently highlighted "critical events," that is, events or decisions during the recruitment process. Our later comparison of these independent analyses showed substantial agreement. We used an iterative process of cycling between data, emerging theory, and relevant literature (Hargadon & Bechky, 2006).

Results

In line with the state of the art of literature, the aim of our study is exploratory and intended to offer an insight on recruitment in the Web 2.0 era to enable a better understanding of the behaviors, habits, and expectations of actors who constitute the job market (i.e., applicants, recruiting specialists, suppliers of web services). To accomplish this objective, data from each type of player in the job market are first described. This evidence is then compared in the discussion section so that we can frame the alignment between perceived needs and services provided as well as future desires and prospective developments in terms of both technological progress and market evolution. This comparison will also allow highlighting the main recruitment opportunities and challenges in the Web 2.0 environment and open the discussion on implications in both theoretical literature on staffing and on managerial practices in relation to brand image and recruitment and selection practices.

Applicants and Web 2.0

The employees selected to be interviewed in our empirical study are part of Gen Y since, as previously discussed, enterprises are increasingly interested in the talented individuals that belong to this generation and because they are described as employees who master and use these new tools most.

This general assumption is confirmed in our research sample. All 26 young employees interviewed confirmed they use social media for fun and personal reasons.

They also all confirmed knowing that companies are increasingly adopting Web 2.0 for employer branding and recruitment purposes, even if some admitted not using these and did not think they would in future job search activities.

> Of course, I'm on Facebook and I know that companies have their official pages there. I use it and social media in general in my spare time for fun! I've never thought of using them to look for a new job. I don't think they can be useful for this purpose. I don't think they are reliable and safe. Traditional recruitment solutions are more effective. I believe word of mouth is the most effective. [Employee no. 15, male, engineer]

> No, I didn't use social media while I was searching for my current job. And I didn't use it for the previous one either. I'm not a good user of social media! ... Mmm ... to be honest I'm on LinkedIn, I think it is useful to build my own professional network that could be important for my future professional career. [Employee no. 3, male, business analyst]

Although there is broad knowledge on the potential of social media, all interviewees agree that more traditional practices for recruitment are still fundamental. In particular, the company website and the university placement and career service are the starting points of their job searching strategy and are perceived as essential. Company recruitment websites are appreciated because they supply information on vacancies with the opportunity to apply for them. Their main limitations are anonymity and the frequent lack of feedback.

> When I apply through the company website, I feel I'm throwing my CV into a black box, where it will be retrieved by chance. [Employee no. 17, female, pharmaceutical chemist]

On the other hand, graduate placement and career services are considered positively since alumni feel the job offers take into account their academic background and the solid reputation of the university. This gives them the impression of a more focused opportunity that is also perceived as limiting anonymity and the lack of responses.

Further practices that are appreciated for the same reasons include specialized online services (e.g., research engines) and dedicated web intermediaries.

> I think the most effective solution to find a new job is the placement and career service of your own university. This is a direct link between the university and companies. ... I particularly rely on job proposals promoted through the placement and career service of my university. I believe that whenever companies use this service, it means that they are specifically looking for people raised in a particular organizational culture, who share certain values and with a specific education. Each university guarantees an audience with a distinctive level of competencies. In this way, I think competition is lower and this results in a higher probability of succeeding. [Employee no. 1, female, psychologist]

In most cases, social media and Web 2.0 recruitment services are considered complementary to other recruitment practices.

First, applicants acknowledge that social media play an important role in employer branding activities since companies can post creative campaigns and initiatives to communicate and emphasize brand values and image, while brand supporters can share their impressions and feelings in relation to these. Effective word of mouth is achieved in this way, also thanks to the contribution of brand supporters resulting in a bottom-up value emphasizing effect.

> I tick the homepages of my favourite enterprises, so that I can receive all updated information. I often comment on novelties to my friends because some are really cool! [Employee no. 6, female, biologist]

Second, young employees appreciate when information and messages published on social media are aligned and complete what they find with other recruitment tools. They expect complete consistency and synchronicity among offline and online recruitment tools and deeply disapprove when this is not the case.

> The official page on Facebook is even more useful than the website to prepare for an interview. Information is more frequently updated. [Employee no. 22, male, information systems specialist]

> I expect firm information and job opportunities published through different channels to be consistent and as regularly updated as possible. In my opinion, companies should avoid adopting Web 2.0 applications if they are not sure that they will be able to cope with the speedy and interactive exchanges that characterize this technology. I would irritate me a lot. Much better not to be on social networks if a company is unable to manage it properly. [Employee no. 4, female, marketing specialist]

Returning to employer branding, partly surprising is also that young people seem to be interested in the social media institutional proposals of companies they most appreciate. Social media do not appear to be greatly considered as a useful way to find new companies. Consistently with the prevalent use of social media, young employees have a mainly curious approach to social media. Therefore, most young people primarily search for and monitor the institutional initiatives of brands they like. This also appears to be confirmed for the more advanced Gen Yer users.

> I tick (like it) the Facebook page of the firms whose brand I particularly like! In this way, I regularly receive information on vacancies. That's the quickest way to be updated on job opportunities. I believe that official pages of companies on Facebook have a greater amount of updated information than any other firm communication channel. [Employee no. 15, male, industrial chemist]

> ... I now realize that I don't use social media to look for firms that I don't know. To be honest, Web 1.0 applications (such as specialized websites or search engines) are OK in this case. [Employee no. 3, male, business analyst]

Most young employees we interviewed mainly use social networks, in particular LinkedIn and Facebook, and videocasts on YouTube to seek and receive information on job opportunities. These can be described as "average" users and number 16 out of 26. Conversely, 10 interviewees can be described as advanced users. They appropriately use a wider range of social media (social networks but also blogs, videocasts, virtual worlds) and demonstrate using them properly. For example, they know that companies with strong brands are on Facebook because this is the most popular social network. Therefore, they "like" the official Facebook page in order to be regularly informed. They recognize Twitter is even quicker and more reactive and allows users to "remain passive." In fact, when choosing to follow the contents of firms or well-known people, messages are received more frequently and are usually shorter, more regular, and effective. Other social networks they use for professional purposes are MySpace and Instagram, although they find them less user-friendly.

In general, they demonstrate knowing the difference between various social networks in terms of professional activities and contents.

> I continue following my favourite companies on LinkedIn, although I know that job opportunities here are more for people that have more experience than I do. [Employee no. 8, female, accountant]

Advanced users also follow the official pages of job intermediaries and labor market specialists on social networks (e.g., Monster, but also job agencies) and know the different types of services they offer. A further feature that distinguishes this group of employees is the fact that they also use other social media in their job-seeking activities. They consider blogs, wikis, and videocasts to find specific and updated information, virtual worlds and virtual environments provided by firms or job intermediaries to train when they are involved in a selection process, but differ from the other group of applicants chiefly because they have an active approach to social media. They ask for information, take part in discussions, contribute to building and developing content related to the social media job market, as well as interacting with professionals and other applicants.

Active applicants also have some suggestions for firms and professionals. They would like Web 2.0 to be further developed in terms of more interactive tools useful in preparing for the selection process (trial tests, simulations, business games but especially case studies).

> I think social media are transforming recruitment and selection. We can now participate in a previously unimagined way to receive responses to specific questions, we communicate in real-time with top managers, we share informal news on working conditions, recruiters and selection processes, we can discuss and take part in building knowledge and best practices useful for job search and selection activities. That's an incredible transformation! [Employee no. 20, male, engineer]

Social media complete the existing panorama of recruitment and selection functionalities and services, contributing in different ways. The use of social media for recruitment has greatly allowed expanding the quantity of information available on firms and on the staffing process. The information provided through social media does not generally overlap with the previously available information; to the contrary, it is additional, particularly "informal communication" on the work climate, on selection practices, and on people. Applicants feel more powerful as a result of having access to this informal information.

Moreover, young employees state they especially appreciate the new applications because they are perceived as richer and allow interaction. In particular, Gen Yers assert that they appreciate interaction, but their habits indicate they predominantly use social media passively to receive information.

Closely linked to this approach, Gen Yers especially value obtaining information through social media because feedback is much quicker and often perceived as personalized. As previously mentioned, applicants consider social media as less anonymous than the company website recruitment area. It is easier for them to receive feedback, they can repeatedly ask specific questions, they can raise new issues, and ask for further explanations. Owing to these functionalities, young applicants think that Web 2.0 recruitment solutions allow developing a deeper relationship than was possible with Web 1.0.

> I think the main novelty of social media in the job searching domain is informal information on recruiters, managers and working conditions within firms. This is information that everyone can easily find now, while before much less was known about these aspects. [Employee no. 19, female, salesperson]

With reference to the adoption of different social media, LinkedIn is in fact considered the most coherent in terms of professional purposes and is also indicated as the most used. With the exception of an educator of disadvantaged adults, all the young employees we met have a LinkedIn account and all confirm this is important for career management. They are very cautious in how they use it because they understand that honesty and the reliability of the information provided are fundamental to social reputation. Moreover, people in the network are perceived as important in terms of the opportunities they may offer.

> LinkedIn is the only social media I use for professional purposes ... I don't use social networks when searching for jobs. To be honest, I use it [i.e., LinkedIn] rarely. I almost always use it for networking, to get in touch with people. [Employee no. 7, female, engineer]

Many respondents state they also use LinkedIn during the selection process. As soon as they know the name of the recruiters they are going to meet, they look for their profiles on LinkedIn. They are interested in the professional career of their interviewers in order to find a way of being in tune with the recruiter. Most Gen Yers who use LinkedIn also check for more informal and personal information on Facebook. In doing so, they believe they can garner some aspects of the recruiter's personality, their experiences, and what they like most.

> When I'm involved in a selection process, I check the LinkedIn and Facebook pages of recruiters and line managers I'm going to meet. I look for information on their experiences, their preferences and passions in order to find a point of contact with them. ... I try to understand what kind of people they are and to figure out the behaviours they prefer during an interview. [Employee no. 16, male, administrative clerk]

Recruiters and Web 2.0

Recruitment experts are aware of the relevance of social media. They acknowledge that social media can play a significant role in employer branding and staffing activities as a result of their widespread use. Following the Web 1.0 revolution, Web 2.0 solutions are presented as the second wave of a changing era. HR departments are defining their employer branding and staffing strategies taking into consideration the opportunities and risks linked to Web 2.0.

> I think companies should be on social media. They are the communication channels young talented individuals prefer and mostly use. ... If we want to attract them, we must be on social media! [Recruiter no. 3, female]

Recruiters consider social media as a double-edged sword: they admit they have great potential, but also perceive them as risky. They think HR departments currently do not have enough resources to implement effective employer branding and staffing strategies.

The foremost opinion is that competencies are lacking. Knowledge on brand communication and recruitment competencies is insufficient. Moreover, generic technological competences are not sufficient while technological and communication knowledge on Web 2.0 applications are more appropriate. On the other hand, technological and communication profiles do not have the professional HR skills that would allow them to respond punctually to the applicants' specific requests and doubts. Social media require integrating the competencies in a job profile that enterprises currently do not have.

Time is the second resource that is lacking. HR professionals claim that nobody in the personnel department would have enough time to take charge of managing the institutional activities on social media.

As a consequence, cautious attitudes prevail and companies currently prefer to opt for a fence-sitting strategy. They have limited experience and experiment little on social media. Large companies particularly want to be present on social media, but are substantially playing a waiting game and prefer to observe how activities and solutions on social media are evolving in the business world. They consider that recruitment activities on social media need to be strictly aligned with Web 1.0 and face-to-face initiatives, thus part of a homogeneous strategy. This need for continuous alignment is a further forewarning that worries HR departments in expanding their presence on social media. Even head hunters and professional recruitment companies are not investing in this direction and want to maintain their equilibrium.

> We currently choose to be only on LinkedIn and Facebook … . We aren't on Twitter yet. It's already a challenge with the official profiles of Facebook and LinkedIn. We wouldn't be able to manage conversations on Twitter with the appropriate rhythm. [Recruiter no. 1, female]

Social Media Professionals and Web 2.0

Social media industry managers observe a wide misuse of social media for professional purposes and, as a consequence, a suboptimal enterprise strategy. The domain is changing continuously, but at present confusion and uncertainty seem to prevail. Scarce investments due to the difficult general economic conditions produce the effect of delaying awareness and the definition of needs and expectations of players in the job market in terms of the functionalities and services on social media. The situation is described as fluid.

> Firms are aware that they must be on social media. But they aren't investing adequately in them. A waiting strategy still prevails. Firms are looking to each other and are substantially copying what their competitors do. … Only a few companies are defining a systematic and complete communication strategy on social media. [Social media professional no. 1, male]

The evolving situation on the user side contrasts with the opportunities that the technology is ready to provide. In fact, technology could push innovation further and offer even more advanced opportunities for social media recruitment activities. Social media professionals state that Web 2.0 is a vastly growing domain from the technological side. Web 3.0 technologies are available and undergoing testing, thus offering great potential also in the employer branding and recruitment domain.

Managers working for social media confirm that culture affects the adoption and use of Web 2.0 technologies. A high rate of use for personal purposes combined with the rapidly growing interest in the marketing potential of social media essentially characterizes the Italian market. Instead, less sophisticated than in other Western countries is the adoption of social media for recruitment and career management purposes.

> Italians use social media intensely. They spend much of their spare time on social media but mainly for fun. Compared with other countries, it's a kind of immature usage. But it's a market with great potential and a challenge for us as professionals. [Social media professional, no. 3, male]

Discussion

The results confirm the popularity of social media among Gen Yers, although they also suggest varied and heterogeneous behaviors when searching for jobs.

There are few advanced users with sophisticated competencies and awareness of social media opportunities to better organize job-seeking activities. On the other hand, participative use of social technologies is not as widespread among our sample and some applicants report mistrust of, or dissatisfaction with, Web 2.0 activities in relation to the professional domain.

The most frequently cited problems concern the amount of time needed to search and verify the reliability of the information collected through social media. On the other hand, the main perceived advantages concern the personalization of relationships and the two-way communication that social media enables, even if the Gen Yers also report their irritation when these two issues are not addressed in the process.

Y Gen Applicants: Social Media Activities

The evidence indicates that Gen Yers use social media for various purposes during their job search. They implement up to five behaviors according to diverse patterns and use different social media for different activities (see Figure 1).

When Gen Yers are looking for new employment opportunities, they use social media to *receive* institutional information and rumors about companies, people, and processes, in accordance with a push logic. This action emphasizes reactive behavior

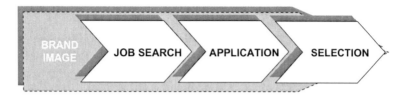

Applicants' activities	Web 2.0 technologies
Receiving	social networks, RSS
Seeking	blogs, social networks, wikis, podcasts, videocasts
Sharing	blogs, social networks, wikis, videocasts, podcasts, virtual worlds, virtual environments
Leading	blogs, social networks, virtual environments
Experiencing	virtual worlds, virtual environments, videocasts, podcasts

Figure 1: Recruitment through social media: the applicants' habits.

that is unaligned with the "participative" nature of the social media environment. Less sophisticated applicants perform only this activity through social media, receiving information from social networks and RSS systems.

A further possibility emerging from our respondents concerns data and opinion *seeking* of job vacancies, recruiter personal profiles, organizational climate, career and reward opportunities, work conditions, and selection processes. This activity is intended to increase awareness, to be updated on job opportunities, and to reduce information asymmetry during the selection phase. This activity, similar to the previous, is also not completely consistent with the potential participative nature of Web 2.0 solutions. Candidates web surf through blogs, social networks, wikis, podcasts, videocasts without actively contributing.

Active contribution begins when applicants start to effectively participate in social media environments, *sharing* information, experiences, and points of views with other users on their knowledge of actual job vacancies, recruitment activities, or work opportunities. Some of our respondents (not the majority) declared participating and actively using a wide variety of social media such as blogs, social networks, wikis, videocasts, podcasts, virtual words, and virtual environments. Users that behave in this participative way, albeit few in our sample, are the most advanced and their expectations about the organization's behaviors through social media are high and sophisticated, confirming that Gen Yers are not automatically Web 2.0 oriented when searching for job opportunities.

Participation through social media could increase when highly developed users decide to implement *leading* behaviors in forums, discussions, communities, and social network groups, developing social environments where they activate and manage exchanges and dialogue on specific work and selection topics. From our exploratory sample, although this type of behavior appears to be rather uncommon, it is feasible for some particularly sophisticated applicants.

Finally, our results show that social media can also be activated by applicants with the aim of *experiencing* virtual activities to implement recruitment activities or to understand the company's cultural values and climate through virtual world experiences, but also through videocasts and podcasts.

Even if applicants declared different behaviors, all five activities are certainly possible through social media. In particular, almost all social media users receive and sometimes seek information and rumors. Actively participative and contributing behaviors are less common when respondents report their professional activities and those specifically related to job searching practices.

Generally, considering the relationship between people and organizations, Gen Yers use social media with the aim of obtaining real-time updates on their favorite brands; this has significant effects on the company's brand image and also — but not exclusively — on the perceived value of employer brands.

The results suggest that during the job search process, Y Gens pursue different aims according to three main phases: searching, applying, and selection.

In the first phase of the job search process, young people seem to pursue two main objectives: (a) to punctually know about job vacancies and (b) to collect rumors about the organizational climate and career opportunities in different companies. Social media enable increasing the quantity and speed of information they receive and also to collect "informal" and unofficial data to better evaluate the person-organization fit that drives their intention to participate (e.g., to apply or to widen their sources of information).

The second phase of the process concerns application. In this phase, Y Gen applicants use social media to find direct and effective channels to reach the companies they have chosen and the right person (i.e., recruiters, HR professionals) within them to apply to. At this stage, young people seem to pursue two main objectives: (a) make direct and less anonymous contact and (b) receive quick and personalized feedback. A correct (i.e., personalized) and prompt response seems to be crucial to maintaining candidates engaged and to sustain the employer brand image.

Finally, applicants also use social media during the selection process to collect formal an informal news about the process and the people involved. At this final stage, young people seem to pursue three main objectives: (a) collect information and rumors about recruiters also from their personal web pages (frequently from LinkedIn), (b) collect information and opinions on the selection process from previous candidates and, finally, (c) collect especially nonofficial rumors about the organizational climate and career opportunities from actual employees.

Y Gen Applicants: Social Media Aims and Needs

The preliminary results underline the different aims and needs of respondents in their use of social media when they contact companies and search for a job. These aims

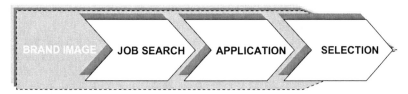

Applicants' needs and aims	1-Realtime updates on favourite brands	1-Punctually knowing about vacancies; 2-Collecting rumours about the organizational climate & career opportunities	1-Making direct and less anonymous contact 2-Receiving quick and personalized feedback	1-Collecting information and rumours about recruiters 2-Collecting information and opinions about the selection process 3-Collecting rumours about the organizational climate & career opportunities

Figure 2: Recruitment through social media: applicants' needs and aims.

vary across the various phases of the searching process and all activities affect the applicants' perceptions of employer branding (see Figure 2).

This preliminary evidence confirms that social media enable prospective employees to collect official information on both the organization and on people related to the staffing process. Furthermore, respondents declare collecting rumors and voices from both internal and controlled organizational sources (e.g., official Facebook pages, institutional videos on YouTube, company LinkedIn profiles), but also, and moreover, from organizational (e.g., actual employees and managers) and external sources (e.g., previous candidates, former employees) that companies do not control directly.

Theoretical and Managerial Implications

Theoretical Implications

Our research is of an exploratory nature and aims at a more in-depth understanding of the habits and expectations of young applicants with reference to Web 2.0 functionalities in recruitment and selection practices. Moreover, the ideas and considerations of Web 2.0 professionals and recruiters were also collected, providing a better understanding of the state of the art of this budding domain. Our results show that Y Gen applicants appear to appreciate Web 2.0 functions, but surprisingly, most young people use them passively, that is, to obtain information and feedback. In this perspective, what they especially appreciate about this new technology seems to be speed and personalization. Gen Yers perceive official company pages on social networks and blogs as more updated than recruitment websites and enthusiastically report that they can obtain direct feedback to their specific questions. Young applicants state they are interested in information on the values of the enterprise, on job requirements, and activities and the work climate. A small number of interviewees appear to be advanced users and pro-actively add content, know the characteristics of social media, and use them for different purposes during recruitment and selection activities coherently with their specificity. This evidence confirms that Web 2.0 can offer new and effective support to subjective P-O and P-J fit (Dineen et al., 2002; Ployhart, 2006). Social media also allow obtaining "informal insights" on recruiters as well as on selection process type and content, thus offering greater opportunities to applicants who are particularly motivated and attracted to the firm. Our study therefore extends the P-O fit framework to staffing activities performed through Web 2.0 technologies.

The personalization of responses and feedback enabled through Web 2.0 functionalities allows extending the concept of designing different E-O relationships even at the very beginning of the recruitment and staffing phase, which applicants would seem to appreciate (Stone & Lukaszewski, 2009).

Our results concerning the widespread adoption of social media and their use in recruitment and selection activities by young applicants confirm the theory that Gen Yers are technology oriented and use these naturally. Future research should investigate the topic of employees from other generations, in particular Gen X and Baby Boomers. This would allow comparing the behaviors and expectations of employees of different generations. Such results would contribute to the discussion around the generational approach and either support the idea that generations vary in their approach to technology or, alternatively, criticize it (Giancola, 2006).

Web 2.0

Considerations on the evidence we provide could also be relevant to the role of Web 2.0 technologies in affecting recruitment and selection processes. If interactions with applicants continue to increase and further evidence supports the value of such functionalities in sustaining applicant attraction, then this could affect decisions on how to design and organize recruitment and selection processes. Companies turn to outsourcing recruitment activities such as updating and managing recruitment channels or CV screening (Ordanini & Silvestri, 2008). Should interactions markedly increase and the personalization of recruitment activities become highly important in defining the attraction of applicants, the current trend could be reversed and companies could think about directly managing recruitment.

On the other hand, the interaction opportunities offered through Web 2.0 technologies could allow carrying out part of the selection phase remotely (e.g., more opportunities to perform tests online), thus contributing to making these activities more efficient.

In sum, Web 2.0 has the potential of customizing recruitment and selection processes so they are more customized and efficient. Applicants and firms could have the opportunity to collaborate in designing the recruitment and selection process, which could assume different forms depending on the contributions and requirements of both parties. Consistently with the Deleuzian perspective of open innovation, Web 2.0 could contribute to transforming such HR activities into a rhizomatic process, where candidates, HR professionals, and line managers cooperate in a nonhierarchical network to shape a continuously innovative, emergent, and nonlinear collective process (Biffi, Bissola, & Imperatori, forthcoming; Deleuze & Guattari, 1987). This could lead to the satisfaction of all parties involved and become a way of engaging employees and sustaining their motivation.

Managerial Implications

The evidence presented, although tentative, suggests various relevant and sometimes unexpected implications for organizations and for employment strategies. Social media seem to offer interesting and valuable opportunities to HR professionals to attract and engage young talented people. On the other hand, they seem to entail some organizational risks and costs, which imply some managerial caution and a change in the prevalent HRM mindset.

As to the opportunities, social media affect both the quantity and quality of communications that organizations could disseminate in the labor market, supporting employer branding and reaching and engaging appropriate target candidates.

First, Web 2.0 solutions enable organizations and recruiters to contact a wider group of potential applicants, even those who are not actively job seeking, with relatively low-cost activities (*relationship quantity*).

Second, via social media, organizations have the possibility of sending and receiving up-to-date information and messages as well as personalizing and targeting potential recipients to focus their employer branding activities and recruitment processes (*relationship quality*).

Furthermore, social media enable recruiters to maintain person-organization relationships with continuity, enabling recipients to use their voice and actively participate. They promote the perception of organizational transparency and fairness, allowing users to share opinions and engage connections (*relationship fairness*).

In terms of costs and potential risks, social media pose new HRM challenges in relation to the need for both new competencies and renewed mindsets.

First, Web 2.0 solutions seem to be popular among Y Gens, despite the inhomogeneous diffusion for professional use. This implies new potential management solutions that need to be integrated with existing and more traditional recruitment practices. Social media impose the design of a differentiated HR architecture according not only to the characteristics of human capital, such as competency, strategic value, and specificity, but also to the individual needs and habits of candidates (*relationship differentiation*).

Second, the new practices require new HRM technical competencies and dedicated organizational roles that are still lacking in organizations. Social media are changing the communication habits and patterns of employees (both actual and potential employees) but they have their own rules that need to be respected to be credible and to avoid potential misuse and negative — even if unintentional — outcomes. Gen Yers request prompt Web 2.0 communication and responses, participative patterns, real time, and updated content and also desire personalized contacts (*relationship personalization*).

Finally, Web 2.0 applications imply a radical change in the traditional approach to organizational control, which is still present in many Italian organizations, often characterized by the total internal control of organizational information, especially in relation to HRM activities. Social media enhance organizational transparency and potentially help organizations support their employer branding and collect accurate and at times low-cost information on potential candidates. Furthermore, social media allow candidates to share and seek information and opinions before and during the staffing process. These possibilities mean that if organizations want to play the social media game, they have to accept losing their "total" control of external communication processes (*reduced control relationships*).

Limitations and Future Research Directions

Our research aims at exploring the role of social media e-HRM systems in shaping the employee–organization relationships of the new workforce. The young people who constitute this workforce are known as Generation Y and differ from the previous generation largely due to their familiarity with technology.

In our study, we first found that most, but not all, employees in our pilot sample have a high level of technology readiness, as the literature on Gen Yers assumes, suggesting new opportunities for employer branding and recruitment strategies that support the quantity, quality, and fairness of employment relationships, albeit imposing an actual transparency mindset on the new HRM department.

The main limitation of this preliminary research is the sample size and the results can thus not be generalized. Consequently, the next step of the research program is to design a wider survey.

Useful suggestions could also ensue from a combinative approach, which assumes that there are no single type of Web 2.0 practices to implement, but that various positive organizational combinations are possible (considering, e.g., degree of technology readiness). Clusters of users could be formed based on different criteria such as the types of social media actually adopted and desired and the technology readiness level.

The research could also evolve into a different domain, considering the types of social media practices that can better support the HR department in performing its activities along with the alternative roles as proposed, for example, in the Ulrich framework (1997). The assumption, in this case, is that different combinations of Web 2.0 HR practices can better suit the needs of the different functions that the HR department aims to perform within the firm.

Finally, the research framework here developed could be adopted to study the influence of social media on all employees, and this would become more relevant especially if Web 2.0 practices continue gaining importance in the HRM of all firms.

References

Alsop, R. (2008). *The trophy kids grow up: How the millennial generation is shaking up the workplace*. New York, NY: Jossey-Bass.

Baumann, M. (2006). Caught in the Web 2.0. *Information Today, 23*, 8–38.

Beer, D., & Burrows, R. (2007). Sociology and, of and in Web 2.0: Some initial considerations. *Sociological Research Online, 12*(5). article 17.

Biffi, A., Bissola, R., & Imperatori, B. (2014). Collaborare per la creatività. Università, aziende e open innovation. In A. Antonietti (Ed.), *Collana di Psicologia dell' Educazione*. Trento, Italy: Erikson.

Bissola, R., & Imperatori, B. (2009). Generation Y and team creativity: The strategic role of e-HRM architecture. In T. Bondarouk & H. Ruel (Eds.), *Human resource information systems* (pp. 59–69). Portugal: INSTICC Press.

Bradley, A. J., & McDonald, M. P. (2011). *The social organisation: How to use social media to tap the collective genius of your customers and employee*. Boston, MA: Harvard Business Review Press.

Bruning, S. D., Dials, M., & Shirka, A. (2008). Using dialogue to build organisation-public relationships, engage publics, and positively affect organisational outcomes. *Public Relations Review, 34*(1), 25–31.

Bunderson, J. S. (2001). How work ideologies shape the psychological contracts of professional employees: Doctors' responses to perceived breach. *Journal of Organizational Behavior, 22*, 717–741.

D'Amato, A., & Herzfeldt, R. (2008). Learning orientation, organizational commitment and talent retention across generations. *Journal of Managerial Psychology, 23*(8), 929–953.

Dearstyne, B. W. (2007). Blogs, mashups and wikis: Oh, my!. *Information Management Journal, 41*(4), 25–33.

Deleuze, G., & Guattari, F. (1987). *A thousand plateaus: Capitalism & schizophrenia*. Minneapolis, MN: University of Minnesota Press.

Dineen, D. R., Ash, S. R., & Noe, R. A. (2002). A web of applicant attraction: Person-organization fit in the context of web-based recruitment. *Journal of Applied Psychology, 87*(4), 723–734.

Dries, N., Pepermans, R., & De Kerpel, E. (2008). Exploring four generations' beliefs about career. *Journal of Management Psychology, 23*(8), 907–928.

Edwards, J. R. (1996). An examination of competing versions of the person-environment fit approach to stress. *Academy of Management Journal, 39*(2), 292–339.

Erickson, T. J., Alsop, R., Nicholson, P., & Miller, J. (2009). Gen y in the workforce. *Harvard Business Review, 87*(2), 43–49.

Furness, V. (2008). The new frontier, *Personnel Today*, January.

Gallagher, N., & O'Leary, D. (2007). *Recruitment 2020: How recruitment is changing and why it matters*. London: Demos.

Giancola, F. (2006). The generation gap: More myth than reality. *Human Resource Planning, 29*(4), 32–37.

Glaser, B., & Strauss, A. (1967). *The discovery of grounded theory: Strategies for qualitative research*. Chicago, IL: Aldine.

Hargadon, A. B., & Bechky, B. A. (2006). When collections of creatives become creative collectives: A field study of problem solving at work. *Organization Science, 17*(4), 484–500.

Henderson, A., & Bowley, R. (2010). Authentic dialogue? The role of "friendship" in a social media recruitment campaign. *Journal of Communication Management, 14*(3), 237–257.

Howe, N., & Strauss, W. (2000). *Millennials rising: The next great generation*. New York, NY: Vintage Books.

Hu, C., Su, H.-C., & Chen, C.-I. B. (2007). The effect of person-organization fit feedback via recruitment web sites on applicant attraction. *Computers in Human Behaviors, 23*, 2509–2523.

Kaplan, A. M., & Haenlein, M. (2010). Users of world, unite! The challenges and opportunities of social media. *Business Horizons, 53*, 59–68.

Kietzmann, J. H., Hermkens, K., McCarthy, I. P., & Silvestre, B. S. (2011). Social media? Get serious! Understanding the functional building blocks of social media. *Business Horizons, 54*(3), 241–251.

Krisof-Brown, A. L., Zimmerman, R. D., & Johnson, E. C. (2005). Consequences of individuals' fit at work: A meta-analysis of person-job, person-organization, person-group, and person-supervisor fit. *Personnel Psychology, 58*, 281–342.

Martin, G., Reddington, M. & Kneafsey, M. B. (2009). *Web 2.0 and human resource management. 'Groundswell' or hype?*. London: CIPD.

Mead, L. (2008). Legal and regulatory updates: Web 2.0 — The key legal questions. *Journal of Direct, Data and Digital Marketing Practice, 9*(3), 298–303.

Miles, M. B., & Huberman, A. M. (1994). *Qualitative data analysis*. Thousand Oaks, CA: Sage.

NM Incite. (2011, April). *State of the media: The social media report Q3*. Retrieved from www.nielsen.com. Accessed in August 2012.

Ordanini, A., & Silvestri, G. (2008). Recruitment and selection services: Efficiency and competitive reasons in the outsourcing of HR practices. *The International Journal of Human Resource Management, 19*(2), 372–391.

Ployhart, R. E. (2006). Staffing in the 21st century: New challenges and strategic opportunities. *Journal of Management, 32*(6), 868–897.

Proserpio, L., & Gioia, D. A. (2007). Teaching the virtual generation. *Academy of Management Learning & Education, 6*(1), 69–80.

Richards, J. (2007). Workers are doing it for themselves: Examining creative employee application of Web 2.0 communication technology. Paper presented at the Work, Employment and Society Conference, September , University of Aberdeen, Aberdeen, Scotland.

Ruel, H., Bondarouk, T., & Looise, J. K. (2004). E-ERM: Innovation or irritation. An explorative empirical study in five large companies on web-based HRM. *Management Revue, 15*(3), 364–380.

Scott, S. G., & Lane, V. R. (2000). A stakeholder approach to organisational identity. *The Academy of Management Review, 25*(1), 43–62.

Stone, D. L., & Lukaszewski, K. M. (2009). An expanded model of the factors affecting the acceptance and effectiveness of electronic human resource management systems. *Human Resource Management Review, 19*(2), 134–143.

Strauss, W., & Howe, N. (1991). *Generations: The history of America's future, 1584 to 2069.* New York, NY: William Morrow.

Strauss, W., Howe, N., & Markiewicz, P. (2006). *Millennials and the pop culture: Strategies for a new generation of consumers in music, movies, television, the Internet, and video games.* Great Falls VA: Lifecourse Associates.

Tapscott, D., & Williams, A. D. (2007). *Wikinomics.* New York, NY: Portfolio.

Twenge, J. M., & Campbell, W. K. (2008). Increases in positive self-views among high school students: Birth cohort changes in anticipated performance, self-satisfaction, self-liking, and self-competence. *Psychological Science, 19,* 1082–1086.

Wandel, T. L. (2008). Colleges and universities want to be your friend: Communicating via online. *Planning for Higher Education, 37*(1), 35–48.

Williams, S., & Verhoeven, H. (2008). 'We-find-you' or 'you-find-us'? Internet recruitment and selection in the United Kingdom. *International Review of Business Research papers, 4*(1), 374–384.

Wilson, M., & Gerber, L. E. (2008). How generational theory can improve teaching: Strategies for working with the "millennials". *Currents in Teaching and Learning, 1*(1), 29–44.

Wong, M., Gardiner, E., Lang, W., & Coulon, L. (2008). Generational differences in personality and motivation: Do they exist and what are the implications for the workplace? *Journal of Managerial Psychology, 23*(8), 878–890.

Chapter 4

Social Media in Internal Communications: A View from Senior Management

Tanja Sedej and Gorazd Justinek

Abstract

Purpose — The chapter presents a senior management view on the role of new and technologically advanced tools, such as social media in internal communications.

Design/methodology/approach — We conducted 23 in-depth interviews with senior managers of large- and medium-sized companies in Slovenia.

Findings — The results obtained in the research confirmed that the senior management possess a strong awareness of the importance of internal communications in managing their organizations. Moreover, many top managers even pointed out that internal communications play a crucial role, and add value to the business performance through more motivated employees and that social media in the context of internal communications are vivid and growing in importance.

Implications — The study provides a starting point for further research in this area. However, the core policy recommendation would mainly be focused on internal communication experts, who must no longer underestimate the urgency of developing communication programs that help employees and senior management start working with social media successfully.

Originality/value — The research presents a new — senior management view on the role of social media in internal communications.

Keywords: Internal communications; social media; management

Social Media in Human Resources Management
Advanced Series in Management, 83–95
Copyright © 2013 by Emerald Group Publishing Limited
All rights of reproduction in any form reserved
ISSN: 1877-6361/doi:10.1108/S1877-6361(2013)0000012008

Introduction

Internal communications represent a vital part of every manager's activities, despite often being neglected through other "priorities." Evidence in support of the first part of this statement can be found in relevant empirical analysis carried out in the past, such as the "Productivity report of 2008," where Parkinson (2008, pp. 64–65) established that a quarter of the managers interviewed had identified internal communication problems as being a critical barrier to improving company productivity, making this the second greatest obstacle cited among all the respondents. Furthermore, in the "European communication monitor," a survey conducted in 43 countries, Zefass, Tench, Verhoeven, Verčič, & Moreno (2011, p. 85) pointed out that internal communication, together with change management, rank fourth among the most important disciplines of communication management. Current trends indicate that by 2014 it will have risen to second place, when it will overtake marketing, brand and consumer communication, which currently holds the second place. Despite the importance ascribed to internal communication, it is often prioritized lower than it should be.

However, we live in a globalized world and in a time of previously unimaginable technological development. One area which is the focus of almost daily rapid development is the social media phenomenon. It "took off" just after the Millennium and so could be defined, in entrepreneurial terms, as a "gazelle" among other media. Social media tools are therefore no longer just used for fun and recreation, nor do they merely serve as useful kit to reach customers and the rest of the external audience. Rather, they are also becoming an increasingly important instrument in reaching the internal audience of companies and institutions.

The purpose of this chapter is therefore primarily to point out the crucial role played by internal communications within organizations from the perspective of senior management. Yet, as change has become the one constant in our life, rapid development has also been recorded in the field of internal communications. Here we mainly refer to the use of new technologies — especially the use of social media. Since social media is also increasingly used in the framework of internal communications, we will continue the chapter with a critical review of some of the main theories and approaches in internal communications and social media as modern tools, which are gaining importance in many organizations.

Despite limited available empirical data on the use of social media in internal communications, some studies on a similar topic have been conducted in the past. Sinickas (2005) analyzed the role of the intranet and other electronic channels in employee communication preferences. The survey resulted from 21 large organizations and revealed that the preferences of employees may vary from commonly believed assumptions. As additional electronic choices become available, the overall preference for electronic channels increases, yet the new electronic options do not replace other existing electronic channels in employee preferences. Ahonen (2011) conducted an online survey among 80 white-collar workers in a company on the topic of social intranet implementation and organizational readiness for change. No significant relationship was established between the four main variables observed (contextual factors, change valence, change efficacy, and perceived readiness for change). Baltatzis, Ormrod, and Grainger (2008), on the other hand, examined the prospect of introducing social networking technology and practices within large organizations. It revealed a very high rate of adoption among recreational users of tools such as Facebook, in comparison to the corresponding rate in businesses.

In order to contribute a piece of puzzle to the literature in this field and provide some new empirical data, we conducted 23 in-depth interviews with senior managers of large- and medium-sized companies[1] in Slovenia[2] on the importance and use of social media in the framework of internal communications.

The main value added of the chapter is therefore in the collection, evaluation, and interpretation of the empirical data gathered through the in-depth interviews performed with senior managers. Through these interviews, our main aim was to confirm that internal communication does indeed represent a vital role in management, and that senior management is aware of this. And, second, social media tools are used more often in the framework of internal communications, since senior management is aware of its positive characteristic, synergies, and outcomes. We would like to highlight that the emphasis of the whole chapter is on the perspective of senior management (CEOs), who are also the key decision makers.

The data collected therefore provide a valuable up-to-date research basis for an analysis of the views held by senior management on the importance of social media in internal communications. It also serves as an interesting perspective on management in a harsh and difficult environment, since the research was carried out during the recent economic crisis, which has still not loosened its grip in some of the eurozone's[3] member countries (such as Slovenia). The results and the main findings of the interviews are presented below, which is also where conclusions and policy recommendations are provided with regard to better and more efficient internal communication in organizations.

The Importance of Managing Internal Communications

It is often said, mostly among experts and those working in the field, that internal communication is important. However, in order to confirm this statement, we first must clarify what we mean when we talk about internal communication. At this juncture, it seems apt to note that many senior managers still have a less-than-clear understanding of its complexities, since internal communication is not just about producing and disseminating information to employees (as is often mistakenly thought). It involves much more than this, and therefore represents a significant

---

[1] In accordance with the definition of the European Commission. More on http://ec.europa.eu/enterprise/policies/sme/facts-figures-analysis/sme-definition/index_en.htm.
[2] An EU and OECD member country from Central Europe, with a population of 2 million.
[3] Member of the European Monetary Union.

challenge for organizations. We fully concur with Barrett (2002, p. 220), who stresses that communication is either everything in the organization (vision, mission, strategy, strategic business planning, management, knowledge management, etc.) or it is nothing more than publications intended to keep communication staff busy and employees up to date with company news. Justinek and Sedej (2011, p. 8) agree and emphasize that internal communication needs to be flexible and must adapt to business needs.

Communication with employees is an issue that is gaining significance as the world shrinks into an ever-smaller global village (Dolphin, 2005, p. 185). Hurley (2008) also agrees with this statement and argues that our hugely complicated organizations, networks, and geographies will become even more complex. As a result, communication is more important now than it ever has been — and this trend will continue.

The employees of today work in a turbulent, ever-changing, and dynamic environment, and this is the main reason why internal communication is becoming not only more significant, but also a complex, broad, and indispensable activity that has to be carefully planned and managed. Orsini (2000, p. 31) emphasizes that we must not forget that internal communication is a vast area, since it can be written, spoken, or virtual — and can take place among individuals or groups in a work environment.

Effective internal communication tends to pave the way toward the main goal of most companies and institutions. In most cases that goal would be represented in the creation of an environment where all employees would contribute to attaining the mission, vision, strategy, and goals of the organization. Or, as Argenti (2007) and Kalla (2005) state, organizations which have developed effective communication strategies are usually also more successful. Orsini (2000, p. 33) adds that successful internal communication is not an easy task, since we are dealing with a fast moving target.

We could summarize the previous findings by saying that effective internal communications is important, but a never-ending challenge, since new and more innovative practices in this field are developed every day. Nevertheless, in order to be effective at communicating with employees, organizations need to enable that a culture of communication pervades the whole organization; one which encourages horizontal and vertical communication, flows across the organization (Asif & Sargeant, 2000, p. 301). Buckingham (2008, p. 7) substantiates this kind of thinking with a comment that internal media, which is out of touch with the true culture of the organization, may dominate the internal airwaves, but sadly just a few people truly listen in.

Communication is indeed a very complex phenomenon and it is true that people often need to hear the same information a few times before they really accept it. In this sense Austin and Currie (2003, p. 236) point out that leaders should use a variety of media, and look for new and innovative ways to connect with their employees. Luss and Nyce (2004, p. 20) add that organizations which communicate effectively use different technologies to amplify their message. A successful communication plan needs to leverage the power of the manager's relationship with his or her employees while duplicating the hierarchy, and get information smoothly to and from everyone in the organization (Austin & Currie, 2003, p. 235).

It is sensible to use different modes of communication tools in internal communications. Nevertheless, despite all the recent advances in technology, personal communication still represents the most efficient tool and, in fact, is sometimes the only tool that can be used in some certain cases. However, in an organization which is geographically dispersed, this is often very difficult to achieve, and consuming in terms of time and cost. This is the main reason why organizations devote more attention to setting up electronic tools in internal communications.

Nevertheless, the way we choose to communicate can be just as important as the message itself Orsini (2000, p. 31). Consequently, organizations have to find the optimum way to use the internal communication tools at their disposal. With the latest developments in technology, a whole new palette of instruments for internal communicators is now available, especially in the field of social media tools, such as social networks, blogs, wikis, podcasts, online videos, etc.

Social Media in Internal Communications

Over the last decade the influence of web-based technological changes has had a significant impact on our lives; it has become widely accessible, and social media has taken off. Moreover, traditional approaches in internal communications are failing to deliver positive outcomes, not forgetting that any technology that becomes commonly used on the Internet will find its way onto intranets sooner or later (Holtz, 2006, pp. 24–25).

Some organizations already acknowledge the value of social media and are taking advantage of its benefits. However, tools such as blogs, wikis, and podcasts have found their way onto only a handful of intranets. Despite this, their eventual assimilation into intranets is inevitable, since social software gives employees a voice and, in this sense, there is still a lot of potential to be used. It is true, however, that most businesses have not yet awakened to just how powerful that voice could be (Holtz, 2006, p. 25). Nevertheless, embracing social software on intranets will probably mean having to convince the management of their value. In order to do so, the way in which these tools could help solve the problems that keep senior managers "awake at night" needs to be explained.

Social media of all kinds in fact represent a great way to establish a two-way dialogue with employees. By their very nature, social media tools are more democratic and are becoming a popular method of not only communicating with employees, but also facilitating the dissemination of information and knowledge within the company. We agree with Briggs (2008, p. 154), who states that the key issue for all internal communicators is to carefully consider how blogs and other forms of social media will complement and enhance the existing internal media mix. We would like to emphasize that they should complement and add to them, but by no means serve as their replacements.

Social media thus brings many benefits. Holtz (2006, p. 24) points out the two characteristics of social software that are pertinent to this discussion: it is web-based, providing an intuitive "point-and-click interface" and is remarkably simple to use. If we take the example of a blog or wiki, we can see that it takes five minutes to set up and requires no special skills or knowledge to do so.

At this point we must not forget the Generation Y[4] phenomenon, which is becoming an important part of communities, and poses a great challenge, especially for the human resources and corporate communications departments in organizations. Social media attracts young and mobile employees, to whom these tools are important part of their business environment, as well as private lives. King (2008, p. 132) states that the traditional model is definitely breaking down when you talk about Generation Y. As they have grown up with a virtual relationship, they simple do not need as much face-to-face time to build trust. In this sense, a profound understanding is vital for the development of an adequate communication strategy and planning.

On the other hand, social media also involves some risks since it is impossible to control every piece of information that gets published. This could probably also be the main reason why many companies hesitate to introduce it into their work environment. Bernoff and Li (2008, p. 40) argue that because social media involve people banding together, social applications often move in unexpected directions. Consequently, in addition to careful planning, social applications also require flexibility and nimbleness on the part of their creators.

We can conclude that social media have gained a significant impact in internal communications (as well as other parts of our lives), providing organizations with new opportunities for information and knowledge sharing, building relationship, and facilitating collaboration between employees. With social media, knowledge and ideas can be more easily captured, while at the same time employees can be more interconnected. However, social media are not suitable for all organizations. They can flourish in organizations with less hierarchical and top-down driven organization and those which have a more open and democratic style of communication.

Views of Senior Management on the Role of Social Media in Internal Communications — Empirical Study

In order to gain primary data on the views of senior management on social media in internal communications, we conducted 23 in-depth interviews with senior managers of large- and medium-sized companies in Slovenia.[5] The interviews were carried out

---

[4]Generation Y — the people born between 1982 and 2000.

[5]Due to the international perspective of the readers we will also shortly present the economic situation in the country of the empirical study. The Slovenian economy in 2012 is again in a demanding period since it is experiencing a decline of GDP (the OECD forecasts a 2% decline). Slovenia was hit very hard by the global economic crisis in 2009, when it recorded a fall of more than 8% of GDP. In 2010 and 2011 the economy recovered, but GDP growth was only minimal — just a few points above zero. It is important for the reader of this chapter to bear this in mind, since the macroeconomic circumstances have undoubtedly had an impact on the perception of the Slovenian business community and actions of senior management (Justinek, 2012).

throughout Slovenia between June and September of 2012 (always conducted at the headquarters of the company interviewed).

At the beginning of the research phase, we looked at the 101 best companies for 2011, as defined by the Slovenia's main economic daily newspaper — *Finance*.[6] We narrowed our research to only large- or medium-sized companies, as defined by the European Commission, and selected 67 companies. We devoted our attention to large- and medium-sized companies since, in smaller companies, communication runs much more simply and is limited mostly to personal communication tools.

Therefore, for the 67 large- and medium-sized companies selected, we prepared and sent a request for a 60-minute (approximately) interview with the CEO or another member of the management board responsible for internal communications. We received 23 confirmations, and, during the summer and early autumn of 2012, conducted interviews with 23 senior managers[7] (17 CEOs and 6 members of the management boards). Among the 23 companies interviewed, 7 were from the ICT sector, 5 from the financial services sector, 4 from the green energies sector, 3 from the industrial sector, 2 from pharmaceuticals, 1 from healthcare/life sciences, and 1 from the media sector. All the interviews took between 45 and 90 minutes.

Since communication is about the creation of meaning and understanding, not simply moving information around (Gray & Robertson, 2005, p. 27), at the beginning of all the interviews we were interested in finding out the managers' views of the importance of internal communications in managing changes in companies. Almost all (22) of the senior managers interviewed acknowledged the importance of internal communication. One top manager even pointed out: "*It is simply not enough to understand the external market. You really have to appreciate and feel the internal reality. People are the audible voice that goes beyond the walls of the company.*" Another CEO added: "*We have to commit to developing an effective internal communication strategy which is based on a two-way communication strategy. Internal communication is not just about giving instructions to employees; it is much more than that. You have to win their hearts if you want to achieve above-average results. And above average is what matters today. If you are average, you are already lagging behind.*"

We can summarize that almost all the senior managers interviewed pointed out that internal communication is a very important discipline in managing their company processes. The only manager who did not see it as a priority area said: "*It could be an important topic, but it is not a priority at this very moment, since times are very hard and we have our human resources people dealing with these issues.*" This kind of perception clearly shows the false understanding of the internal communication concept, since senior managers are usually viewed as the primary communicators in every company. Gray and Robertson (2005, p. 28) even believe that there is much evidence that we can get a bigger "bang for our buck" by putting efforts into improving executive communication.

---

[6]More on www.finance.si.

[7]The names of the companies and members of senior management interviewed are known to the authors. However, the members of senior management interviewed were assured complete anonymity.

As previously mentioned, Slovenia is still in the grip of recession. Despite this, it was interesting to note that the majority of senior managers interviewed did not see that as a particular distraction or a setback for prioritizing internal communications. One senior manager even said: "*On the contrary, investments in people and top internal communication are essential, especially at a time of recession and financial crisis. If you cut people and internal communication resources, and, as a result, resources for the 'internal community' you are dead already in the mid-term, not to mention the long-term.*"

What about the use of social media in this context? Holtz (2006, p. 24) argues that intranet take-up is always slower because business leaders tend to dismiss new technologies with contempt, viewing them as nothing more than diversions for youngsters and computer geeks. Bernoff and Li (2008, p. 41) share a similar opinion, since they believe that social applications frequently elicit resistance from senior management. However, the research we have conducted has presented us with different conclusions. Only five senior managers agree with the statements provided above. One senior manager even said: "*In my opinion social media does not belong in workplace. It has no practical use in the business world. It is time consuming and does not provide any results.*"

Yet, a majority (18) of the senior managers interviewed disagreed and believed it is actually a great way to facilitate the flow of information, ideas and knowledge throughout the company. One stressed: "*We introduced social media tools in our company only four years ago. I have to admit I was a little sceptical as to whether it would really serve to support and meet our business goals. Today, I see it was the right decision because it encourages engagement and collaboration. Employees can get a bigger picture on emerging issues than was possible before with the use of only traditional tools.*" Another manager argued: "*Social media helps me to keep in touch with internal reality. Meeting employees online results in more regular discussions and a better understanding of some current issues.*"

Nevertheless, social media has not (yet) found its way into every company. There are many reasons for this, but some are probably down to the company's culture. One senior manager confirmed our thesis, stating: "*You must know who your people are and the best ways to communicate with them. If this means that we — the 'old habits die hard' CEOs — have to learn to use these new techniques, then so be it.*" Another senior manager was unequivocal: "*It is clear that company performance rests on the shoulders of its employees, and all these new age tools help to share information more effectively, and create an environment where social relationships develop across the globe. They also contribute to an organisational culture with a more democratic style of communication and encourage employees to be more open, collaborative and innovative; in other words, to be their very best.*"

It is clear that the use of different techniques and modes of communication in an organization are contingent on the openness of senior management. Once senior management clearly sees the value in social media and how it can contribute to achieving business goals, their support and cooperation is no longer in question. Most of the senior managers (19 in total) agreed and one even said: "*New projects (no matter how ill-advised they might seem at the outset) always have my support if they bring measurable results which ultimately manifest themselves in increased revenues and profit.*"

What about the role played by social media in the working environment? A majority (15) of the managers interviewed pointed out that one of the main goals of social media is, in fact, knowledge sharing — eight managers, however, did not. We could conclude that the awareness of knowledge sharing in companies is still not common. However, one senior manager interviewed mentioned: "*The top down model of spreading information is ancient history, and publishing must be democratised. Employees support one another by sharing information, opinions, ideas, knowledge and contacts. Today, the success of an organisation depends more than ever on the commitment, engagement and motivation of its employees.*" Another CEO added: "*Knowledge sharing is the key argument in favour of social media. Someone might already have knowledge or experience in some specific field and employees can find this through messages posted on the intranet, which can often be quite valuable. In this way we can maintain the history of conversions and, consequently, even review them on occasion in the future.*"

At this point we must not forget that good communication involves (at least) two sides. Therefore, it is not just about the employees, who need to listen, but it is also about the management. Nevertheless, employees want and need to be heard. Briggs (2008, p. 13) believes that opening up the internal communication network can help keep rumor and speculation to a minimum and allow employees to share frustrations and solutions with each other when they most need to. One CEO interviewed stressed: "*You have to answer two questions. How would employees like to get information? What is the most appropriate tool, or, maybe, what is the best mix of tools to do so? Most of all, ultimately, it is important to create a climate which is conducive for daily two-way communication, taking into account the whole range of face-to-face, printed or electronic tools available.*" Another senior manager added: "*In this computer and internet era, employees spread over large distances are far better informed, and personal communication is often disregarded. Moreover, it is becoming the norm for individuals sitting in offices just a few metres away from one another to communicate through electronic communication tools. Even employees who sit in close proximity to one another usually go online to discuss details about their plans for lunch (when to go, where to go, and to post the available menus), and invite other colleagues to come along. This is much easier and less time consuming than going physically from one office to another, then returning and discussing with others if someone would like to go somewhere else, etc.*"

However, as already mentioned, we have to keep in mind that social media can be an interesting ingredient in the communication media mix of an organization, but cannot represent the sole method for communication. In this regard, D'Aprix (2005, p. 34) emphasizes the influence of social demographics on the predisposition of an individual toward the absorption of information.

The difference in communicating with different generations and age groups is important and has to be kept in mind when using and developing the right communication mix. Social media are easily accepted by young people, while older people struggle, not only with new technologies, which they have to learn, but also with the bigger issue of trust. One manager stated: "*Younger generations are becoming a significant part of the workforce and we need to consider the relatively new, more interactive methods of internal communication. Social media should not be under-estimated.*" Another CEO expressed concerns: "*The acceptance of social media can be difficult for older generations. It is important to create an atmosphere that encourages the dissemination of information and knowledge. Technology itself cannot facilitate it, but can create numerous possibilities. Nevertheless, trust is essential.*" King (2008, p. 132) also agrees with the last sentence and says that a lack of trust is the major drawback to virtual teaming. If the trust does not exist, virtual team cannot do their job successfully.

Although trust is indeed important, education and the right training are equally crucial. Younger generations, who have practically grown up with these tech-nologies, usually do not have any problems using them, but for all others, the right training should be in place before introducing them into their working environments (also for senior managers). Nevertheless, only one of the managers admitted his troubles and struggle with these new ways of communicating. Consequently, he recommended: "*Providing an educational programme about tools, tips and techniques to managers and employees is essential for the creation and facilitation of mutual dialogue and discussion through social media.*" Another manager pointed out: "*Promotion, education and support of the use of social media was essential when we were introducing it in our work environment. Our communication professionals put a lot of effort in to encouraging employees to participate in improving and developing our organisation. A specific programme was developed because we really wanted to establish content that was rich and would represent a result derived from a diverse range of employees.*"

The interviews performed and the data gathered provided us with many relevant findings and important confirmations. They provide empirical evidence for many of the "hot" discussions currently taking place among the internal communicator network, like the benefits and drawbacks of the use of social media in the workplace.

Conclusion

We have pointed out several times during this chapter that there is a broad understanding of the key contribution made by social media in internal communica-tions toward organizational efficiency. However, until now, we have not had relevant empirical data from the perspective of senior management to support this thesis. As outlined in the introduction to this chapter, there have been some analyses carried out in the past, but mostly among communication professionals, and with the focus on other issues.

With our research we have presented a new view from senior management on this topic. Through the results obtained from the 23 in-depth interviews conducted with senior managers, we confirmed that they possess a strong awareness of the importance of internal communications in managing their organizations. Moreover, many top managers even pointed out that internal communications play a crucial role, and add value to the business performance through more motivated employees.

Thus, with our research, we can confirm the findings of D'Aprix (2005, p. 36), who explained that the employees of the future will increasingly require seamless information flows as complexity and information overload increases. But understanding the role of internal communications in the sense of disseminating information is now a thing of the past. We therefore agree with Dolphin (2005, p. 185), who stated that the key to success in employee relations in the future will predominantly involve building relations. In this sense, effective internal communications align communication within a company with the main goals of the business. It is therefore no surprise that senior management considers internal communications to be important and closely intertwined with the success of any organization, as also proven with our analysis in many statements by the members of senior management interviewed.

Nevertheless, the world really is "turning faster and faster" and we have to adapt to numerous changes in every aspect of our lives on almost a daily basis (Justinek & Sedej, 2012). Taking all that into account, companies also need to take better advantage of the modern tools at their disposal, which can become a part of solutions for improving internal communications and, as a result, business efficiency. Holtz (2006, p. 25) supports our findings in stating that not one of the companies that have introduced these new technologies into their work environments have done so for the "coolness" factor. Rather, they saw how these tools could make them more competitive and, ultimately, more profitable.

The use of social media is clearly on the rise, mainly because it has potential to improve information sharing, knowledge sharing, relationships, and collaboration. Although we must not forget that social media can never replace personal communication, they can serve as an excellent complement to other internal communication tools and management practices. Our research demonstrates that social media in the context of internal communications are vivid and growing in importance. Moreover, a significant proportion of senior managers recognize the importance of social media in internal communications. An open organizational culture and support from management are the key factors that determine the success of introducing social media.

In this framework, our core policy recommendation would mainly be focused on internal communication experts, who must no longer underestimate the urgency of developing communication programs that help employees and senior management start working with social media successfully. In a way it is sad that social media in internal communications is still sometimes overlooked (although this was not the case in our study). As a result, there is a clear need for further research in regard to this development. Further research could help ascertain what kind of organizational culture is required in order for social media in internal communications to flourish. Potential difficulties (trust in social media, generational differences, and the loss of control) in accepting new technologies might well be another area that warrants future research.

There are also some limitations to our research. First of all, the interviews have been carried out only in Slovenia and therefore represent a view of senior management from only one country. However, all the companies interviewed were internationally engaged, and their comments are therefore influenced heavily by the international and global environment. Another issue would be that the research was limited to only large- and medium-sized companies, since the internal communications processes in smaller companies run differently and are usually based on a personal approach. It would be very difficult to elaborate on any coherent findings due to the organizations compared being too different. The research was also carried out at a time of recession in Slovenia, and, prior to the interviews being conducted, we feared that senior management could have pushed internal communications to the background due to the other "more important" issues at hand. However, the readiness exhibited by senior managers to be interviewed demonstrated their awareness of the topic and their answers additionally confirmed their commitment to the topic analyzed.

We can conclude that, through our research, we have been able to confirm the importance of internal communications in managing organizations, and the high and positive levels of awareness of the use of new technology within this framework — like social media, as perceived by senior management. Although social media can bring many positives to the table: heightened cooperation, improved dissemination of knowledge and information, better connectivity, etc., they should mainly be used as a complementary tool and not as a replacement for other communication tools. On the other hand, there are also some drawbacks, the biggest of which would be the lack of trust in social media, and the huge intergenerational differences that exist when it comes to using and working with social media. Nevertheless, effective and improved internal communication can be achieved through the use of social media, as proven by the many statements in support from the senior managers interviewed and also, for this reason, organizations can achieve better business results. Despite this, the success of its implementation is very much tied to the clear support of senior management and its readiness to implement these changes.

References

Ahonen, J. (2011). *Implementing a social intranet: A study of organizational readiness for change.* Aalto, Finland: Aalto University School of Economics.

Argenti, P. A. (2007). *Corporate communication.* New York, NY: McGraw-Hill.

Asif, S., & Sargeant, A. (2000). Modeling internal communications in the financial services sector. *European Journal of Marketing, 34*(3–4), 299–318.

Austin, J., & Currie, B. (2003). Changing organisations for a knowledge economy: The theory and practice of change management. *Journal of Facilities Management, 3*(2), 229–243.

Baltatzis, G., Ormrod, D. G., & Grainger, N. (2008). Social networking tools for internal communication in large organizations: Benefits and barriers. The 19th Australasian Conference on Information Systems (ACIS 2008), Christchurch, New Zealand, 03–05 December 2008/Annette Mills and Sid Huff (eds.), pp. 76–86.

Barrett, D. J. (2002). Change communication: Using strategic employee communication to facilitate major change. *Corporate communications, 7*(4), 219–231.

Chapter 5

Integration of Social Media in Recruitment: A Delphi Study

Aurélie Girard, Bernard Fallery and Florence Rodhain

Abstract

Purpose — The development of social media provides new opportunities for recruitment and raises various questions. This chapter aims to clarify areas of agreement and disagreement regarding the integration of social media in recruitment strategies.

Methodology/approach — A Delphi study was conducted among a panel of 34 French experts composed of 26 practitioners and 8 academics.

Findings — Three quantitative results and five qualitative results are presented. Social media appear as an opportunity to raise the strategic role of HR professionals through employer branding strategy, internal skills development, and a greater involvement of managers within the sourcing process.

Practical implications — This study points out several barriers and limits regarding the integration of social media in recruitment strategies and encourage HR professionals to take up the challenge. Multiple recommendations are addressed to HR professionals.

Originality/value of chapter — This chapter is based on an innovative application of the Delphi method. Moreover, it offers a more comprehensive and critical look on the integration of social media in recruitment strategies.

Keywords: Social media; recruitment; employer branding; Delphi; e-HRM

Introduction

In 2011, 77% of French Internet users were members of at least one social networks site (IFOP, 2011). This number has risen sharply: they were only 27% in 2008 (IFOP,

Social Media in Human Resources Management
Advanced Series in Management, 97–120
ISSN: 1877-6361/doi:10.1108/S1877-6361(2013)0000012009

2008). For several years, the term "social network" is therefore widespread in the Internet sphere. When users talk about "social networks," they refer to sites "2.0," such as Facebook, Twitter, LinkedIn, and YouTube. Many terms are used by the media and researchers: Web 2.0 (O'Reilly, 2005), social network sites (Boyd & Ellison, 2007), social media (Kaplan & Haenlein, 2010) …. We will use the term "social media" to characterize these tools (it includes social network sites but also blogs).

The rapid development of social media opens up new opportunities for businesses, particularly in e-HRM area (Barker, 2008; Heikkilä, 2010; Joos, 2008; Kaplan & Haenlein, 2010; Martin, Reddington, & Kneafsey, 2008; Welbourne, 2010). Bondarouk and Ruël (2009) define e-HRM as *"an umbrella term covering all possible integration mechanisms and contents between HRM and Information Technologies aiming at creating value within and across organizations for targeted employees and management"* (p. 507).

Recruitment is one of the main HR activity impacted by the rise of social media. According to a French survey (RegionsJob, 2011), 49% of French recruiters are now using social media to recruit. Forty-three percent of them admit to *"google"* applicants and 8% say they had already rejected someone based on the results obtained though the search engine.

These e-recruitment strategies remain largely unstudied in the literature. After conducting four case studies at two recruitment agencies and two companies that have developed innovative strategies through social media, we decided to realize a Delphi study to gather expert judgments and clarify points of agreement and controversy regarding these new approaches.

First, based on a literature review we demonstrate that social media represent an important issue for recruitment.

Then, we present a Delphi study conducted among 34 experts of social media and recruitment. Three quantitative results and five qualitative results are highlighted.

Finally, we discuss the results and provide suggestions for further research.

Social Media and Recruitment: Literature Review

The use of social media within recruitment strategies seems to be an important issue for two main reasons:

- to reduce the "noise" caused by previous e-recruitment tools;
- to face the "war for talent" and adapt the communication to new Internet users' behaviors.

To Reduce the Noise Caused by Previous E-Recruitment Tools

Since the late 1990s, Internet has taken an important place within the recruitment process. It has enabled organizations to extend their CV databases through three main instruments: job boards, careers websites, and recruitment software applications. According to a recent survey conducted by the French association for executive employment (APEC, 2010), almost all executives job offers are broadcast on the Internet (through job boards or careers websites), of which 81% exclusively online.

Despite the widespread use of technology in the recruitment context, research is scarce and mostly applicants-oriented (Lievens, Dam, & Anderson, 2002). From the employer perspective, Parry and Tyson (2009) demonstrate that the use of both career websites and recruitment systems has several benefits: cost reduction, efficiency gains, improved service to clients, and improved strategic orientation. Indeed, Internet has brought various benefits to recruiters in terms of job offers broadcasting (fast, large-scale, and cheaper), CVs access, and application management.

However, although the labor market has become more transparent, it has also become noisier. Fondeur (2006a) calls this phenomenon the dilemma "transparency–noise." Internet has led to a trivialization of the act of application, lowered the level of self-censorship of the applicants, and encouraged increased "unqualified" applications (Dineen, Ling, Ash, & DelVecchio, 2007; Fondeur, 2006b).

Today social media offer an opportunity for companies and applicants to solve this problem of noise induced by previous e-recruitment tools.

The literature has already demonstrated that "offline" social network, and thus the mobilization of social capital, do play an important role particularly within the recruitment process (Bourdieu, 1986; Lin, Ensel, & Vaughn, 1981). Granovetter (1973) used the job market to illustrate "*the strength of weak ties*" that enables to get in touch with a large number of people and to access new information and opportunities. From an applicant's point of view, mobilizing a social network makes it possible to obtain more information about the company and the job (Holzer, 1988; Lin et al., 1981; Rees, 1966). This method may also enable applicants to acquire better wages (Granovetter, 1995; Holzer, 1988). From an employer's perspective, according to Rees (1966), making use of one's own network or that of the staff should limit the number of applications while simultaneously ensuring their quality and also reduce absenteeism and turnover. This method is both less expensive and more effective because of the confidence put in the applications (Holzer, 1988).

Social media, and SNS in particular, multiply the possibilities of interpersonal contact and exchange (Roberts & Roach, 2009). Both applicants and employers can maintain, mobilize, and develop their social network more efficiently thanks to SNS. They can filter out relevant information and access new collaboration opportunities (DeKay, 2009; Girard & Fallery, 2011).

To Face the War for Talent and Adapt the Communication to Internet Users' Behaviors

According to the Resource-Based View (Barney, 1991; Prahalad & Hamel, 1990; Wernerfelt, 1984) a firm's human resources, or human capital, is an important potential source of sustained competitive advantage (Wright, Dunford, & Snell, 2001). Recruiting is the first step to obtain such an advantage. Nevertheless, today the nature of work presents many challenges (Ployhart, 2006): knowledge-based work places greater demands on employee competencies; demographic, societal, and cultural changes are widespread and are creating an increasing global shortfall in the number of qualified applicants; the workforce is also increasingly diverse. Several authors use the term "war for talents" to describe this phenomenon (Chambers, Foulon, Handfield-jones, Hankin, & Michaels, 1998; Guthridge, Komm, & Lawson, 2008). Companies are thus in competition and must implement effective strategies on one hand to detect talents and appreciate their skills, and on the other hand to attract, acquire, and retain them in the organization.

Moreover, in line with the increasing use of social media, Internet users' behaviors have evolved (as for applicants). Internet users are no longer spectators, they have become true "consum'actors" (de Rosnay, 2006) or "prosumers" (Toffler, 1980). They create, share, and exchange many contents. They no longer hesitate to express their opinions online on many platforms and call into question the traditional broadcasters of information. Empowered by social media technologies, customers are now connecting with and drawing power from each other (Bernoff & Li, 2008). They gain knowledge through Internet and social media in particular before making a decision, to forge an opinion about a brand, a company, and why not about their future employer.

In parallel, they can also use social media to manage their online presence and develop their "personal branding" (Dutta, 2010; Malita, Badescu, & Dabu, 2010). They can get in touch with other professionals, share their experiences, and thus develop their professional network and improve their employability. These behaviors are supposed to be characteristic of the so-called "Generation Y" (born between the late 1970s and mid-1990s) considered as interactive, impatient, and demanding with employers and society in general (Hewlett, Sherbin, & Sumberg, 2009; Tapscott, 2008).

Either way, these new behaviors seem to force companies to rethink the way they communicate. Social media bring the opportunity to develop their employer brand and to monitor they reputation. Backhaus and Tikoo (2004) define employer branding as "*the process of building an identifiable and unique employer identity.*" The concept of employer reputation "*is based on what one does as an employer plus what one says one is doing*" (Hepburn, 2005). In other words, the employer brand is the desired image by the company, while the employer reputation is the projected and interpreted image by particular candidates. Social media appear to be an interesting mean to improve both branding and reputation by being active and engaging the conversation with potential applicants and other stakeholders (Girard & Fallery, 2011).

The Research Approach

Origin and Rationale of the Approach

As a first step, we conducted case studies at two recruitment agencies and two companies that have developed recruitment and employer branding strategies on social media (Girard, Fallery, & Rodhain, 2011). Two main types of data were collected: secondary data (internal and external documents) as well as semi-structured interviews with actors being primarily involved (26 interviews conducted between September 2009 and February 2011, 24 hours of recording). After a content analysis, it appeared some differences of views among the various actors interviewed.

As a second step, we therefore wanted to clarify points of agreement and disagreement about social media and recruitment. Delphi method proved to be appropriate to achieve this goal. Indeed, this method was originally developed by Norman Dalkey and Olaf Helmer (from RAND Corporation) in the 1950s to obtain and organize a group of experts' opinions on issues of prospective military operations (Dalkey & Helmer, 1963). It permits to collect experts' opinions through a series of questionnaires (2–3 in general) iteratively. Delphi method is very adaptable and used in many fields for decision making, to explore a topic, to build models, or to perform scenarios and forecasts (Linstone & Turoff, 1975; Okoli & Pawlowski, 2004).

There are no set rules for Delphi study, however, Rowe and Wright (1999) characterize the classic Delphi method by four main features:

1. Participants' anonymity: it allows participants to express themselves freely and to avoid any influence based on respondents' personality or status.
2. Iteration: it enables participants to refine their views round by round.
3. Controlled feedback: it indicates to participants the ratings of others, and provides them the opportunity to clarify or modify their views.
4. Statistical aggregation of responses: it allows a quantitative analysis and the interpretation of data (Schmidt, 1997).

The aim of a Delphi study is usually to reach a consensus, through successive iterations, but in some cases, consensus is not necessarily the main goal. Therefore, our study is close to the "Argument Delphi" as defined by Kuusi (1999). Indeed, our approach encourages discussion and aims to highlight relevant arguments rather than just consensus.

Implementation of the Approach

Based on the literature review and case studies, we formulated 20 proposals: 12 "validation proposals" (affirmatives), and 8 "prospective proposals" (written in the future). Proposals have been formulated to lead the experts to argue their position and answers (formulation not "consensual"). For example, the term "indispensable" has been preferred for proposal 4 (cf. Table 2) to the term "useful" to encourage experts to discuss. Quite categorical words have been used (e.g., insufficient, forces, clearly, significantly...).

A pretest was previously performed. Proposals were reviewed by several colleagues (4) to ensure their understanding. This resulted in a few changes in the wording of some proposals. In general, the pretest encouraged us to use a simple vocabulary and add some details in brackets when necessary.

We opted for Likert scales ranging from 1 (strongly disagree) to 7 (strongly agree). We selected seven points under the criteria of Cox (1980) and Preston and Colman (2000). Moreover, it allows participants to provide more flexibility in their answers. Questionnaires were sent by email as a Word document as shown in Table 1.

Selection of experts and data collection.   The selection of "experts" is an essential element that determines the quality of results (Adler & Ziglio, 1996; Bolger & Wright, 1994). We selected experts following the three components suggested by Larréché and Montgomery (1977): industry experience, familiarity with the object of study, and knowledge of the characteristics of the object. Thanks to our case studies and our professional use of various SNS, we have been in contact with a number of social media and recruitment experts. Their identification was thus facilitated. In order to achieve a sufficient sample we contacted 44 experts; 34 of them agreed to participate and did respond to the first questionnaire (final response rate: 77%). Our panel consisted of 8 academic researchers who have published and/or participated in seminars on the topic, and 26 "practitioners": consultants working in recruitment agencies (8), consultants working in management and HR consulting agencies (7), HR corporate managers (5), and job boards or SNS managers (6).

A three round Delphi.   The Delphi study was conducted between March 28 and June 20, 2011 (12 weeks).

At *the first round*, we asked the experts to rate each proposal from 1 to 7, to comment on their vote if they wished, and to write any other proposals at the end of document (proposal 21 was thus added). Answer time ranged from 1 day to 3 weeks and one reminder was sent.

At *the second round*, we indicated to each expert for each proposal, the median, the histogram of the answers, and their positioning in red. Experts had to:

- Confirm or change their rating for each proposal (given the discovery of other experts' opinions)
- Comment on their position, especially if they changed their vote.
- Give a rate to each proposal, from A (very important) to D (not important).

This second round took 4 weeks and two reminders were needed.

At the third and last round we identified and communicated three groups of proposals:

- Group 1: proposals with a low level of consensus but judged as important to very important.
- Group 2: proposals with a high level of consensus and judged as important to very important.
- Group 3: proposals with a low level of consensus but considered as few or not important.

Table 1: Extract of the questionnaire.

We submit for your expert assessment a list of 20 proposals on the topic of social media and recruitment.
Please assess each proposal according to the following indicators (put an "X" next to the rating chosen):
1: Strongly disagree, 2: Disagree, 3: Rather disagree, 4: Neutral 5: Somewhat agree, 6: Agree, 7: Strongly agree
Feel free to add your comments on each proposal (right column)
You can write any other proposals at the bottom of the table
Please return the completed word document at:....

Proposals on Social Media and Recruitment - First Round

University logo

Proposals	Rate From 1 (strongly disagree) to 7 (strongly agree)	Your comments on the proposal and your assessment
1. Careers websites and job boards are essential but with social media development, they are now insufficient to recruit.	1 2 3 4 5 6 7	
2. With the development of interaction through social media, companies and recruitment agencies have lost control of information; they must agree to interact with potential applicants.	1 2 3 4 5 6 7	
3. Social media use by applicants has amplified the demand for a more personalized, balanced and transparent relationship with the company / the recruitment agency	1 2 3 4 5 6 7	
4. Social media have become essential to develop long term relationships with "pre-candidate" who listen to the job market.	1 2 3 4 5 6 7	

Regarding group 1 proposals, we asked the experts to explain why the level of consensus was low while proposal were classified as "important to very important." The median, the histogram of the answers, and the positioning of the expert were reported. This last round took 5 weeks and two reminders were also necessary. Contrary to previous rounds, all experts did not respond. We obtained a response rate of 70% (24 of 34 experts) (Table 2).

Results

Numerous assessments and comments were collected along the three rounds. Data collection, descriptive statistics, and comment analysis were performed with Excel. Statistical test were determined with SPSS. All the study was carried out in French, proposals and comments have been translated in English for this article. Three quantitative results and five qualitative results emerged.

Three Quantitative Results

(1) *All proposals combined, the global level of consensus is low*
The global level of consensus is relatively low. Indeed, we used Kendall's W to measure this level and its robustness (statistical significance). Kendall's W ranges from 0 (no consensus) to 1 (total consensus) (Schmidt, 1997) (Table 3).

Second round W is equal to 0.337 with a high degree of significance. This level corresponds to a relatively low level of consensus according to Schmidt (1997).
(2) *Two main groups of proposals are distinguished: with a high level of consensus and with a low level of consensus*
Therefore, two main groups of proposal can be distinguished: proposals with a relatively high level of consensus and proposals with a low level of consensus.

To measure the degree of consensus for each proposal we use the level of MAD (Isaac, 1996; Vella, Goldfrad, Rowan, Bion, & Black, 2000; Zenou, 2004), refined through another measure of dispersion (% IM1).

We present the quantitative results in summary tables indicating for each proposal:

- Me: The median.
- MAD (Round 1 and 2): The mean absolute deviation around the median, for the two rounds.
- %IM1: The percentage of answers in the range [median −1, median +1].
- % changes: The percentage of changes by proposal between round 1 and round 2.
- Importance: The assessment of importance: + (important to very important); − (few important to not important) (Table 4).

Some proposals seem to reach a high level of agreement (median from 6 to 7): 8, 11, 6, 3, 4, 13, and 2. Others seem to reflect more balanced positions (median

Table 2: List of the 21 proposals submitted to experts' judgment.

1. Careers websites and job boards are essential but with social media development, they are now insufficient to recruit.
2. With the development of interaction through social media, companies and recruitment agencies have lost control of information; they must agree to interact with potential applicants.
3. Social media use by applicants has amplified the demand for a more personalized, balanced, and transparent relationship with the company/the recruitment agency.
4. Social media have become essential to develop long-term relationships with "pre-candidate" who listen to the job market.
5. To manage its digital identity (managing its online presence, be able to communicate on itself, to interact) has become a sought, valued, and essential skill.
6. Although Generation Y is well known for his personal use of social media, professional use of social media is not a matter of age.
7. We must clearly distinguish between professional social networks used for the recruitment and other social media used to develop the employer brand.
8. It is necessary to adopt differentiated and targeted strategies (between tools, topics people) to implement actions on social media.
9. Social media monitoring (observations and reactions) is the most important to develop an employer brand strategy.
10. The practice of social media forces to create new positions in companies (Head of the Employer Brand, HR Community Manager).
11. With the use of social media, internal–external boundaries are increasingly blurred (role of Community Manager, intranet/Internet tools, private–professional repercussions …).
12. Social media are just complementary tools to improve recruitment and manage the employer brand.
13. Social media will change considerably applicant relationship management (with relations established in the long term, based more on exchange, with more proximity …).
14. Social media will give HR professionals a greater role in strategic decisions.
15. Social media use for recruitment will concern only specific profiles (some sectors, some professional status, some age groups …).
16. Even if a formal piloting/management of communities on social media is initially required (Community Manager), in the future communities will have more open structures with a voluntary commitment of members inside and outside the company.
17. Because of difficulties in mastering social media, companies will increasingly outsource their recruitments to experienced recruitment agencies.
18. By extending the possibilities of co-option, social media will lead to greater decentralization of recruitment responsibilities to managers and employees.
19. Applicants' use of social media will lead to a zapping (switching) behavior in professional careers (high turnover).
20. With the development of applicants' activity on social media (interactions, blogs...), companies will pay more attention to competencies than to job profiles (competencies more visible …).
21. Social media development favors the appearance of unethical behavior by the recruiters.

Table 3: Kendall's W of the first and second round.

Kendall's W — First round	0.241
Kendall's W — Second round	0.337
Asymptotic significance	.000 ($<1\%$)

Table 4: Group of proposals with a high level of consensus.

	Me	MAD round 1	MAD round 2	% IM1	% changes	Importance
p8 — Differentiated and targeted strategies	7	1.15	**0.79**	79%	11.8%	+
p11 — Internal–external boundaries are increasingly blurred	6	1.09	**0.82**	88%	17.6%	+
p5 — Managing his digital identity has become a skill sought, valued, and essential	5	1.06	**0.88**	71%	14.7%	+
p6 — Generation Y/not a question of age	7	1.06	**0.88**	79%	14.7%	+
p3 — Increasing demand for a more personalized, balanced, and transparent relationship with the company/recruiter	6	1.09	**0.94**	91%	11.8%	+
p9 — Social media monitoring is the most important/employer branding	4	1.00	**0.97**	85%	17.6%	+
p4 — Long-term relationships	6	1.32	**1.03**	85%	20.6%	+
p10 — Creation of new jobs	5	1.09	**1.09**	68%	0.0%	+
p13 — Will change dramatically the applicant relationship management	6	1.12	**1.09**	82%	11.8%	+
p18 — Will lead to greater decentralization of recruitment responsibilities	4.5	1.18	**1.12**	62%	8.8%	+
p1 — Careers website, job boards, are a must but are now insufficient	5	1.26	**1.18**	50%	8.8%	+
p2 — Loss of control/must interact	6	1.44	**1.18**	71%	20.6%	+
Mean of all answers:				75%	13.2%	

from 4 to 5): 5, 9, 10, 18, and 1. Comments analysis allows us to clarify these positions (Table 5).

The proposals regarding the future are the most represented (6/8). Comments analysis allows us to better understand the various experts' arguments.

Table 5: Group of proposals with a low level of consensus.

	Me	MAD round 1	MAD round 2	% IM1	% changes	Importance
p16 — Formal piloting/ more open structures	5	1.26	**1.21**	**68%**	**20.6%**	+
p21 — Appearance of unethical behavior	4	NA	**1.21**	**59%**	NA	+
p17 — Outsourcing	4	1.35	**1.29**	**68%**	2.9%	−
p20 — More attention to skills/competencies	5	1.41	**1.35**	**65%**	14.7%	+
p7 — Distinction between professional social networks and others social media	3	1.56	**1.41**	**59%**	8.8%	+
p14 — Greater HR role in strategic decisions	4	1.53	**1.56**	**50%**	5.9%	+
p19 — Zapping behavior	3	1.62	**1.59**	**44%**	14.7%	−
p15 — Only concern particular profiles	3.5	1.65	**1.65**	**24%**	8.8%	+
p12 — Just additional tools	3	1.88	**1.74**	**35%**	**17.6%**	+
Mean of all answers:				**52%**	**11.8%**	

(3) *Opinions converged from round one to round two*

Several elements allow us to affirm that opinions converged between round 1 and round 2 thanks to the Delphi process.

First, Kendall's W of round 2 is higher than the W of the first round (0.337 > 0.241). The global level of consensus is still low but has improved between the two rounds.

Moreover, the number of proposals with a high level of consensus has increased between the two rounds. Proposals number 1, 2, and 4 moved from a low level of consensus to a high level of consensus, especially proposals 2 and 4 which have led experts to revise their assessments (over 20% of changes).

Finally, the Wilcoxon signed-rank test enables us to test the significance of answers convergence between the two rounds. Indeed, this nonparametric test measures the convergence or divergence of the assessments. We perform this test on the distribution of mean absolute deviation from the median (MAD) of all proposals (Table 6).

In line with the Wilcoxon signed-rank test, answers convergence between the two rounds of Delphi is significant at a high confidence level (i.e., distribution of MAD2 < MAD1).

Five Qualitative Results

(1) *Social media do not replace other e-recruitment tools and they can either be used to develop employer branding or to recruit.*

Table 6: Wilcoxon signed-rank test.

		N	Rank sum	Z	Asymptotic significance
MAD2−MAD1	**Negatives ranks**	17[a]	168.50	−3.622[d]	.000
	Positives ranks	1[b]	2.50		
	Ex aequo	2[c]			
	Total	20			

[a]MAD Round 2 < MAD Round 1.
[b]MAD Round 2 > MAD Round 1.
[c]MAD Round 2 = MAD Round 1.
[d]Based on positive ranks.

Comment analysis of proposals number 1, 7, and 12 allow us to support this result

Regarding the first proposal: "*Careers websites and job boards are essential but with social media development, they are now insufficient to recruit*" ($Me = 5$), a form of consensus is reached. Indeed, the large majority of experts agree with the essential character of careers websites and job boards but most of them consider social media as more dynamic and relational tools. However, the term "insufficient" is often regarded as too categorical. Some experts stress that job boards are also evolving to incorporate social networking features.

> Corporate sites may be the place that provides information and so on. But social media allows sharing and virality, in short, a more extensive and efficient distribution. (no. 23)

> For recruitment, professional social networking sites expand sourcing and introduce another form of relationship with the applicants. (no. 29)

> From the "active applicant" perspective, job boards are essential. From the "passive applicant" perspective, job boards seem inefficient and social media have become essential to create development opportunities. (no. 15)

> They (job boards) are insufficient in their current form but get better by providing social networking features. (no. 31)

A majority of respondents tends to reject proposal 12: "*Social media are just complementary tools to improve recruitment and manage the employer brand*" ($Me = 3$) and do not perceive social media as "just complementary tools" but as more and more important tools for recruiting and employer branding strategies and having a significant organizational impact.

> On the contrary, they become more and more essential tools not only "gadgets" in charge of interns. (no. 23)

> "In fact I have a problem with" complementary "because they are more than that due to the skill they require to develop, the time they take to manage, the impact they can have internally and externally." (no. 24)

> No, they change the mode of seduction, recruitment, retention. (no. 26)

Indeed, social media may enable a better fit, notably by a better visibility of applicant's competencies, however, positions differ regarding proposal 20: "*With the development of applicants' activity on Social media (interactions, blogs...), companies will pay more attention to competencies than to job profiles/descriptions (competencies more visible ...)*" (Me = 5). Many experts consider that social media allow going beyond the simple resume, but the majority put forward different limits: organizational barriers, lack of flexibility in the selection process, or potentially superficial nature of "personal branding."

> Consideration of the individual applicant as a whole (competencies, network, recommendations, online engagement, opinions, personality, behaviour...). (no. 19)

> I confirm my vote because I am a typical example of this phenomenon because I was recruited to duplicate my techniques of personal branding to the company (employer branding). (no. 1)

> It's a fundamental shift ... but it faces certain inertia of companies. I think this will happen but not in the short term (no. 10)

> [...] but it is still necessary that the recruiter has the possibility of varying the "bounds" of the profile he is looking for. (no. 25)

> Possibly, but social media enable also to "build" a profile ("personal branding") [...]. (no. 23)

Proposal 7 tends to be rejected: "*We must clearly distinguish between professional social networks used for the recruitment and other Social media used to develop the employer brand*" (Me = 3). Most experts believe that it is not possible to categorically distinguish these two categories of social media and that all social media can be used both for employer branding and recruitment. Various reasons are evoked for rejecting this distinction: the symbiotic relationship between social media; the "war of positioning" of social media; others possible distinctions in terms of use, strategies, and levels of communication.

> Today it is very difficult, if not impossible, to cleave its different practices and keep waterproof its diverse networks. (no. 1)

> For me, the network is all the networks, so there is no distinction. (no. 21)

> I do not think we should separate as much the two types of tools because we are in a war of positioning of these tools. On the other hand, it will depend on the users and we are only at the early beginning. (no. 3)

> You must distinguish what you broadcast, what you do and the levels of confidentiality. [...] You can recruit via Twitter and Facebook by communicating your recruitment needs, and you can also be "conversational" on Linkedin and Viadeo through discussion groups. (no. 25)

(2) *In the short term social media can meet the demands of exchange; in the long term the change of applicant relationship will depend on the labor market and the appropriation of these tools.*

Comment analysis of proposals 2, 3, 4, 13, 20, and 21 allow us to support this result.

Regarding proposal 2: "*With the development of interaction through social media, companies and recruitment agencies have lost control of information; they must agree to interact with potential applicants*" (Me = 6), the majority of respondents actually think that recruiting agencies and companies do not — really — have the control of information and must exchange more with applicants through social media. Many argue that applicants have access to much more information via social media and that relationships are more balanced between recruiters and applicants.

> It's one of the major impacts that companies have to deal with. (no. 8)

> Companies do not have lost control of the information on their brand ... they never really had it. However, today, the applicants' speeches can be read and be seen more quickly. So we need to establish the dialogue. (no. 3)

> Indeed, it has become very easy for an applicant to inquire about a company, a recruiter, his future manager, through networks or by contacting directly current or former employees. The relationship has been balanced. (no. 32)

> A company that does not play the "game of conversation," will damage its brand image and will be deprived of applications for which the "social media" identity is important. (no. 1)

A majority of experts agree with proposal 4: "*Social media have become essential to develop long-term relationships with 'pre-candidate' who listen to the job market*" (Me = 6). Social media are thus considered as essential or at least "very useful" due to several advantages: construction of an applicant pool, management of online communities, enhancement of the company, and development of a "conversational" employer brand.

> This logic of community enables to be proactive in terms of talent identification and recruitment rather than being in a reactive mode. (no. 9)

> Sourcing and conversational employer brand. (no. 19)

> I think social media make it possible to get in touch before and after stay in touch, even in case of non recruitment. In other words, to extend the life cycle of the prospect-applicant. (no. 34)

Indeed, most experts agree with proposal 3: "*Social media use by applicants has amplified the demand for a more personalized balanced and transparent relationship with the company/the recruitment agency*" (Me = 6). This demand is considered by many experts as legitimate and transversal. Several emphasize the need for organizations to be more transparent and to adopt a less conventional discourse.

> Companies must become more transparent and limit conventional speech. It is necessary to communicate and to talk straight with applicants: promotion of the company's values, adequacy with the applicant's values... (no. 3)

> Yes. This demand first appeared in the relationship "customer-seller" or "consumer-brand/ manufacturer." Many of these players have been able to respond. It is natural that this expectation is also brought by other sectors, including recruitment. (no. 10)

> Social media is not the only item: the tense market, the CSR, diversity policies are also a pressure. Social networks are a digital representation of societal demands. (no. 2)

More than half of the experts are in total agreement with proposal 13: "*Social media will change considerably applicant relationship management (with relations established in the long term, based more on exchange, with more proximity ...)*" (Me = 6). Indeed some believe that there will be more proximity and more dialogue but another part believes that this change will depend both on the evolution of the labor market and the real appropriation of these media by recruiters (real exchanges, relational approach, ethical behavior ...).

> Yes because the applicant is better informed, he has more relational power. (no. 23).

> Social media enable us to create more links. [...] Now, regarding the long term, I confess being more sceptical by now. (no. 3)

> Potentially, but it involves some additional costs. Probably this vision will be limited to niche segments (specific expertise, high potential, etc.). (no. 33)

> Yes, if companies and recruiters use what these tools are offering more and better. But this will not prevent some recruiters using only social media to build a pool (as they would do with a job board) and missing the relational aspects. (no. 25)

> [...] The employer will remain still in a position of strength in most cases especially with difficult economic conditions as currently. (no. 13)

At the end of the first round, several experts stressed that this evolving relationship also includes ethical issues. We have thus submitted proposal 21 to experts' opinions: "*Social media development favors the appearance of unethical behavior by the recruiters*" (Me = 4). Most experts believe that social media can facilitate (and not favor) unethical behavior, these behaviors being more related to the recruiter than to social media themselves. It is worth noting that one expert wishes to stress the responsibility of applicants and three others even consider that social media will make unethical behaviors more visible.

> Unethical behaviour comes from people, not from tools implemented. (no. 3)

> [...] however, the applicant shares the responsibility for what happens to him. (no. 30)

> [...] On the contrary, social networks help identify these recruiters and to make known it at the speed of light. (no. 24)

(3) *New behaviors become widespread independently of applicants' age and carriers strategies.*
Proposals 5, 15, 6, 19 allow us to achieve this result.

The majority of experts had a balanced position regarding proposal 5: "*To manage its digital identity (managing its online presence, be able to communicate on itself, to interact) has become a sought, valued, and essential skill*" (Me = 5). The management of its "online traces" is seen as a generic skill (to be developed by all applicants), while the management of its online presence (be able to communicate on itself) is seen as a more specific skill currently restricted to certain occupations. Yet, most experts agree that these skills will involve a growing number of jobs and become more and more important, if not a norm.

> It depends on the position you are looking. In any case it has become essential for positions in communications, marketing, HR and web. (no. 5)

> It is generally true and it will be increasingly. It's a way to make a difference between two profiles a priori equivalent. But for certain qualifications or certain areas, it matters less (e.g., for construction and public works). (no. 10)

In and of itself the answer is "a big Yes" for digital identity, but concerning the "be able to communicate on itself and to interact" (which does not fall within digital identity) I'm not sure. The majority of Internet users do not express themselves. (no. 2)

[...] This might evolve from a distinctive competence to a key success factor. (no. 13)

By consequences proposal 15 "*Social media use for recruitment will concern only specific profiles (some sectors, some professional status, some age groups ...)*" (Me = 3.5) has a low level of consensus. A majority of experts think that the use of social media for recruitment will concern more and more profiles but the disagreement lies in the assessment of this generalization importance. Indeed, some consider that social media already concern very different profiles, while others believe some profiles will never be concerned.

The trend is democratizing, and today we find already people from diverse backgrounds. (no. 9)

It reminds me discourses at the beginning of job boards = where nobody believed that we would recruit non-executive ... With 20 million members on FB, 4M on Viadeo, the market is there ... (no. 29)

Even if the trend pushes more and more diverse backgrounds to come on social networks (different experience, education, age groups ...), it is true that at first glance it will always concern profiles with a computer access at their workplace. (no. 15)

Moreover, generation Y is often evoked regarding the use of social media but the vast majority of experts agree with proposal 6: "*Although Generation Y is well known for his personal use of social media, professional use of social media is not a matter of age*" (Me = 7). Indeed, they recognize that the younger generation has abilities but does not have a very professional approach of these tools. Other factors of use are underlined such as curiosity, experience, and interpersonal skills. Some experts even directly challenge the very existence of "gen Y."

Absolutely, Gen Y has de facto developed abilities to manage multiple profiles, communicate in real time and in a transversal way, and to use mobility services but does not necessarily have a professional and entrepreneurial approach of these technologies. (no. 2)

[...] The proper use of social media goes beyond mere technical knowledge, and also requires common sense, experience, interpersonal skills, qualities that do not belong to a generation. (no. 10)

Studies on uses (we have done a lot ...) show significant standard deviations within this "Generation Y." (no. 28)

Besides, information and opportunities provided by social media activity could lead to a higher turnover; this idea is also widespread in the media. Yet experts are quite negative about proposal 19: "*Applicants' use of Social media will lead to a zapping (switching) behavior in professional careers (high turnover)*" (Me = 3). Indeed, the majority tends to reject the term "lead." One half of experts do not consider social media as the triggers of change but as enablers that can accentuate this phenomenon. The other half does not link the practice of social media and zapping behavior. Some even think that social media could favor a better match between the applicant's project and the strategic project of the company. Many also stressed the importance of employee retention, with or without the help of social media.

The switching already exists, social networks could perhaps act as amplifiers. (no. 17)

[...] Ultimately, the challenge is reversed: how to use it to keep applicants. But the tool can only be at the service of a policy ... that still remains to be built. (no. 30)

On the contrary, transparency that social media entails rather could even curb this behaviour. Similarly, being less in a selling behaviour, but rather in the search for a fit between strategic business project and personal/professional project should enable a healthier and long-term collaboration. (no. 9)

(4) *Social media will enable either a greater involvement of employees in the sourcing or an outsourcing toward new types of recruitment agencies*

Proposal 17 and 18 allow us to formulate this result.

Only one expert totally agrees with proposal 17 "*Because of difficulties in mastering social media, companies will increasingly outsource their recruitments to experienced recruitment agencies*" (Me = 4). One-third totally disagree with the proposal and think the opposite situation will occur, that is, a greater internalization of recruitment activity for various reasons: cost reduction, facilitated sourcing through social media, outsourcing difficulty related to the need of interactivity, and transparency.

On the contrary, companies want to capitalize on the opportunity to save outsourcing costs by internalizing the sourcing. (no. 32)

I do not think, on the contrary. It seems to me more difficult to outsource under these conditions (immediate reactivity, transparency, proximity and knowledge of the company ...). (no. 34)

I think it would be wrong because if we are talking about recruitment with dialogue and exchange is that we want to recruit people with the best profile and meet the company's values. [...]. (no. 3).

The opinions of the remaining two-thirds are more nuanced. Several experts believe that recruitment via social media can be outsourced, subject to the emergence of new types of agencies: providing a real added value, specializing in certain jobs, and developing approaches and skills about social media.

I confirm my vote but subject to the emergence of new types of recruitment agencies — because I still believe that traditional agencies will themselves have as much trouble (or more) than companies to turn to social media for carrying out their mission. (no. 1)

I hope so, but I do not believe it ...;) mainly because of the previously mentioned job aspect ... or via recruitment agencies specialized in specific jobs. (no. 9)

Opinions are also nuanced regarding proposal 18: "*By extending the possibilities of co-option, social media will lead to greater decentralization of recruitment responsibilities to managers and employees*" (Me = 4.5). Some (7) strongly agree and think this is a logical evolution. However, the majority actually believe that there will be a greater involvement of managers, more actors involved in the sourcing process, but that the rest of the recruitment process will remain rather centralized.

This is a just reward — we have disempowered managers of recruitment for 20 years. We were giving an unlikely profile to HR professionals who had to cope with it. (no. 27)

I 100% agree concerning the sourcing. For the rest of the recruitment process, including selection, this does not change much (except for references). (no. 9)

> Greater involvement rather than greater decentralization. (no. 25)

It is worth noting that many experts mention organizational and French cultural barriers about the system of co-option by itself.

> It is hoped — it makes sense — but organizations do not like cronyism ... (no. 7)

> We have seen that the French market, except some well-known sector, was not ready for co-optation ... Important ... but so very complicated. (no. 30)

(5) *Social media provide an opportunity to raise the strategic role of HR professionals; if indeed HR professionals take up the challenge.*

Proposals 10, 8, 9, 16, 11, and 14 allow us to support this result.

In order to manage HR social media strategy, some companies have already created new positions. Proposal 10 addresses this issue: "*The practice of social media forces to create new positions in companies (Head of the Employer Brand, HR Community Manager)*" (Me = 5). A majority of experts consider that social media use can lead to create new specific positions, but most emphasize that this can be achieved also by an evolution of employees' roles and in addition to another position. Thus, many consider that the creation of specific jobs depends on the company size and the magnitude of the task. Some even argue that, in the long run, everyone will have to assume a part of these new roles.

> New skills in existing jobs and sometimes indeed new positions. (no. 26)

> In the short/mid-term only. Then this will be part of the role of everyone. (no. 30)

> (...) The efficiency of this role will depend above all — on the capacity of employees to play a part of this role. Education and engagement is therefore fundamental. (no. 9)

Others consider that this evolution is still ongoing, and highlight different barriers: resistance to change, organizational, and cultural barriers.

> 5 in 2011, six in 2012: currently, companies should no longer be afraid of these tools, and select the ones they need according to their target. [...]. (no. 24)

> HRD is often hostile to social media, like the Legal Department, as they have a culture of "regulations" and "codes" while social media require a lot of creativity and risk. (no. 23)

Besides, regarding proposal 8 "*It is necessary to adopt differentiated and targeted strategies (between tools, topics people) to implement actions on social media*" (Me = 7) a large majority advices HR professionals to distinguish media and targets, to adapt and personalize content but many emphasize that this must be done within the framework of a broader HR strategy and be consistent with it.

> First, we must observe each media to choose how to interact and what to put inside according to what we like to say, transmit, and who we want to touch. This is the marketing side of HR communication. (no. 25)

> Yes, but within the framework of a global strategy, otherwise it will be fragmented. (no. 26)

Moreover, regarding proposal 9, "*Social media monitoring (observations and reactions) is the most important to develop an employer brand strategy*" (Me = 4), most experts consider social media monitoring as an important element in developing an employer brand strategy, but not as the most important.

> [...] the most important is the real HR offer of the company, social media are a medium to communicate about this offer, without offer, no message. (no. 8)

Proposal 16 addresses the possible distribution of roles and trigger debates on participation and animation of "communities" gathered via social media: "*Even if a formal piloting/management of communities on social media is initially required (Community Manager), in the future communities will have more open structures with a voluntary commitment of members inside and outside the company*" (Me = 5). Majority of experts believe that ultimately much more employees should participate through social media communities but several admit that some kind of management and support will remain necessary.

> Community management biodegradable. (no. 26)
>
> A regulation and moderation on these media seems indispensable. (no. 5)
>
> It is desirable because the current position of community manager in some companies makes them run a huge operational risk, in which the community manager attaches to his own name all communities! More than his employer!!! (no. 9)

Different barriers are once again mentioned:

> Currently, companies are afraid of what they cannot control, but gradually, the greater use of social media will allow them to soften their point of view and accept that people outside the HR department express themselves. (no. 15)
>
> I'm uncertain that our corporate cultures lead us in this direction so quickly. Uncertain that employees will want to get involved more, either ... (no. 30)

With these new practices, internal–external boundaries seem to be increasingly blurred. A majority of experts agree with proposal 11: "*With the use of social media, internal–external boundaries are increasingly blurred (role of Community Manager, intranet/Internet tools, private–professional repercussions ...)*" (Me = 6). Most experts consider that the use of social media tends to make the internal–external boundaries increasingly blurred and flexible. They regard this as both an opportunity and a matter of concern. Some stress the importance of establishing rules, social media guidelines.

> Strong porosity which begins to be confirmed in most studies [...]. (no. 13)
>
> [...] it is both an opportunity and a real concern. A risk. Properly position the cursor is essential. (no. 30)
>
> Yes this is the main problem. There is no longer hours to deliver a message, and public/private distinction is unclear. It is within the practice of networks that ambiguity must be removed (e.g., do not diffuse messages after 8pm!!!!). (no. 7)
>
> [...] It is important to set some rules about this, guidelines are welcomed. (no. 25)

Finally, all proposals lead us to proposal 14: "*Social media will give HR professionals a greater role in strategic decisions*" (Me = 4). Majority of experts

References

Adler, M., & Ziglio, E. (1996). *Gazing into the oracle: The Delphi method and its application to social policy and public health.* London, UK: Jessica Kingsley Publishers Ltd.

APEC. (2010). Sourcing cadres/Baromètre annuel de l'Apec. Survey from the Association Pour l'Emploi des Cadres (pp. 1–6).

Backhaus, K., & Tikoo, S. (2004). Conceptualizing and researching employer branding. *Career Development International, 9*(5), 501–517.

Barker, P. (2008). How social media is transforming employee communications at Sun Microsystems. *Global Business and Organizational Excellence, 27*(4), 6–14.

Barney, J. B. (1991). Firm resources and sustained competitive advantage. *Journal of Management, 17*(1), 99–120.

Bernoff, J., & Li, C. (2008). Harnessing the power of the oh-so-social web harnessing the power of the oh-so-social web. *MIT Sloan Management Review, 49*(3), 36–42.

Bolger, F., & Wright, G. (1994). Assessing the quality of expert judgment. *Decision Support Systems, 11*(1), 1–24.

Bondarouk, T. V., & Ruël, H. J. M. (2009). Electronic human resource management: Challenges in the digital era. *The International Journal of Human Resource Management, 20*(3), 505–514.

Bourdieu, P. (1986). The forms of capital. In J. Richardson (Ed.), *Handbook of theory and research for the sociology of education* (pp. 241–258). New York, Greenwood.

Boyd, D. M., & Ellison, N. B. (2007). Social network sites: Definition, history, and scholarship. *Journal of Computer-Mediated Communication, 13*(1), 210–230.

Chambers, E. G., Foulon, M., Handfield-jones, H., Hankin, S. M., & Michaels, E. G., III. (1998). The war for talent. *McKinsey Quarterly, 3*, 44–57.

Cox, E. (1980). The optimal number of response alternatives for a scale: A review. *Journal of Marketing Research, 17*(4), 407–422.

Dalkey, N., & Helmer, O. (1963). An experimental application of the DELPHI method to the use of experts. *Management Science, 9*(3), 458–467.

DeKay, S. (2009). Are business-oriented social networking web sites useful resources for locating passive jobseekers? Results of a recent study. *Business Communication Quarterly, 72*(1), 101–105.

de Rosnay, J. (2006). *La révolte du pronétariat: des mass média aux médias des masses.* Paris: Fayard.

Dineen, B. R., Ling, J., Ash, S. R., & DelVecchio, D. (2007). Aesthetic properties and message customization: Navigating the dark side of web recruitment. *Journal of Applied Psychology, 92*(2), 356–372.

Dutta, S. (2010). What's your personal social media strategy? *Harvard Business Review, 88*(11), 127–130.

Fondeur, Y. (2006a). Le recrutement par internet: Le dilemme transparence/bruit. *Personnel, 472*, 46–48.

Fondeur, Y. (2006b). Internet, recrutement et recherche d'emploi: Une introduction. *Revue de l'IRES, 52*(3), 3–10.

Girard, A., & Fallery, B. (2011). e-Recruitment: From transaction-based practices to relationship-based approaches. In T. V. Bondarouk, H. J. M. Ruël, & J. Looise (Eds.), *Electronic HRM in theory and practice* (Vol. 8, pp. 143–158). Advanced Series in Management. Bingley, UK: Emerald Group Publishing Limited.

Girard, A., Fallery, B., & Rodhain, F. (2011). The development of social media in the field of e-HRM: Employer branding and e-recruitment. *Proceedings of the 16th AIM conference 2011*, Association Information Management, Saint Denis, Reunion, France (p. 18).

Granovetter, M. S. (1973). The strength of weak ties. *American Journal of Sociology*, *78*(6), 1360–1380.

Granovetter, M. S. (1995). *Getting a job: A study of contacts and careers*. Chicago, IL: University of Chicago Press.

Guthridge, M., Komm, A. B., & Lawson, E. (2008). Making talent a strategic priority. *McKinsey Quarterly*, *1*, 48–59.

Heikkilä, J. P. (2010). A Delphi study on E-HRM?: Future directions. *Proceedings of the third European academic workshop on electronic human resource management*, Bamberg, Germany (pp. 229–249).

Hepburn, S. (2005). Creating a winning employer reputation. *Strategic HR Review*, *4*(4), 20–23.

Hewlett, S. A., Sherbin, L., & Sumberg, K. (2009). How Gen Y and Boomers will reshape your agenda. *Harvard Business Review*, *87*(7–8), 71–77.

Holzer, H. J. (1988). Search method use by unemployed youth. *Journal of Labor Economics*, *6*(1), 1–20.

IFOP. (2008, December). Les internautes et les réseaux sociaux. Survey from the Institut Franç ais d'Opinion Publique (pp. 1–10).

IFOP. (2011, November). Observatoire des réseaux sociaux, vague 6. Survey from the Institut Français d'Opinion Publique (pp. 1–28).

Isaac, H. (1996). *Ethical codes, a tool for quality management in professional services*. PhD thesis in Management Science, University Paris Dauphine, France.

Joos, J. G. (2008). Social media?: New frontiers in hiring and recruiting. *Employment Relations Today*, *35*(1), 51–59.

Kaplan, A. M., & Haenlein, M. (2010). Users of the world, unite! The challenges and opportunities of social media. *Business Horizons*, *53*(1), 59–68.

Kuusi, O. (1999). *Expertise in the future use of generic technologies. Epistemic and methodological considerations concerning Delphi studies*. Helsinki: Government Institute for Economic Research VATT.

Larréché, J., & Montgomery, D. (1977). A framework for the comparison of marketing models: A Delphi study. *Journal of Marketing Research*, *14*(4), 487–498.

Lievens, F., Dam, K. V., & Anderson, N. (2002). Recent trends and challenges in personnel selection. *Personnel Review*, *31*(5), 580–601.

Lin, N., Ensel, W. M., & Vaughn, J. C. (1981). Social resources and strength of ties: Structural factors in occupational status attainment. *American Sociological Review*, *46*(4), 393–405.

Linstone, H., & Turoff, M. (1975). *The Delphi method: Techniques and applications* (Vol. 18). Reading, MA: Addison-Wesley.

Malita, L., Badescu, I., & Dabu, R. (2010). Culture tips of online job searching. *Procedia — Social and Behavioral Sciences*, *2*(2), 3070–3074.

Martin, G., Reddington, M., & Kneafsey, M. (2008). *Web 2.0 and HRM: A discussion document*. Chartered Institute of Personnel and Development. London, UK.

Okoli, C., & Pawlowski, S. (2004). The Delphi method as a research tool: An example, design considerations and applications. *Information & Management*, *42*, 15–29.

O'Reilly, T. (2005). What is Web 2.0: Design patterns and business models for the next generation of software. *O'Reilly Media Inc*. Retrieved from http://oreilly.com/web2/archive/what-is-web-20.html. Accessed on April 2, 2010.

Parry, E., & Tyson, S. (2009). What is the potential of E-recruitment to transform the recruitment process and the role of the resourcing team? In T. Bondarouk, H. Ruel, K. Guiderdoni-Jourdain & E. Oiry (Eds.), *Handbook of research on E-transformation and human resources management technologies: Organizational outcomes and challenges* (pp. 202–217). New York, NY: IGI Global.

Ployhart, R. E. (2006). Staffing in the 21st century: New challenges and strategic opportunities. *Journal of Management, 32*(6), 868–897.

Prahalad, C. K., & Hamel, G. (1990). The core competence of the corporation. *Harvard Business Review, 68*(3), 79–91.

Preston, C. C., & Colman, A. M. (2000). Optimal number of response categories in rating scales: Reliability, validity, discriminating power, and respondent preferences. *Acta Psychologica, 104*(1), 1–15.

Rees, A. (1966). Information networks in labor markets. *American Economic Review, 56*(1–2), 559–566.

RegionsJob. (2011). Enquête emploi & réseaux sociaux, deuxième edition. Survey from Regionsjob.com (pp. 1–17).

Roberts, S. J., & Roach, T. (2009). Social networking web sites and human resource personnel: Suggestions for job searches. *Business Communication Quarterly, 72*(1), 110–114.

Rowe, G., & Wright, G. (1999). The Delphi technique as a forecasting tool: Issues and analysis. *International Journal of Forecasting, 15*, 353–375.

Ruël, H. J. M., Bondarouk, T. V., & Looise, J. (2004). E-HRM: Innovation or irritation: An explorative empirical study in five large companies on web-based HRM. *Management Revue, 15*(3), 364–380.

Schmidt, R. C. (1997). Managing Delphi surveys using nonparametric statistical techniques. *Decision Sciences, 28*(3), 763–774.

Tapscott, D. (2008). *Grown up digital: How the net generation is changing your world.* McGraw-Hill.

Toffler, A. (1980). *The third wave. Blueprint* (p. 544). New York, NY: Morrow.

Vella, K., Goldfrad, C., Rowan, K., Bion, J., & Black, N. (2000). Use of consensus development to establish national research priorities in critical care. *British Medical Journal, 320*(7240), 976–980. Clinical research ed.

Welbourne, T. M. (2010). New media: Opportunity or curse for HR? *Human Resource Management, 49*(1), 1–2.

Wernerfelt, B. (1984). A resource based view of the firm. *Strategic Management Journal, 5*(2), 171–180.

Wright, P. M., Dunford, B. B., & Snell, S. (2001). Human resources and the resource based view of the firm. *Journal of Management, 27*(6), 701–721.

Zenou, E. (2004). *How to integrate the value created by a CEO within a firm's global value creation? Contribution to the investigation of a CEO's value assessment. An application within the French market.* PhD thesis in Management Science, University Jean Moulin, Lyon 3.

Chapter 6

Social Media as a Mechanism for Engagement?

Emma Parry and Adriano Solidoro

Abstract

Purpose — This chapter examines the use of social media within organizations in order to engage with both current and potential future employees.

Design/methodology/approach — It is commonly claimed that social media technologies can help organizations to engage with both current and potential employees. This chapter examines these claims through an examination of the use of social media within two organizations: a UK television company and an international UK telecommunications company. Data was gathered from the company websites and via 34 semi-structured interviews.

Findings — The two case studies confirm that social media has promise with regard to facilitating the engagement of existing employees. However, the findings suggest also that the use of social media to engage employees will not be successful unless the culture and leadership of the organization already embraces open communication and participation.

Research limitations/implications — The findings are limited in that they rely on two case studies and therefore might not be applicable to other organizations. Despite the limitations, this chapter has significant implications for organizations considering the adoption of social media as a means to improve employee engagement. It suggests that when adopting social media for organizations, the very first step should be to assess the organizational readiness with a focus on culture and people rather than on the technology itself. This is because managerial behaviors and styles are central to the level of engagement individuals feel with an organization. For the same reason leaders need to be trained to lead collaboratively, and to be able to understand the new social practices.

Originality/value — The chapter makes an important contribution to an extremely sparse literature on social media as a means for engaging with employees through the

Social Media in Human Resources Management
Advanced Series in Management, 121–141
ISSN: 1877-6361/doi:10.1108/S1877-6361(2013)0000012010

provision of rare empirical data and is therefore valuable both for managers and for HR scholars and practitioners.

Keywords: Social media; Web 2.0; employee engagement; recruitment; employee communication

Introduction

One of the commonly espoused uses of social media for employers is to help them to engage with both existing and potential employees. The precise definition of "engagement" is much debated in the literature and might also vary among organizations. However, employers do agree that engagement of employees is essential if organizations are going to be successful and create competitive advantage (IABC, 2011), Engaged individuals are described as being attentive, emotionally connected, integrated, focused in their performance (MacLeod & Brady, 2008), involved with enthusiasm, and willing to exert greater discretionary effort in his or her work. The engaged employee will typically demonstrate initiative, proactively seeking opportunities to contribute, be willing to share information with colleagues while speaking up for the organization, and trying harder to meet customers' needs.

The contribution of engaged employees is particularly indispensable during a turbulent period of economic recession such as that currently experienced within much of the Western world, since they have a strong emotional sense of ownership and are willing to do whatever is needed to support the organization MacLeod & Clarke, 2011). Numerous studies (CIPD, 2008; IABC, 2011) show a direct relationship between employee engagement and business results. Engagement contributes significantly to an organization's performance, leading to improvements in service quality, customer satisfaction, as well as higher productivity and financial results. By contrast, when employees are disengaged, organizational performance declines. Engagement also serves the individual, fulfilling a basic human need to be connected to worthwhile endeavors and make a significant contribution. Since individuals often prefer to be involved (engaged) in meaningful and challenging work, employee engagement is therefore a classic win–win initiative since it is associated with employee satisfaction as well as organizational success.

Typically, engagement of employees is discussed at two stages of the employment cycle. First, job seekers or potential employees need to engage with an organization in order to feel attracted to that organization and to decide to apply to work there. Second, once employed by the organization, individuals need to develop high levels of engagement with their employer in order to facilitate the outcomes discussed above. At both stages, engagement can be driven by an individual's perception that they are involved and listened to, and that they have a role to play in the organization. With regard to existing employees, the literature has focused on the need to promote dialogue within the organization in order to facilitate employee participation and involvement and therefore improve engagement. For job seekers, dialogue is also important in order for the job seeker to perceive a fit between their needs and that of the organization and to understand what the employer can offer them. At both stages of employment therefore, engagement is about building a relationship between the individual and employer. It has been claimed that social media can provide the means by which dialogue and therefore this relationship can be developed. Social media therefore provide a new dimension to the building of relationships between employees, their line managers, and senior management.

Social media may therefore support more collaboration, greater transparency, and increased trust between employees and the organization, becoming an important vehicle for many aspects of internal communications that are relevant to employee engagement. For these reasons, the intersection between digital communication's omnipresence and the emerging culture of deeper engagement provides many opportunities to organizations. Thus, more and more companies are recognizing social media and social networks as valuable tools for refining employee engagement, responding to the greater than ever need to deliver information to employees in a way that creates a sense of community. New social and networking media provide a valuable opportunity for companies to increase engagement with employees through facilitating dialogue, and to integrate employees into the culture of the organization by creating a sense of community. Internal social groups can be connected and engaged through the effective use of social media giving the opportunity to employees to share ideas, replacing the old style suggestion boxes with a more interactive process.

In successful organizational use of social media, social and business functions intertwine: forums spring up to connect people in similar job functions or expertise areas but different locations; people can ask for and quickly get help from peers, or brainstorm ideas; employees are empowered as authors post useful reference material and share their expertise. These corporate social networking platforms offer a variety of engagement and productivity benefits from employee brainstorming, increased collaboration, and knowledge transfer. Therefore, these enabling technologies can have an effect on employee satisfaction levels while creating value for the organization. All of this could be essential to an engaged and productive workforce.

The little research that is available about social media and employee engagement bears this idea out. In 2008 an Aberdeen Group (2008) reported that organizations using blogs, wikis, and social networking tools achieved an average year-on-year improvement in employee engagement of 18%, compared with 1% for organizations that do not use social networking tools. The study reported that organizations that achieved the leading performance designation in the use of blogs, wikis, corporate social networking, and other online collaboration tools throughout the talent management life cycle demonstrated a 39% reduction in training costs while simultaneously improving engagement and quality of hire by 33%. A 2012 study by APCI and Gagen McDonald (2012) reveals how internal social media use can bring major benefits to a number of employee engagement areas, and isolates the key attributes that such programs require. They found that 58% of the workers polled would prefer to work at a company that uses social media; 86% would refer others for employment; 61% felt it became easier to collaborate, while 60% were likely to feel their company is innovative. Employees were 60% more likely to give their company the benefit of the doubt in a crisis, and two-thirds of employees were likely to support government policies their company supports. They are also 78% more likely to purchase the company's stock. It seems evident, then, that social media platforms and social intranets can offer some positive solutions to the complex problem of employee engagement.

Despite the two consultancy-based studies above, academic research into the use of social media for engaging with potential and current employees is sparse. In particular, there is little in-depth research that looks at the ways in which companies are using social media tools for these purposes and whether these social media satisfy their objectives with regard to improving engagement. This chapter will therefore examine the use of social media for engagement with existing and potential employees through the use of two organizational examples. We will proceed by discussing in more detail the literature on employee engagement and social media before describing our organizational examples.

Background and Literature Review

In order to study the literature relevant to the focus of our chapter, we will concentrate first on what is known about employee engagement generally. We will look at what is known about engagement of both existing employers and of potential employees through a brief analysis of the literature on employee branding, employee value propositions, and the psychological contract. We will then move onto to examine the role of social media in engaging both current and potential future employees.

Employee Engagement

Employee engagement has emerged relatively recently as a concept within human resource management (HRM) and therefore has, so far, been subject to only a small amount of empirical research. Despite this, the idea of employee engagement appears to have resonated with employers, and so it has already become prominent in the world of HR practice and within organizations (Vance, 2006). Employee engagement can be defined as "the extent to which an employee is psychologically present in a particular organizational role" (Saks, 2006, p. 604). Robinson, Perryman, and Hayday (2004) suggested that engagement is a positive attitude that employees have toward their organization and its values.

Khan (1990) was one of the first scholars to discuss the notion of engagement in relation to employees and HRM. Khan suggested that people have various degrees of engagement or disengagement at work. The consequence of this is that people use various amounts of their personal selves (cognitive, emotionally, and physically) in their working lives and roles. High employee engagement is characterized by high levels of activation and identification with the organization and employer. Alternatively, Schaufeli, Martinez, Pinto, Salanova, and Bakker (2002) suggested that high levels of engagement are represented by "a positive, fulfilling, work-related state of mind that is characterized by vigor, dedication and absorption" (p. 72). More recently, Macey and Schneider (2008) divided the concept of engagement into three components: trait engagement, focusing on personal level attributes such as personality; behavioral engagement, focusing on the actions of employees; and psychological state engagement, represented by affect and feelings of energy.

Engagement has been adopted by HR practitioners as a characteristic of employees that is related to high productivity. Specifically, recent research in the United Kingdom suggested that high levels of engagement can lead to lower sickness absence, higher customer service, and better retention, as well as higher innovation and better overall performance (MacLeod & Clarke, 2009). Therefore most of the attention in discussions of engagement has focused on how employers might develop high levels of engagement in their workforce. As with engagement more broadly, empirical research in this area is generally sparse. However, what research there is has suggested a connection between effective performance management systems and high employee engagement, and in particular one aspect of engagement — employee commitment (Gardner, Moynihan, Park, & Wright, 2001). In addition, work climate has been suggested as having a relationship with employee engagement. Indeed, work climate, defined as a combination of factors such as perceived organizational justice and trust in their employer, has long been seen as important in affecting employee outcomes (Greenberg, 1990; Macky & Boxall, 2007). One factor that has been related to both work climate and employee engagement, and is of particular interest to this study, is that of communication (Cartwright & Holmes, 2007; Lockwood, 2007). Indeed, Ruck and Welch (2012) connect engagement to effective internal communication, underlying the fact that organizations need to evaluate and improve communication especially in increasingly difficult economic pressures. If communication is an important antecedent of employee engagement, then it might be that information-communication technologies (ICT), such as social media, can also be used to promote employee engagement within organizations. In fact one of the most commonly espoused advantages of social media is that it can facilitate more effective communication and collaboration, and therefore has the capacity to build relationships between employees and their employers (and therefore potentially improve engagement). The next section of this chapter will focus on the use of social media for communication and collaboration and therefore its potential affect on employee engagement.

Social Media and Employee Engagement

Since a changing communication environment calls for new approaches with an emphasis on communities, content, and dialogue rather than volume and channels, opportunities for employee voice and participation can be significantly improved by taking more account of the impact of social media. Groysberg and Slind (2012) indicated that such a more collaborative approach to leadership might be a prerequisite for the improvement of employee engagement and alignment in today's more and more networked (also through social media) organizations. Martin, Reddington, and Kneafsey (2009) provided examples of social media corporate applications to key functions in HR and people management as a benchmark for more effective listening to understand employees and other internal stakeholders. These included the promotion of the use of employee blogs and online discussion forums to raise issues that are important to employees, in order to surface authentic employee voice rather than responses to attitude surveys.

Murphy (2010) reviewed this ability of social media technologies and mobile computing devices to facilitate and encourage knowledge sharing between "silo'd" groups. The cases analyzed indicated that the collaborative and interactive characteristics of social media had provided organizations with increased capacity to share information to facilitate problem solving, reduce duplication of effort, and increase business agility, as well as bringing the side benefits of stronger employee engagement with senior members of the workforce, and the development of a competitive advantage in new talent acquisition. Through social media, leaders can facilitate two-way communication while employees engage in a bottom-up exchange of ideas, and interact with colleagues through blogs and discussion forums.

By allowing employees to voice their concerns and communicate with employers, social media applications can therefore contribute to the improvement of employee engagement. Indeed, Dahl, Lawrence, and Pierce (2011), who took into account the increasing use of social media to broaden the approach to idea generation and innovation both within and outside the walls of the organization, suggested that this provided intangible benefits such as improved internal processes, increased customer satisfaction, as well as employee engagement. Doherty (2010) provided practical advice for HR professionals, suggesting that social media represented a great opportunity for organizations to create a sense of community among employees. Social media allow HR to promote communication and the sharing of knowledge and ideas and, as a result, boost employee engagement and ultimately enhance the internal employer brand, as well as attracting and retaining the most talented individuals.

The potential benefits of social media for communication (and therefore employee engagement) are therefore strongly promoted in the literature. However, these espoused benefits have been cast into doubt by an increasing literature that suggests that achieving improved communication, collaboration, and engagement through social media might not be as easy as suggested. Interactivity is not just a matter of finding and deploying the right technology, equally if not more important is the need to buttress social media with social thinking, in order to avoid that an organization's prevailing culture works against any attempt to transform corporate communication into a two-way affair.

When using social media to better engage employees, managers can tend to focus on installing the technology, rather than on designing a socio-technical system that can meet the organization's goals and foster authentic participation. Therefore, only organizations that learn how to constructively engage their workers are likely to enjoy distinct competitive advantage. Taking a more extreme position, MacCormick et al.

(2012) question whether the increase in the use of social media via mobile devices could actually lead to conditions under which connectivity was problematic for engagement. However, McCormick et al.'s empirical research suggested that the use of a Smartphone appeared to amplify work engagement behaviors, mainly, but not exclusively, in functional ways.

A number of authors have suggested that the use of social media can only mirror the existing structure of power and politics within an organization and will not transform communication in organizations in which openness and trust are not already a feature of the climate. More specifically, Hodgkinson (2007a, 2007b) suggested that organizations must ask themselves whether they are truly ready to collaborate, create, and exploit knowledge and whether existing social interactions are open or closed. Hodgkinson also proposes that social media will mean an inevitable loss of control in an organizational environment, and recognizes that the cultural aspects, particularly those regarding hierarchy, power, and politics are very different to the peerless, self-managing communities observed in the consumer domain. Although the technology provides an opportunity to build identity, meaning, and trust, he questions whether organizations have the critical mass of users that can spark and subsequently sustain interaction, suggesting that not everyone will be prepared, or able, to participate — a key factor in creating a truly collaborative environment. Tapscott and Williams (2007, p. 276) also recognized that social media, with its sense of openness, democratization, and the ceding of control to the organization at large, all present challenges to the established cultural and leadership norms, asking whether the minds of leaders are truly "*wired*" for Wikinomics.

Hodgkinson (2007a, 2007b) suggested that the change must be managed using different approaches and that by addressing the psychological and social aspects of communication (and engagement) organizations could truly unlock the benefits of community and collaboration. In order to address the more prominent cultural aspects, Hodgkinson (2007a, 2007b) suggested that organizational leaders needed to provide a facilitative and moderating environment to secure success, suggesting leaders must "*let go*" of their traditional tight controls, and work to foster collaborative use of social media platforms.

These assertions lack empirical support, therefore we will investigate these ideas in this chapter through the use of a detailed case study of the use of social media within an organization.

Social Media and Recruitment

So far, we have focused on the engagement of existing employees. Indeed, the sparse literature on employee engagement also focuses on the engagement of current employees. However, employers also spend a lot of time and money engaging with potential future employees, or job seekers. We often talk about "engaging" with potential employees or job seekers, but recruitment is rarely thought of in terms of employee engagement. In fact, recruitment is the first step on the journey to engaging with employees as the perceptions that potential employees form about the values of an employer and what an organization can offer them are vital in developing the psychological contract between employer and employee. It is through the recruitment process that a (potential) employee forms the seeds of their relationship with an employer and also "buys in" to the role that they will adopt. It can be suggested therefore that the recruitment process lays the foundations for whether an employee is "psychologically present" (Saks, 2006) in the role that they may eventually adopt in the organization. It can therefore be suggested that the recruitment process provides the basis for an employee's engagement with a role and organization. Within this chapter, we will therefore also investigate the use of social media for engaging with potential employees as part of the recruitment process.

In fact, much of the attention given to the use of social media within HRM has focused on the use of social media tools for engaging with potential future employees. Social media potentially could have a significant impact in changing the nature of the recruitment process, by allowing recruiters access to a wider pool of passive, as well as active, job seekers. Girard and Fallery (2010) have described "e-recruitment 2.0" as using social capital to tap into both active and passive job seekers' online social networks through the use of social media such as Facebook or LinkedIn, as well as other Web 2.0 tools such as blogs, RSS feeds, and virtual worlds. Social media allows employers to directly contact individuals who are not actively seeking work. The evolution of social media means that employers now have easy access to a wide variety of social networks, without the need to employ an executive search agent. Websites such as Facebook, LinkedIn, and Twitter contain a significant amount of information about potential employees that can be accessed relatively easily.

Miller-Merrell (2012) also underlined the attractiveness of employer branding promoted through social media, since it gives significant opportunities for HR professionals to get involved in activities beyond their traditional HR tasks. Also recruiting can become more interesting and efficient by tweeting a job opening; head hunting can be facilitated by the vast number of Linked profiles; and allowing employees to blog about how it is to work in that company could enhance the organizational image, thus increasing the number of applications interested in that company. The outcomes and benefits of social media diffusion of information could therefore be of major interest for companies willing to establish a strong employer branding reputation in order to influence engagement with both employees and applicants. Recent studies suggest the reasons a company should engage in recruiting and employer branding via social media: 43% of recruiters who use social recruiting saw an increase in candidate quality; and 31% of recruiters using social recruiting have seen a sustained increase in employee referrals (Jobvite, 2012). In other research, 62% of employer information in social networks was considered useful and a third of all online connections with a company happened because of an interest in company culture (eMarketer, 2010). In combination, these data illustrate how, when used effectively, social media are a powerful tool for improving reputation and a stronger employer brand, for both internal and external marketing.

Since members of the newest generation of job seekers and employees constitute the future largest segment in the workforce, it is important for employers to research, plan, and engage in new ways to reach the most skilled members of this generation because they will be the ones who steer the future of the most competitive organizations. For this reason, Rai (2012) attempts to understand concepts of employee engagement and social media while presenting an outline into the characteristics of Generation Y and their influencing factors in the organizational context. Rai (2012) investigated how specific characteristics of Gen Y and their connectivity to a digital world impact organizational processes like workplace environment, internal communication, employee well-being, in turn impacting their commitment levels and perception toward their organizations. These are all processes vital for the success of employee engagement. Organizations, thus, might have significant benefits to realize through the use of social media in recruitment, particularly in recruiting generation Y.

Research Questions

Based on the discussion above we have two areas of interest: first is how organizations are actually using social media to engage with both existing and potential future employees. We are also interested in how effective these methods are. For this second question we will focus on existing employees due to the ease of obtaining feedback from these individuals. Therefore, we have three overarching research questions:

1. How can an employer use social media to engage with potential employees?
2. How can an employer use social media to engage with existing employees?
3. How effective is social media as a means of improving employee communication and collaboration and therefore promoting employee engagement?

The Case Studies and Method

In order to investigate the research questions above, we collected data from two organizations. The first, a UK television company, has adopted social media extensively as a tool for recruitment. The second, an international UK telecommunications company, uses social media to facilitate communication and collaboration among existing employees and managers. For the purpose of this chapter, these companies will be called TVCo and Telco respectively. We will first describe the two organizations and the method used to collect data from each below. We will then take each of the three research questions above in turn and address each question using data from the appropriate organization.

UK Television Company (TVCo)

TVCo is the largest commercial television network in the United Kingdom. It operates a family of channels and delivers content across multiple platforms.

TVCo Studios produce and sell programs and formats across the United Kingdom and worldwide. Following the Television Act of 1954 which made commercial television in the United Kingdom possible, TVCo first began broadcasting in 1955 in the London area, before moving country-wide. TVCo has recently expanded its family of channels with the launch of new channels in 1998, 2004, 2005, and 2006. TVCo has around 4000 employees on permanent or fixed-term contracts and another 2-300 contractors.

TVCo is governed by a management team who is overseen by a Board of Directors. Human Resource Management is headed by their Group HR Director who sits on the Management Board. Each business area has an HR representative at HRD, Head of HR, and HR Manager level. Centers of Expertise exist within the HR Business Partner structure in Pensions, Reward, Operations and Systems, Learning and Development, Internal Communications, and Recruitment.

Up until 18 months before this case study, TVCo did not have a recruitment function. Recruitment of fixed term and permanent paid employees was undertaken by line managers with support from the HR department and relied heavily on the use of agencies. A new Head of Recruitment was employed in 2010 in order to review recruitment practices within the organization. She created an in-house recruitment team (of nine people at the time of data collection) and facilitated the move from agency recruitment to direct sourcing. The decision to move to direct sourcing was made for a number of reasons: to reduce costs; to ensure ownership of recruitment; and to create a robust recruitment process. In addition, the move represented a desire to take a longer-term view of recruitment and recruit employees for future as well as current company requirements. At the time of writing, 97% of recruitment was undertaken directly rather than via the use of agencies.

Data about TVCo was gathered from the internet and via an interview with the Head of Recruitment. A semi-structured interview protocol was used to gather data about the organization's use of social media for recruitment, the reasons for the adoption of this technology, and the perceived impact of the use of social media. Unfortunately access to job seekers/candidates was not available; therefore data from this organization will be limited only to the use of social media rather than the reactions of candidates.

UK Telecommunications Company (Telco)

Telco provides communications and IT solutions and services to consumer, small medium enterprise businesses, corporate customers, and communications providers in over 170 countries worldwide and employs around 150,000 people. Telco was originally a (once nationalized) UK plc that has experienced significant changes in a relatively short space of time and has been particularly hard hit by the global financial crisis. Telco has long been associated with innovation and the adoption of new technologies, places great emphasis on knowledge work, and has a history of facilitating communities of interests and collaborative working.

Three business units from Telco were selected to be included in this research. The three business units were selected based upon their use of the technology and their overall level of employee engagement in decision making. This allows us to obtain a range of responses to the social media. The first business unit had relatively high use of technology and relatively low employee engagement. This business unit is responsible for IT and network development, employs approximately 18,000 largely desk-based knowledge workers, and comprises of a management team who have pioneered the use of social media both within and outside the organization under study. The second business unit had a relatively moderate use of technology and relatively modest employee engagement. This business unit was responsible for IT and network operations and employs approximately 18,000 people, including a substantial field-force. The final business unit had a relatively minimal use of technology and relatively high employee engagement. This business unit is a market-facing unit discharging the organization's wholesale business, and employs approximately 4000 people including a mix of sales, marketing, product, operational, and customer service agents. A unit with high employee engagement and high use of technology could not be found in the case study organization.

These data were collected as part of a larger study into the impact of social media (see Denyer, Parry, & Flowers, 2011). In order to allow us to investigate the effectiveness of social media technology for communicating and engaging with employees, 33 semi-structured interviews with individual respondents were undertaken. First, 12 interviews were conducted with individuals responsible for policy and business direction to understand the strategic importance of social media and its role within the organization. Second, 21 face-to-face interviews were carried out with members of the three business units, using a standard interview protocol developed from a literature review. These interviews were recorded and transcribed. The interview data was then analyzed with the support of NVivo in order to identify emerging themes about the perceptions of the use and impact of social media within Telco.

Findings

Information from the two case studies will now be discussed in relation to the three research questions.

1. *How can an employer use social media to engage with potential employees?*

The recruitment process in TVCo relies heavily on social media tools, specifically LinkedIn and Twitter. The choice of social media tools was based upon the need to communicate the company's brand. It was felt that TVCo had a well-known brand generally, but not as an employer. The primary driver for using social media was to access passive as well as active job seekers.

TVCo subscribe to LinkedIn so that they have access to the profiles of all LinkedIn members. In addition to this access, they have developed a number of careers pages on LinkedIn. The pages contain information about the employer brand, the jobs that are available, and testimonials from employees. These pages are bespoke to particular job roles or areas. People entering the TVCo careers pages will automatically be directed to the page that is relevant to their work experience (based on an analysis of the information on their profile). TVCo can also search profiles for particular skills and contact LinkedIn members directly. They allow applicants to apply for jobs via their careers website using their LinkedIn profile, rather than having to create a separate CV. The company's use of LinkedIn has been very successful. The company now has over 16,000 "followers" and is the second most popular company with students on LinkedIn.

TVCo also has a careers page and account on Twitter. They regularly "tweet" content and news via this account and link readers to their careers website. They use a Twitter scheduling tool to send previously created tweets at particular times. They also encourage candidates to tweet about their experiences. The tweets are then re-tweeted regularly; the company also makes sure that they use popular hash tags (subject areas) so that they are found by people searching Twitter. For example, TVCo launched a recent graduate recruitment scheme on Twitter, by sending two tweets a day about the scheme for two weeks prior to the launch and then encouraging both recruiters and candidates to tweet during the assessment process. They also provided a number of 30-minute Twitter "chats" for potential applicants. Twitter has also proved to be a successful tool for recruitment. In particular, it is very cheap. Twitter itself costs nothing to use and the scheduling tool costs very little.

The use of social media is supported by an applicant tracking system and company careers website. The company also uses Google Analytics in order to track where applications have originated and therefore assess the success of their social media promotions and has done a lot of work on search engine optimization in order to ensure that they are located by search engines. It is the combination of social media tools and online support mechanisms such as these that allows TVCo to use social media effectively.

2. How can an employer use social media to engage with existing employees?

Telco has made increasing use of social media since 2004, following the appointment of a new CEO for the business unit responsible for IT and network development and operations. For example, blogs and podcasts are frequently used by senior leaders for the purpose of corporate communications, corporate blogging policies have been developed, social media guidelines and tools have been established, and standardized tools have been selected and deployed across the organization to support project or organization-based wiki's. Existing communication channels have been extended to include RSS news-feeds. Other interventions include an internal version of Wikipedia, an internal version of MySpace, and the extension of the online news service to include spaces for discussion. Many of these tools can be accessed directly from the organizations' intranet homepage. The professional communities of interest have also extensively deployed social media technologies to share information and create communities of interest and more recently an initiative to encourage people to create video podcasts as part of the learning and development agenda has been piloted. Second Life style avatars are being used as part of a Web 2.0 talent academy. In addition, a number of campaigns have been launched to encourage usage and a range of social media was used during a recent consultation on the future of the company pension scheme.

Interviewees described a number of uses of social media technologies, mainly within professional communities of interest. These included collaboration, maintaining contact between individuals, learning, and professional development. Interestingly for this chapter, none of the interviewees saw social media as a means by which to engage employees.

3. *How effective is social media as a means of improving employee communication and collaboration and therefore promoting employee engagement?*
Despite the extensive development of social media tools the success of these tools within Telco has been mixed. In some departments, web social media have proved to be a cost and time efficient means of promoting communication and collaboration and therefore might have promoted employee engagement. However, in other departments, little evidence of any positive impact of the technology on communication and employee engagement was found. This was due to a number of reasons.

In all three business units, some of the interviewees were reluctant to speak up because they were not convinced that it was "safe" to express their opinions without any negative consequences.

> It all depends what you mean by safe ... I still think people tend not to because they are not confident it is safe. It's encouraged obviously but people would think twice about posting certain things I would have thought.

In addition, the level of comfort that employees felt in speaking up was dependent on the leadership style of both their line manager and senior leadership. So in some, cases, interviewees felt that social media were used as a vehicle for propaganda from management. In particular, people commented on the way in which some individuals exploited the channel to serve their own purposes, and the way in which the technology was treated as part of a "corporate machine" so that "*leaders get to tell you what they want you to know*" and the "*party line*." Leaders, too, acknowledged that social media were used to distribute propaganda, with one stating that some blogs are:

> clearly a management propaganda tool. It is like [newsdesk] on the web, you know it is sunny and upbeat and it never rains ... people just see it as just another media medium for management to get the message across.

In other cases managers suppressed debate. One leader explained:

> We generally try to close things down. What we will try to do is answer in such a way that no one else feels that they should comment on it, or ask another question. Generally the response has been to try and close it down rather than allow it to run and let people have their say.

In other cases, interviewees explained that conversations that managers were not happy with had been continued offline. It was also noted that managers tended to select the topics included in any debate so that they were setting the agenda. In other cases, leaders chose to avoid the conversation completely by not engaging with the technology. Other interviewees suggested that many leaders felt the need to be "*seen to be doing something,*" so tended to adopt the technology for the sake of it, or because it was fashionable. One middle-manager felt that

> people hardly left any comments, but I think that was done for the wrong reasons, I think it was trying to get discussion taking place without any compelling subject matter.

A number of interviewees suggested that even when workers did engage with the technology, it was to discuss topics that were not of any great importance to the organization. It can therefore be seen that overall many interviewees were of the opinion that workers were not engaged with the technology in such a way as to make use of it in the way that was intended.

Some differences were observed based upon the level of engagement of the employees in each business unit. In the business unit with high levels of employee engagement people suggested that a key reason for implementing social media was to help leaders to be more open and accessible. Many of them argued that using social media to engage employees was "*the right thing to do.*" However, in the business unit perceived by actors to already have low levels of employee engagement, little interest in the use of social media for the purpose of increasing employee participation in decision making was described. Indeed, many people felt that the technology was used to inform employees, rather than to facilitate two-way conversations and that the organization itself, rather than the employees, was the ultimate beneficiary of social media. It is of course difficult to establish cause and effect between these attitudes, but these observations do suggest that it is impossible for social media to facilitate improved employee engagement in departments or organizations where the will to engage with employees through increased communication or participation is not already present.

Discussion

This chapter has examined the use of social media within organizations in order to engage with both current and potential future employees. An increasing number of companies use social media such as Facebook, Twitter, and LinkedIn to promote communication and collaboration among employees, announce job openings, and search for potential qualified personnel as well as marketing their employer brand both internally and externally. We have examined how two UK companies are using social media for the engagement of current and potential future employees and also examined the effectiveness of social media for internal engagement.

Social media can allow organizations to promote themselves externally to a large number of potential employees with little effort or expense. In contrast to more traditional recruitment advertising techniques, social media can allow companies to access passive as well as active job seekers, as our examination of practice in TVCo showed. Indeed, the experience in TVCo appears to show, anecdotally, a certain degree of success in engaging with potential employees via the use of LinkedIn and

Twitter. The Head of Recruitment in TVCo suggested that the use of social media had enabled the company to move from recruiting predominantly via agencies to a system whereby 97% of recruitment was conducted in-house, therefore reducing costs substantially. Unfortunately, little empirical data is available regarding the actual success of recruitment via social media or the impact of using this media of potential employees, but the TVCo experience seem to suggest that this provides valuable alternative to more expensive traditional methods of engaging with job seekers.

TVCo have focused their recruitment efforts to date on just two social media channels — Twitter and LinkedIn. They could of course expand this to other channels such as Facebook, the use of YouTube to post original and creative videos on YouTube about the everyday life of an employer within that company, or creating a blog for the current employees and management to post stories about the company. These factors could all represent a successful employer branding strategy. Indeed, information about a company as reported through any media outlet, including social media sites can have an influence on public perception and help an organization to engage with potential employees.

Of course, the impact of social media in creating an employer brand is not limited only to potential future employees. As social media becomes integrated commonly into employee engagement strategies the differences between internal and external communication are blurring. Organizations that communicate effectively through social media might find that it enhances a positive workplace culture and improves employee engagement as well as enforcing a positive external reputation. Also for this reason and in order to gain competitive advantage, more companies are investing in creating an identity inside and outside the company. The basic principle of employer branding is therefore that all employees are consumers who must be recruited and retained. This is because existing employees (as well as customers) like to be associated with distinctive organizations. One aim of employer branding should be then to distinguish the employer in the minds of the employees, creating commitment, satisfaction, and developing emotional attachment — and employees who are committed and satisfied also create better relationships with customers.

In the future, social media may not only influence recruiting processes and employer branding value proposition, but also internal marketing, making it become a more effective back-up for external marketing. Through social media employees can be ambassadors of the organization, agents of the company who make part of the employer branding outside the company in way which are not even always conscious.

Moving on to focus on the role of social media in engaging with existing employees, the popular media has espoused that social media can increase the degree of involvement and engagement of employees, by creating an open, inclusive, and collaborative environment, as well as a sense of belonging to a community, identity, and organizational citizenship. Making employees feel a part of the company and a part of the decision-making process has been suggested to have a large impact on the employees' behavior.

We took a more in-depth focus on the use of social media to promote the engagement of current employees. Popular media has suggested that social media can improve employee collaboration and communication and promote employee participation, therefore leading to higher levels of employee engagement. Indeed, our examination of the use of social media within Telco demonstrated that this company had widely introduced social media, including blogs and wikis, with the purpose of increasing employee collaboration and communication, building a greater sense of community within the organization and therefore ultimately improving employee engagement.

However, and more importantly, our analysis of social media use within this organization showed that the introduction of social media technologies does not necessarily lead to increased engagement, or indeed collaboration, even in an organization such as Telco that has a long history of using cutting edge technology. In Telco, despite several campaigns to promote and encourage the use of social media, use of these tools was still patchy at best and there was little, if any, evidence that the widespread introduction of social media for employees had any great impact on collaboration, communication, or employee engagement.

Our examination of social media use within Telco demonstrated that the success of social media in increasing employee engagement is dependent on the existing culture of the organization and the attitudes and behavior of the organization's leaders. Our interviewees suggested that employees were not embracing social media technologies because they did not feel safe to speak up openly without retribution, because the tools were being used to facilitate propaganda and promote company messages rather than genuinely create two-way communication channels and because, in some cases, leaders were actively suppressing or controlling the online debate. Our evidence from Telco suggests that social media can only be effective in promoting employee engagement and communication if the existing culture and leadership style is already conducive to employee voice and participation. In fact, it appears to be impossible for social media to facilitate improved employee engagement in organizational environments where the will to engage with employees through increased communication or participation is not already present.

This is not to say that social media cannot improve communication processes and therefore also have a positive impact on employee engagement. The fact that social media can allow employees and managers to communicate quickly and easily can have a positive effect on organizations. Indeed, in Telco, we saw that social media were being used within communities of practice to maintain contact between individuals and for learning and professional development. This is in support of the idea that social media tools and technology can enhance internal communications, while supporting the development of internal communities. Indeed, communication between employees pursuing similar interests and the creation of internal workplace communities can spur innovation, improve processes, and help to break down "silos." We might also expect that this would contribute to a high sense of engagement. Indeed, effective communications processes have been suggested as a key driver of employee engagement (Cartwright & Holmes, 2007; Lockwood, 2007; Ruck & Welch, 2012). However, no real impact of the use of social media for communication and increased employee engagement was obvious within Telco. It is likely that this is because of the tension between the ethos of social media and the culture and leadership of the organization, as described above. Indeed, it appears that social media cannot work miracles but can only operate within the existing organizational culture. If open communication and employee participation is not already part of this culture then the impact of social media will be limited.

Conclusions

This chapter has provided some evidence of the way in which social media can be used within organizations in order to engage with both existing and potential future employees. For engaging with potential employees, anecdotally at least, social media appear to be a useful means of reaching a large number of both active and passive job seekers in a cost-effective manner. We provided a more in-depth analysis of the use of social media for engaging with existing employees and found that, while this technology had the potential to increase internal communication among employees and managers, this did not necessarily translate into increased employee engagement. In fact, the culture of the organization and style of the leaders were more crucial than the technology itself in dictating whether employees engaged both with the social media and at a wider level with the organization.

This chapter has provided only an initial exploratory analysis of these factors in two organizations. Indeed the use of only two organizations means that our findings might not be applicable to other organizations and other adoptions of social media. In particular, the information about TVCo was based only on secondary information available from the website and an interview with the Head of Recruitment. Further research should provide a more in-depth analysis of the actual effectiveness of social media in recruitment and should also examine the reactions of job seekers to the use of social media for recruitment. Future research could also compare the effectiveness of these channels at engaging with potential employees with other methods such as headhunters, agencies, or more traditional recruitment advertising. With regard to the use of social media to engage with existing employees, it would be interesting to examine the use of these technologies across other organizations, particularly those with a more participatory culture.

Despite the limitations and need for future research above, this chapter makes an important contribution to an extremely sparse literature. The popular media has espoused the impact of social media as revolutionary with regard to communication and collaboration and therefore potentially employee engagement. Our contribution has been to add an important note of caution to these claims. Employers cannot expect social media to have a significant impact on the participation and engagement of their employees unless they are also willing to create an organizational culture that promotes open communication and employee voice.

Practical Implications

This chapter has significant implications for organizations considering the adoption of social media as a means to improve employee engagement. We might suggest that the social media can enhance employee engagement when it is aligned with the organizational culture and vision. Indeed, social media provide organizations with the means to share knowledge and expertise, enabling people to communicate directly with each other and cross boundaries between different departments. But when adopting social media for organizations, the very first step should be to assess the organizational readiness with a focus on culture and people rather than on the technology itself.

Not all companies are comfortable with a world where employees can speak so freely with each other, express their thoughts, and where management has increasingly less control over the information available within the organization. This is a matter of leadership attitude, as well as organizational culture. Our findings confirm that managerial behaviors and styles are central to the level of engagement individuals feel with an organization. Social media technologies enable forms of communications and collaborations that are much more pervasive, fluid, free, and transparent. And increasingly, this calls for the creation of collaborative cultures, and, thus, of a collaborative leadership. So far few leaders have been trained to lead collaboratively, and in many cases the culture and reward systems in organizations discourage collaboration. Senior management might not engage in social media for reasons such as being reluctant to give away their power, not knowing how their actions relate to larger changes in an organization or not understanding the new social practices. Thus, success in social media adoption depends on creating an environment of trust, mutual respect, and shared aspiration in which all can contribute openly. Many companies are just now recognizing the need of a new mindset and different skills, as well as a consistent set of systems and processes that enable participants to communicate, learn, and work together.

Employee engagement depends on strong, effective communications. Furthermore, senior management communication and open, effective communication strategies are recognized as having a crucial role in the development of positive employee engagement (Bakker, Albrecht, & Leiter, 2011; Bindl & Parker, 2010; Saks, 2006). Nevertheless, top managers are too often out of the conversations, and while they may use a wide array of communication methods, including social media, these are often in the form of "top-down" communication, rather than giving employees a voice. It is important for employee to have their contributions recognized by their superiors and to receive credit for any ideas they share in the organization. Previous studies, for example, indicate that employee recognition from senior management directly motivates people to share knowledge (Oliver & Kandadi, 2006). Inclusive leaders, by including employees among relevant organization stakeholders, turn those employees into experienced conversation partners, enabling them as frontline content providers, and raising thus the level of employee engagement.

Social media is in fact not something that can be managed by just a dedicated team or a department. Every individual can play a role in the social media arena, in facilitating participation, communication, and sharing. The use of social media as a tool for employee engagement should not be perceived as a matter of exclusive interest of a charismatic and visionary leader or of a specific and determined organizational function. Notwithstanding, the adoption of social media by the organization might have a big impact on the way that HR professionals perform their duties therefore needing different capabilities, skills, and knowledge. HR professionals should enhance their communication, IT, Internet, social, and business knowledge and, in particular, an in-depth knowledge of the social media concept, what can and cannot be achieved with it, and how it can be used effectively. Through the use of social media to attract and recruit candidates, some HR departments have already understood the power of information sharing. To make sure the capabilities and skills to use social media are truly embedded in an organization, HR needs to think innovatively and coach the entire organization in social media use. They should also provide precise guidelines and teach employees how to behave in the social media space. Therefore, HR has to be a role model for their employees on how to use social media devices effectively.

The evolution of social media both outside and within organizations represents an exciting time that could have a great positive impact on organizations and employees. Our research has shown, that in relation to communication, participation, and employee engagement, achieving this positive impact is not simple or revolutionary as some media suggest, Instead, it requires significant work on the part of the organization to ensure that the culture and leadership of the organization supports the effective use of social media to improve employee engagement.

References

Aberdeen Group. (2008). *Web 2.0, talent management and employee engagement*. Retrieved from http://www.Aberdeen.com. Accessed on 4 July 2013.

APCI and Gagen McDonald. (2012). Retrieved from http://www.apcoworldwide.com

Bakker, A. B., Albrecht, S. L., & Leiter, M. P. (2011). Key questions regarding work engagement. *European Journal of Work and Organizational Psychology, 20*(1), 4–28.

Bindl, U. K., & Parker, S. K. (2010). Feeling good and performing well? Psychological engagement and positive behaviors at work. In S. L. Albrecht (Ed.), *Handbook of employee engagement: Perspectives, issues, research and practice*. Cheltenham: Edward Elgar.

Cartwright, S., & Holmes, N. (2007). The meaning of work: The challenge of regaining employee engagement and reducing cynicism. *Human Resource Management Review, 16*(2), 199–208.

CIPD Staff. (2008). *Employee engagement*. London: CIPD. Retrieved from http://www.cipd.co.uk/subjects/empreltns/general/empengmt.htm. Accessed on September 18, 2012.

Dahl, A., Lawrence, J., & Pierce, J. (2011). Building an innovation community. *Research Technology Management, 54*(5), 19–27.

Denyer, D., Parry, E., & Flowers, P. (2011). "Social", "open" and "participative"? Exploring personal experiences and organizational effects of Enterprise 2.0 use. *Long Range Planning, 44*(5–6), 375–396.

Doherty, R. (2010). Engage with your talent through internal social networking. *Strategic HR Review, 9*(1), 39–40.

eMarketer. (2010). *Reasons for friending or following companies through social media according to US consumers*. Retrieved from http://www.emarketer.com

Gardner, T. M., Moynihan, L. M., Park, H. J., & Wright, P. M. (2001). *Beginning to unlock the black box in the HR firm performance relationship: The impact of HR practices on employee attitudes and employee outcomes.* CAHRS Working Paper No. 1–12, Cornell University, Ithaca, NY.

Girard, A., & Fallery, B. (2010). Human resource management on internet: New perspectives. *The Journal of Contemporary Management Research, 4*(2), 1–14.

Greenberg, J. (1990). Organizational justice: Yesterday, today and tomorrow. *Journal of Management, 16*(2), 399–432.

Groysberg, B., & Slind, M. (2012). Leadership is a conversation. *Harvard Business Review, 90*(6), 76–84.

Hodgkinson, S. (2007a). *Does your enterprise need Web 2.0?* Boston, MA: Ovum.

Hodgkinson, S. (2007b). *What is Web 2.0?* Boston, MA: Ovum.

IABC Research Foundation and Buck Consultants. (2011). Employee engagement survey. San Francisco: Buck Consultants.

Jobvite. (2012). *Social recruiting survey.* Retrieved from http://recruiting.jobvite.com/resources/social-recruiting-survey.php Accessed on September 24, 2012.

Khan, W. A. (1990). Psychological conditions of personal engagement at work. *Academy of Management Journal, 33*(4), 692–724.

Lockwood, N. R. (2007). *Leveraging employee engagement for competitive advantage: HR's strategic role.* Alexandria, VA: Society for Human Resource Management.

MacCormick, J. S., Dery, K., & Kolb, D. G. (2012). Engaged or just connected? Smartphones and employee engagement, *Organizational Dynamics, 41*(3), 194–201.

Macey, W. H., & Schneider, B. (2008). The meaning of employee engagement. *Industrial and Organizational Psychology, 1*(1), 3–30.

Macky, K., & Boxall, P. (2007). The relationship between high performance work practices and employee attitudes: An investigation additive and interaction effects. *International Journal of Human Resource Management, 18*(4), 537–567.

MacLeod, D., & Brady, C. (2008). *The extra mile: How to engage your people to win.* Harlow, UK: Prentice Hall.

MacLeod, D., & Clarke, N. (2009). *Engaging for success: Enhancing performance through employee engagement.* Report to BIS. Retrieved from www.bis.gov.uk. Accessed on September 22, 2012.

MacLeod, D., & Clarke, N. (2011). *Engaging for success: Enhancing performance through employee engagement.* Retrieved from http://www.bis.gov.uk/files/file52215.pdf. Accessed on 4 July 2013.

Martin, G., Reddington, M., & Kneafsey, M. B. (2009). *Web 2.0 and human resource management: Groundswell or hype?* London: CIPD.

Miller-Merrell, J. (2012). The workplace engagement economy where HR, social, mobile, and tech collide. *Employment Relations Today, 39*(2), 1–9.

Murphy, G. D. (2010). Using Web 2.0 tools to facilitate knowledge transfer in complex organizational environments: A primer. In *ICOMS asset management conference* (*ICOMS 2010*), June 21–25, University of Adelaide, South Australia.

Oliver, S., & Kandadi, K. R. (2006). 'How to develop a knowledge culture in organizations? A multiple case study of large distributed organizations'. *Journal of Knowledge Management, 10*(4), 6–24.

Rai, S. (2012). Engagement, social media and gen Y: Connecting the dots. *Procedia — Social and Behavioral Sciences, 37*, 257–266.

Robinson, D., Perryman, S., & Hayday, S. (2004). *The drivers of employment engagement.* Report No. 408, Institute for Employment Studies, Brighton, UK.

Ruck, K., & Welch, M. (2012). Valuing internal communication; Management and employee perspectives. *Public Relations Review, 38*(2), 294–302.

Saks, A. M. (2006). Antecedents and consequences of employee engagement. *Journal of Managerial Psychology*, *21*(7), 600–619.

Schaufeli, W. B., Martinez, I. M., Pinto, A. M., Salanova, M., & Bakker, A. B. (2002). Burnout and engagement in university students: A cross-national study. *Journal of Cross Cultural Psychology*, *33*(5), 464–481.

Tapscott, D., & Williams, A. D. (2007). *Wikinomics: How mass collaboration changes everything* (Hardback ed.). London: Atlantic Books.

Vance, R. J. (2006). *Employee engagement and commitment. A guide to understanding, measuring and increasing engagement in your organization*. Alexandria, VA: SHRM Foundation.

Chapter 7

Managing Entitativity through Social Media

David A. Askay, Anita Blanchard and Jerome Stewart

Abstract

Purpose — This chapter examines the affordances of social media to understand how groups are experienced through social media. Specifically, the chapter presents a theoretical model to understand how affordances of social media promote or suppress entitativity.

Methodology — Participants ($N = 265$) were recruited through snowball sampling to answer questions about their recent Facebook status updates. Confirmatory factor analysis (CFA) was used to examine the goodness of fit for our model.

Findings — We validate a model of entitativity as it occurs through the affordances offered by social media. Participant's knowledge that status update responders were an interacting group outside of Facebook affected their perceptions of interactivity in the responses. Interactivity and history of interactions were the strongest predictors of status update entitativity. Further, status update entitativity had positive relationships with overall Facebook entitativity as well as group identity.

Practical implications — To encourage group identity through social media, managers need to increase employees' perceptions of entitativity, primarily by enabling employees to see the interactions of others and to contribute content in social media platforms.

Originality/value — This is the only study we know of that empirically examines how groups are experienced through social media. Additionally, we draw from an affordance perspective, which helps to generalize our findings beyond the site of our study.

Keywords: Technological affordances; workgroups; group identity; identification; entitativity; computer-mediated communication

Social Media in Human Resources Management
Advanced Series in Management, 143–165
Copyright © 2013 by Emerald Group Publishing Limited
All rights of reproduction in any form reserved
ISSN: 1877-6361/doi:10.1108/S1877-6361(2013)0000012011

Introduction

Social media sites like Facebook, Google+, Twitter, and LinkedIn offer unprecedented levels of participation, interaction, and communication, and have rapidly been adopted by organizations to complement existing work practices. In many work environments, computer-mediated communication (CMC) has supplemented face-to-face (FtF) communication, reducing the constraints of time and space on organizing. The adoption of social media in organizations, however, is increasing rapidly while empirical understanding of how these technologies may influence organizational processes remains understudied (Raeth, Smolnik, Urbach, & Zimmer, 2009).

These advances in social media have challenged scholars' conceptions of groups. For example, an employee can post a status update about a problem with statistical program on Facebook and colleagues can respond with both agreement and suggestions on how to solve it. Thus, employees can communicate with each other on social media in ways that overlap their formal and informal work groups. But are these truly groups? How do the employees experience these communications as groups and what effect, if any, does it have on their psychosocial attachment to each other as well as their productivity?

The complexity of interactions on social media highlights the role of entitativity — the cognitive assessment of how much a group feels like a group (Campbell, 1958; Lickel et al., 2000). Entitativity is a fundamental antecedent of both group processes and group outcomes including group membership (Sherman, Hamilton, & Lewis, 1999), identity (Castano, Yzerbyt, & Bourguignon, 2003; Yzerbyt, Castano, Leyens, & Paladino, 2000), commitment (Castano et al., 2003; Ogungbamila, Ogungbamila, & Adetula, 2010), and group trust among other constructs and processes (Hamilton, 2007; Lickel et al., 2000; Spencer-Rodgers, Hamilton, & Sherman, 2007). Indeed, entitativity has recently been called the heart of group social psychology (Igarashi & Kashima, 2011). Consequently, fostering higher levels of entitativity through social media results in important outcomes for organizations, including improved employee attachment and productivity.

This chapter addresses the management of groups through social media by examining their entitativity. One frequent use of social media is microblogging, in which an author posts a short message in the form of text, images, videos, and/or other media to which other people can respond. Facebook status updates and tweets on Twitter are popular examples of microblogging. Responses to these instances of microblogging by others can, possibly, create and reinforce groups. Therefore, using responses to Facebook status updates, this chapter empirically investigates and presents a theoretical model for understanding how affordances of social media promote or suppress entitativity. The practical applications of this model are highlighted to provide managers with direction for managing groups via social media.

Background

Entitativity has predominately been studied in FtF groups, where members physically meet in time and space to work on a common goal. This research demonstrates that entitativity is not a simple binary conception of "this is a group" or "this is not a group." Rather entitativity exists on a continuum. A person passing a bus stop and seeing five people waiting for the bus, all facing the same direction and not interacting would not consider that grouping of people as highly "groupy." However, a person could observe the same five people at a café, sitting around a table in close contact with each other, actively interacting while sharing coffee and pastries. An observer would likely consider that grouping as being much "groupier."

What does this mean for how groups are experienced through social media? It suggests that fostering highly entitative groups is not so much a matter of adding someone to a "friend's list" — which is a social media equivalent to seeing noninteracting people at a bus stop — but rather stresses the importance of perceiving interactions as a basis for experiencing "groupyness." In other words, it is not simply that people are using social media, it is *how* they are using social media that influences how much they perceive groups. When there are links between three or more people on social media, there is potential for a group.[1] The entitativity among mere links, though, is likely to be very low. It is when people interact through social media — when there are activities and responses to these activities — that there is the potential for a group to develop and for its corresponding entitativity to increase.

Social media, however, enable significantly different ways of interacting than FtF settings. Recently, Treem and Leonardi (2012) identified some of the novel features of social media that fundamentally alter the way that social media permit people to communicate in organizations. They suggest that features (e.g., affordances) of social media — such as the increased visibility of knowledge and communication, persistence of contributions, and articulation of links between people and content — create a work environment where group processes likely function differently than in FtF settings. These scholars assert that these affordances fundamentally change the ways in which employees socialize, share information, and influence others. To this, we add that the affordances of social media also change the way in which groups are experienced in organizations.

Understanding when and how interactions through social media are experienced as groups opens up important new analytical and managerial domains. First, given the increased ability of organizational members to self-organize through social media, managers need "to accurately perceive the network relations that connect people, and to actively manage these network relations" (Balkundi & Kilduff, 2006, p. 419). Knowledge of how to influence and enhance group processes and outcomes in organizational members is one such way of managing network relations. Indeed, promoting strategic use of social media may simultaneously expand the effectiveness of groups while also making them easier for managers to facilitate. Second, the relative novelty of adopting social media in organizations creates some level of uncertainty of how to best manage employees. Indeed, this study seeks to identify dysfunctional social media practices that may actually undermine the functioning of

---

[1]We consider communication between just two people to be a dyad, not a group.

groups, informing managers what behaviors and actions should be reinforced and which should not.

The first step to advancing the theoretical and practical domains of managing entitativity through social media is testing the extent to which existing FtF research extends into a social media setting. To this end, we will summarize the literature on entitativity and present a model for testing how groups are experienced through social media.

Face-to-Face Group Entitativity

Despite the original conceptualization of entitativity by Campbell (1958), it is only recently that research on entitativity in FtF groups has grown and developed. This research focuses on identifying the characteristics of groups that affect entitativity as well as understanding how entitativity affects people's impressions of groups (Crump, Hamilton, Sherman, Lickel, & Thakkar, 2010; Hogg, Sherman, Dierselhuis, Maitner, & Moffitt, 2007; Lickel, Hamilton, & Sherman, 2001). The characteristics of FtF groups that affect their entitativity include group member interaction, common goals, common outcomes, importance of group to members, group member similarity, interdependency among members, group boundaries, internal structure, group size, and the duration of the group (Hogg et al., 2007; Lickel et al., 2001).

Of these, interactivity is the strongest antecedent of entitativity for the groups about which we are theorizing (Rutchick, Hamilton, & Sack, 2008). Further, recent experimental research on perceptions of entitativity in social network graphs demonstrates that interaction become very important as social networks get larger (Igarashi & Kashima, 2011). Indeed, as social networks get bigger, it requires fewer interactions for people to perceive a group with strong entitativity as compared to smaller social networks.

However, as with much of the research on entitativity, this previous research assesses people's reactions to other groups, not their own groups. One reason is that it is easier to experimentally manipulate people's perceptions of groups in which they have no interactions. However, in the groups about which we theorize, people are within the group and have substantially more knowledge about the group members. Therefore, the antecedents of member similarity and a history of interactions may become more relevant for both managers and scholars to consider.

As for the outcomes of entitativity, researchers have also found relationships between entitativity and group identity, the in-group/out-group effect, stereotype formation, and other general perceptions of group members (Gaertner, Iuzzini, Witt, & Oriña, 2006; Hamilton, Sherman, & Lickel, 1998; Hogg et al., 2007; Spencer-Rodgers et al., 2007). We focus on group identity as an outcome of entitativity. Group identity has been theorized and studied both as an important organizational outcome (e.g., Ashforth, Rogers, & Corley, 2011) and as an important outcome in online groups (Postmes, Spears, & Lea, 1998). Specifically, group identity — the individual's deeper affiliation with other group members — is known to have important relationships with many other important group and organizational outcomes. Thus, by showing a relationship between entitativity and group identity we are able to place entitativity in the larger program of group and organizational research.

Technological Affordances of Social Media

Social media offer fundamentally new possibilities for employees to interact and communicate with each other. Yet a significant limitation of research about social media is a focus on specific "new" technologies that become obsolete (e.g., Friendster). Theories and studies that focus on specific technologies may then be inherently limited in their longevity. In an effort to develop more generalizable research about social media, Treem and Leonardi (2012) systematically developed four general technological affordances of social media that together provide unique ways of interacting between employees. Affordances refer to the capacities for interaction enabled by a technology.

These four affordances include visibility, persistence, editability, and association. While previous information and communication technologies (ICTs) may have had one or more of these affordances, social media bring all four together at a greater extent and it is because of this that social media hold promise to alter organizational processes. By framing our studying within this affordance framework, it is our goal to create generalizable findings that extend beyond the site under study. Additionally, understanding these affordances will help managers understand how various social media tools can be used to manage entitativity.

Visibility.   Treem and Leonardi (2012) use visibility to refer to the increased capacity of information and behaviors of individuals to be seen by others in the organization. Whereas once one's actions in an organization might have been mostly invisible, actions occurring through social media (e.g., posting a photo, posting a status update, etc.) are available to be seen by anyone who has access. This provides additional opportunities for employees to learn about the backgrounds, interests, and activities of co-workers (DiMicco et al., 2008), which, in turn, can enhance perceptions of such antecedents to entitativity as common goals and member similarity.

Persistence.   Communication occurring through social media produces a record that remains available to others. As these records of communication and interaction can be searched, viewed, and browsed outside of boundaries of space and time, it is likely to have significant impacts on organizational practices (Erickson & Kellogg, 2000). For the entitative feelings of groups, persistent records of activity (and inactivity) by individuals have promise to enhance (or suppress) group experiences of membership. Scholars have noted, however, that over time the buildup of content can become overwhelming and actually discourage use of social media (Ding, Danis, Erickson, & Kellogg, 2007; Grudin & Poole, 2010).

Editability.   Treem and Leonardi (2012) define editability as the ability to take time to craft, revise, and respond to messages. Compared to FtF settings, group communication through social media allows members to strategically craft messages, target specific audiences, and possibly even increase the quality of information submitted. These features emerge as a particularly attractive quality for employees, as they have increased perceptions of control and coordination (Arazy, Gellatly, Jang, & Patterson, 2009; Danis & Singer, 2008).

Associations.   The fourth feature identified by Treem and Leonardi (2012) is that social media show explicit connections between employees and between employees and content. By making these networks of connections and interactions public, it enhances the degree to which people can understand and express the nature of relationships — who knows who and who has produced what. Indeed, associations with information arguably provide a novel way of showing connections which, in turn, may provide additional ways in which co-workers can interact with each other, enhancing the capacity to develop of entitativity.

  While recognizing that other ICTs incorporate some of these features, social media generally encompasses all four. Asserting that the combination of all four of these affordances inherent in social media represents a fundamental change in interacting, Treem and Leonardi (2012) recommend updating the theorization of key organizational processes. We integrate the literature of FtF entitativity with that of technological affordances to develop and test a model of how entitativity develops on social media and affects an important employee outcome: group identity.

Entitativity in Social Media

We are interested in the feelings of entitativity that may develop for users among employees' co-workers, followers, and friends. Specifically, we examine feelings of entitativity within microblogs, through which employees can post information, news, or witticisms about one's thoughts or current behaviors to thoughts of one's co-workers. We examine status updates on Facebook, as it is a very common activity for Facebook members (Hampton, Goulet, Rainie, & Purcell, 2011) and many organizations have adopted Facebook or similar platforms for use among employees. We argue that groups emerge and are reinforced through the process of co-workers posting on and responding to microblogs.

  As exemplified by the technological affordance framework described above, affordances of social media differ from other kinds of ICT. On Facebook, status updates embody the affordances of visibility, persistence, editability, and associations. These affordances inform our hypotheses and the construction of our model for entitativity. Our literature review on FtF entitativity indicates that the primary antecedents to entitativity include the level of activity within a group, the level of interactivity between members, the similarity of members, a history of interaction, and knowledge that members are a group. Using the affordance approach above, we will translate these antecedents to a social media context. In doing so, we will highlight aspects of social media that make group identity different in social media and reveal ways in which managers can use these differences to manage group identity formation.

Activity. This refers to activities that occur between an individual and others. Because of the affordances of visibility and persistence in social media, any of one's connections can respond to a microblog post with a variety of actions. These responses usually take the form of some kind of written dialogue, photos, videos, or "Likes" or "+1." Unlike most FtF settings, these interactions are recorded, made public, and even computed into a running total (e.g., 10 Likes). These various types of responses represent relatively permanent and tangible exchanges between an individual and co-workers, which therefore will likely lead to feelings of entitativity. This leads to our first hypothesis:

> **Hypothesis 1.** Greater activity (number of likes, comments, and commenters) will be positively related to greater entitativity on status updates.

Interactivity. Interactivity is one of the strongest previously identified antecedents of entitativity. It does not refer to the interactions between an individual and a group (which is activity), but rather it is the perception by an individual that a grouping of others interact with each other. For example, it is a belief that "I think these people read each others' messages." Interactivity is important because it distinguishes between an individual having several dyadic relationships with people compared to a group of people that all interact with each other.

How do status updates have interactivity? Affordances of visibility and persistence of social media again allow an employee to be more aware of the interactions that occur between co-workers. Status updates provide an accessible way that an employee can be made aware of these interactions when they may not have been present. For example, a status update on Facebook can make visible photos, social tagging, comments, check-ins, etc. that show interactions between co-workers, which would, in turn, increase entitativity. Moreover, employees viewing these interactions have the ability to respond to them with comments or "liking" them, thereby having a belated level of activity with that group.

The increased capacity to see interactivity has important implications for group duration and its boundaries. First, the group is potentially very short-lived and, indeed, ephemeral. Status updates happen very frequently, and although people update their statuses at varying frequencies, it is unlikely that any feeling of entitativity for a particular status update will last for more than a day, much less for weeks. However, we would expect that repetitive experiences of entitativity on status updates could lead to feelings of overall entitativity. That is, feeling entitativity multiple times with multiple status updates would lead the updater to perceive a continuous, interactive presence of others on the social medium, and thus higher entitativity for the social medium. This connection, should it exist, is quite important because it suggests that group theories could then be useful and appropriate for active participants of social media. This leads to our second hypothesis:

Hypothesis 2. Greater perceived interactivity will be positively related to greater entitativity on status updates.

Similarity. Similarity is another strong antecedent of FtF entitativity. Similar people responding to a status update would represent a typical categorization of "alike members" of a group, whereas diverse respondents would violate this categorization. When a co-worker posts a status update on Facebook, any of their connections can then read and respond to it. Moreover, through the affordance of association, Facebook often provides many additional cues to similarity of responders: education, photos, preferences, and how two people know each other.

This suggests that the similarity of people who respond can vary. For example, if the updater posts comments about a work issue (e.g., a comment about using particular software) and colleagues also respond about using this software, the updater will perceive greater similarity than if the updater's high school friends or family also respond. If this is the case, there may be a trade-off between the access to extra-organizational knowledge afforded by social media and the development of group identity — if a co-worker feels like an "outsider" when a group is formed around a status update, they would be less likely to participate in it and contribute their own knowledge.

Further, the content of the responses from the perspective of social processes may form another dimension of similarity that can affect the updater's entitativity. Comments which remain relevant to the original topic may demonstrate a commonality among the responders which can enhance the entitativity of the status update group. Responses that diverge from the topic, are unsupportive of the topic, or devolve into a dyadic conversation between responders are likely to detract from feelings of entitativity. Therefore leading to our third hypothesis, similarity of responders should be related to higher entitativity whereas diversity of responders should be related to lower entitativity:

Hypothesis 3. Greater perceived similarity will be positively related to greater entitativity on status updates.

Interaction history. Finally, the history of the group — its duration across time — is an important antecedent of entitativity. Knowing that the group has a history of interactions has been important when people make the decision of "How groupy is that group over there?" For example, in FtF entitativity research, knowing that the group has existed for several years leads to greater feelings of entitativity than knowing a group has existed for only a few days.

However, in social media, any single status update is unlikely to have a long duration of interactions. Nonetheless, the affordance of persistence can increase the awareness of groups that have had a history of continually responding to the person's status updates (i.e., the "same old gang" always responding). Therefore, for status updates, history of interactions may mean that the same group of responders form and re-form over time.

Hypothesis 4. The history of interactions of the responders is related to greater entitativity on status updates.

Model of Entitativity in Social Media

We use this information to create a model of entitativity for Facebook status updates (see Figure 1). To summarize, the research and theory in terms of our model, activity, interactivity, similarity, and a history of interaction are consistent antecedents of FtF entitativity and, thus, are likely to be important on social media. Activity refers to the number of responses (i.e., the number of likes, comments, and commenters) on a status update that an employee receives from co-workers, while interactivity an employee perception that a grouping of co-workers interact with each other. Similarity refers to how similar the people are who respond to the update. The responders could be accountants, runners, or family members, or some combination of these groups. Finally, although status updates may not have a long life, it is possible that the same group of people make responses over time, thus creating a history of interactions for status updates.

We hypothesize the relationships between these antecedents to entitativity. In doing this, we also want to account for the possibility that a grouping of co-workers interact outside of Facebook (via FtF or other social media). If an employee is aware that a group interacts outside of Facebook, then social presence theory predicts that they would have a better understanding of why the group is there and what they are supposed to do (Biocca, Harms, & Burgoon, 2003). In turn, knowledge of a grouping interacting outside of Facebook would likely affect their perceptions of interactivity and similarity.

In our model, updater knowledge about the responders, particularly if they are a group that interacts outside of Facebook, affects their perceptions of interactivity in the responses and their perceptions of similarity of the responders. This knowledge

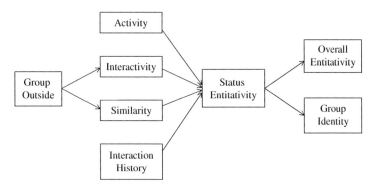

Figure 1: Hypothesized model of entitativity on Facebook.

strengthens the relationship of perceived interactivity and similarity to entitativity through the behavioral intentions inferred of the responders. This particular knowledge about the responders may be particularly relevant to organizations, since their employees may expect that their colleagues interact with each other outside of the social media. Therefore, our next hypotheses are:

Hypothesis 5a. Believing that the responders interact outside of Facebook as a group is positively correlated with perceived interactivity in responses.

Hypothesis 5b. Believing that the responders interact outside of Facebook as a group is positively correlated with perceived similarity in responders.

Hypothesis 6. Perceived interactivity and similarity mediate the relationship between being a group outside of Facebook and status update entitativity.

Finally, we hypothesize a link between these antecedents, entitativity, and group identity. Our model predicts that these antecedents will contribute to status update entitativity, which then predicts overall entitativity and group identity. Entitativity is a fundamental component of groups and group processes; therefore, it should be related to important group processes. FtF entitativity researchers have found a strong link between entitativity and identity with the group (Abrams & Hogg, 2008; Hogg, Abrams, Otten, & Hinkle, 2004). Group identity has been well-studied in online groups as an important predecessor to other group processes and outcomes. For managers, in particular, identity with the members of one's work group is very important (Ellemers, De Gilder, & Haslam, 2004; Van Knippenberg, De Dreu, & Homan, 2004). It is related to group member intentions to remain in the group, information elaboration (Van Dick, Van Knippenberg, Hägele, Guillaume, & Brodbeck, 2008), team conflict, information processing, and workgroup performance (Van Knippenberg et al., 2004; Zellmer-Bruhn, Maloney, Bhappu, & Salvador, 2008). So, by showing a link between entitativity and group identity we can provide additional support for the importance of entitativity in social media.

Hypothesis 7. Perceptions of status update entitativity are positively related to overall entitativity.

Hypothesis 8. Entitativity in status updates is positively related to group identity with these status updates.

Methods

Participants

Participants are $N = 362$ Facebook users recruited through snowball sampling by undergraduates for course credit. Students were required to ask 10 of their Facebook friends to voluntarily participate in our research. Those who responded were included in our study. Students obtained full credit by demonstrating that they asked people to participate, not by the number of people who actually responded.

Participants were composed of 70% female with a mean age of 29 years (SD = 11.91). There were 68% Caucasian, 21% African-American, 6% Asian-American, and 3% Latino respondents as well as 2% who self-identified as other.

Participants were asked to go to their Facebook profile page while they were filling out the survey. They were then asked if they updated their status in the last week. Only those who responded positively continued in our study. Next, they were asked if they had a status update with two or more responses (i.e., likes or comments). If they responded yes, they completed the rest of our questionnaire. Our goals here were to have participants focus on particular, recent status updates for which they could report accurate responses instead of stereotypes (Fowler, 1995) and which we could be sure reflected group instead of dyad perceptions. Two hundred and sixty-five participants met the requirement of having a status update with two or more responses in the last week.

Measures

Activity.   Activity was measured by asking participants to go to their last status update with two or more responders and to report the number of likes, responses, and unique responders.

Interactivity.   Interactivity was measured using three items: I think these responders are close with each other; I think these responders read each others' messages; and I think the way one individual responds has a significant impact upon other responders. Responses varied from 1 = Strongly Disagree to 7 = Strongly Agree.

Similarity.   Similarity was measured using three items: I think the responders are similar to each other; I think the responders have much in common; I think the responders are very different from one another (Reverse). Responses varied from 1 = Strongly Disagree to 7 = Strongly Agree.

Interaction history.   Interaction history was measured using one item: How often do these same general responders respond to your Facebook status updates? Responses varied from 1 = Never to 5 = Always.

Group outside of Facebook.   Perceptions that the responders interact as a group outside of Facebook was measured by one item: The responders to this status update interact with each other as a group outside of Facebook. Responses varied from 1 = Not at all like a group to 7 = Very much like a group.

Entitativity.   Our entitativity measure expanded on the one-item measure used by Hogg et al. (2007). We measured entitativity using three items: These responders are a group; These responders feel like a group to me; These responders are just individuals (reverse coded). Responses varied from 1 = Strongly Disagree to 7 = Strongly Agree.

Group identity.   Group identity was measured using eight items adapted from Hogg and Hains (1996). An example item is, "In terms of general attitudes and beliefs, I am very similar to the group as a whole." Responses varied from 1 = Strongly Disagree to 7 = Strongly Agree.

Overall entitativity.   We used Hogg et al. (2007) one-item measure of overall entitativity, modifying it for Facebook: Overall, how much does Facebook feel like a group?. This measure has been used previously for assessing feelings of entitativity for larger, noninteracting groups (e.g., political parties). Responses varied from 1 = Not very much like a group to 7 = Very much like a group.

Results

First, we conducted a confirmatory factor analysis (CFA) using MPLUS to test that our measures adequately and uniquely loaded upon their constructs. The first CFA did not have adequate fit, χ^2 (160) = 612.22, p = < .001, RMSEA = .10 (with a CI from .10 to .11), CFI = .85, TLI = .82, and SRMR = .07. We examined error residuals for inappropriately covarying items (indicating multiple items asking essentially the same information) and items inappropriately loading onto other constructs (indicating overlap between constructs). Three of the group identity items had high error variances indicating that they were measures of the same information. One similarity item, "I think the responders are very different from one another" (Reverse coded), was inappropriately loaded onto the entitativity scale. Therefore, these items were deleted from our measures. The final CFA model provided evidence for adequate convergent and divergent validity for our measures: χ^2 (94) = 165.61, p = < .001, RMSEA = .05 (with a CI from .04 to .07), CFI = .96, TLI = .95, and SRMR = .06.

The estimated descriptive analyses of our latent measures are presented in Table 1. Several observations can be made about the descriptive analyses. First, the mean perceptions of interactivity, group outside of Facebook, and entitativity of status updates are low on seven-point scales. While the variance of perceived interactivity is low (i.e., respondents converge on a low level of status update interactivity), there is much higher variability on group outside of Facebook and entitativity of status updates, suggesting a wide range of perceptions on these variables. Perceptions of similarity and actual activity (likes, responses, and responders) also have high variability, suggesting a range of perceptions and activities on status update responses. Perceptions of overall Facebook entitativity and group identity for the status update are relatively high with both scoring over four on a seven-point scale.

Table 1: Descriptive data and correlations for the study variables.

Variable	Mean	SD	1	2	3	4	5	6	7
1. Active	6.14	11.9							
2. Interactive	2.97	0.67	0.3						
3. Similar	3.99	2.24	0.1	0.6					
4. Continuity	3.48	0.48	0.1	0.2	0.1				
5. Group outside	2.98	3.51	0	0.7	0.4	0.2			
6. Update entitativity	2.87	2.27	0.2	0.6	0.5	0.2	0.5		
7. Overall FB entitativity	4.15	2.99	0.1	0.2	0.2	0.2	0.1	0.4	
8. Group identity	4.95	0.89	0.1	0.3	0.3	0.3	0.1	0.3	0.3

Note: $N = 295$. As correlations of latent constructs, p values are not applicable.

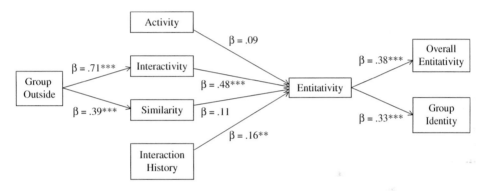

Figure 2: Model of entitativity on Facebook.

We tested the model using structural equation modeling on MPLUS. Our first model showed some room for improvement, χ^2 (145) = 313.346, $p = <.001$, RMSEA = .07 (with a CI from .06 to .08), CFI = .92, TLI = .90, and SRMR = .09. Specifically, RMSEA and SRMR were slightly higher than acceptable and CFI and TLI were slightly lower than acceptable (Kaplan, 2009). Modification indices showed a missing path between similarity and interactivity; because we did not expect a directional relationship between these two latent variables, but could perceive a relationship, we added a correlation between them. Subsequently, our model obtained adequate fit statistics, χ^2 (144) = 272.604, $p = <.001$, RMSEA = .06 (with a CI from .05 to .07), CFI = .94, TLI = .93, and SRMR = .08. The results are presented in Figure 2.

The results generally support our model. First, we start with the direct antecedents of entitativity. Perceptions of interactivity ($\beta = .50$, $p < .001$) and a history of interactions (i.e., that the responders to this particular status update have responded before; $\beta = .15$, $p < .01$) were significantly related to entitativity. Activity on the status updates ($\beta = .09$, $p = .11$) and perceptions of similarity between responders ($\beta = .11$, $p = .19$) were not. We found that the correlation between similarity and interactivity is quite strong at $\beta = .53$, $p < .001$. Therefore, Hypotheses 2 and 4 are supported and Hypotheses 1 and 3 are not.

Next we determined that perceptions that the responders are a group outside of Facebook are strongly related to perceptions of interactivity ($\beta = .71$, $p < .001$) and similarity ($\beta = .39$, $p < .001$). This indicates that both Hypotheses 5a and 5b are supported. Finally, entitativity is significantly related to group identity ($\beta = .33$, $p < .001$) and to overall entitativity ($\beta = .38$, $p < .001$), indicating that both Hypotheses 7 and 8 are supported.

To test that perceived interactivity and similarity mediated the relationship between a group outside of Facebook and entitativity on the status update, we requested that the indirect effects be calculated for these paths by MPLUS. These results indicate that believing that the responders are an interacting group outside of Facebook has an indirect effect on both entitativity through the perceived interactivity but not through similarity, partially supporting Hypothesis 6.

Because of the very strong relationship between group outside and perceived interactivity, we conducted one additional analysis. We wanted to ensure that our measure of interacting as a group outside of Facebook did not inappropriately load onto our perceptions of interactivity among the status update replies. We reran the CFA forcing this item to load on the interactivity latent variable. The resulting CFA fit $\chi^2 (109) = 184.68$, $p = < .001$, RMSEA $= .05$ (with a CI from .04 to .06), CFI $= .96$, TLI $= .95$, and SRMR $= .06$ yields a $\Delta\chi^2 (15) = 19.07$, n.s., which indicates that including this item in the latent measure of perceiving interactivity is not an improvement in the CFA and it should be considered as a separate measure from perceived interactivity.

Finally, our model explained the following amounts of variance in our latent variables: interactivity 51%, similarity 15%, entitativity 37%, and group identity 11%.

The model reveals both commonalities and some unexpected departures from purely FtF entitativity. It also reveals clues for how to activate desired group identities.

Implications for Practice

These results provide guidance for practitioners wishing to use social media to manage group identity. Specifically, by connecting these findings to the affordances provided by status updates, it is our goal to make these recommendations generalizable to other and future social media platforms.

This perspective also emphasizes an important consideration for managers — social media is not technological deterministic. Simply deploying a social media platform that provides the affordances that we discuss in this chapter is not sufficient. Rather practitioners need to manage *how* users of social media use these affordances. For example, imagine the limited ways that one can interact with a co-worker on a blank Facebook page: without wall posts, there is nothing to "like" or comment on; without a filled out profile, there is less information to make judgments of association on. From this it becomes clear that the primary concern for organizations is to manage employees to use social media in ways that further organizational goals.

Direct Antecedents of Entitativity

Implications of interactivity.   In this model, interactivity emerged as the strongest antecedent to entitativity on status updates and can be understood as "the people that responded to me also interact with each other." This finding emphasizes that it is not sufficient for an employee to interact with members of a group to form a group identity — he or she must also know that these members also interact with each other. This highlights the importance of the affordances of visibility and persistence on social media and provides directions for managers wishing to promote group identity through social media.

Coordinate interaction.   The typical role of management is to coordinate the actions of individuals and groups to achieve a common goal. Our model suggests that managers need to not only coordinate action, but also coordinate interaction between members of a group. This goes beyond adding members to "friends lists." It requires managers to create opportunities that allow group members to have meaningful exchanges that are visible to other group members.

Within social media, this can be accomplished by encouraging employees to make visible their FtF and online interactions with others. For example, Google+ can make public when people have interacted during a "hangout" and Facebook enables people to "check-in" themselves and others at physical locations. Other ways of making visible interactions are to encourage the social tagging of photos, comments, and information, which consist of indexing this content with relevant names or ideas that can attract the attention of others (Thom-Santelli, Muller, & Millen, 2008).

Social monitoring.   Along with coordinating interaction among group members, managers need to encourage members and facilitate their ability to become aware of these interactions. The affordance of association is elevated here, as group identity formation on social media is as much about having personal interactions with members as it is about seeing the interactions of other members. Employees need time to view the associations between people. Indeed, a recent study found that time spent on viewing the profiles of co-workers enhanced closeness between co-workers (Wu, DiMicco, & Millen, 2010). Likewise, another study found that reading the messages of a microblogging tool at IBM facilitated affiliation and interaction between employees by helping them feel more connected to what was going on (Ehrlich & Shami, 2010).

While perspectives are changing, many organizations perceive the use of social media during work hours as a waste of time. While this is certainly a valid concern, organizations may also be missing out on opportunities to foster group identity of employees and enhance group performance and outcomes. Therefore, managers can help to enhance group identities by providing time and support for employees to monitor social media.

Avoiding perceived ostracism and token interactions.   Just as perceptions of interactivity can enhance group processes, it also has the potential to undermine them (Kassner, Wesselmann, Law, & Williams, 2012). The ease at which interactions are possible on social media can also facilitate the production of arbitrary interactions with random people. Indeed, employees can feel overwhelmed by the amount of available information in social media (Günther, Krasnova, Riehle, & Schöndienst, 2009). An employee may see such arbitrary and random interactions and interpret them as a form of ostracism, even with minimal (e.g., token) interactions with those members.

For example, early studies of FtF and online co-worker ostracism involved passing a real (Williams & Sommer, 1997) or virtual (Williams, Cheung, & Choi, 2000; Williams & Jarvis, 2006) ball between members of a zero-history group, where all but one member were confederates. In the ostracism condition, each confederate passed the ball only once to the participant and ignored them for the duration of the experiment. In light of seeing the continued interaction of the confederates, participants in these studies reported feeling disidentified from the group.

While our model shows that perceived interactivity among one's respondents can promote entitativity, we also believe that perceived interactivity of others can lead to feelings of fostering ostracism when they are not included in these interactions. The consequences of such ostracism can include aggression (Warburton, Williams, & Cairns, 2006), social loafing (Williams & Sommer, 1997), and disidentification (Matschke & Sassenberg, 2010). Moreover, feelings of ostracism may be attributed to racism (Goodwin, Williams, & Carter-Sowell, 2010) or social categories (Spencer-Rodgers et al., 2007). For a review of ostracism literature, see Williams (2007) and Smart Richman and Leary (2009).

It is a challenge for practitioners to manage the balance between useful and excessive interactions through social media, as too much or too little may undermine the development of group processes. Being aware of the implications of perceptions of ostracism, managers should also monitor interactions among group members to ensure that members are not being left out and if they are, devise ways of fostering online interactions with these members.

Implications of history of interactions.   The second direct antecedent of entitativity is a history of interactions. That is to say, fostering entitativity is not a matter of simply creating a link between people (e.g., adding to a "friends list"), but maintaining interactions over time. In the context of our study it refers to consistent responses to an individual's status updates over time; however, we expect this to generalize to other microblogging platforms (e.g., Google+, Twitter, etc.) as the affordances of persistence and visibility of interactions lies at the heart of this finding. Group identity, then, is promoted when individuals perceive that specific employees consistently respond to their social media content over time. Research has found two key predictors in promoting contributions to organizational social media: managerial buy-in and incentives.

Managerial buy-in.   Studies have found that managerial support and activity on social media promote participation in employees (Brzozowski, Sandholm, & Hogg, 2009; Yardi, Golder, & Brzozowski, 2009). Indeed, these studies found that opinions of social media from one's direct manager are more important than corporate-level policy of promoting social media contributions. Perhaps, most importantly, the data show that managers' participation in social media is a key motivator to getting employees to *start* contributing, while comments from co-workers are key in sustaining these contributions (Brzozowski et al., 2009). This indicates that managers need to participate in social media themselves, producing content and providing feedback to demonstrate managerial buy-in. Without this support, it is possible that employees will not adopt social media in the first place.

Incentivizing content production.   While many organizations are enthusiastic about adopting social media, this enthusiasm is not always reflected in organizational policies and incentives. Rather, organizations frequently create disincentives to contribute to social media (Hinds & Pfeffer, 2003; Paroutis & Al Saleh, 2009). It takes time to produce social media content. While outside of organizational boundaries people may be motivated by self-interest, inside an organization employees often work under time constraints. Employees, then, need time and incentives to produce content.

Managers need to consider meaningful incentives, such as criteria on performance evaluations or recognition. Indeed, one study examining employee contributions to social media found through interviews and log file analysis that one of the strongest predictors of sustaining social media contributions in an organization was the perception that others were reading their content (Yardi et al., 2009). Likewise, another study found that employees that believed they could increase their reputation through social media contributions were more likely to post content (Schoendienst, Krasnova, Günther, & Riehle, 2011). This suggests that a mechanism for managers to promote group functioning through social media is to reward not only the contributions of content, but also the contributions of feedback, comments, and likes to others.

Training.   Research suggests that lack of training also acts as a barrier to contributing to social media in the workplace, due to fear of violating policies, publishing confidential information, or simply lack of knowledge about how to use them (Paroutis & Al Saleh, 2009). As these barriers inhibit the production of content, the organization is missing out on the opportunity to promote group identity. Indeed, as norms to avoid contributing to social media become ingrained in organizations, it may eventually be more difficult to implement organizational strategies to foster contribution.

Indirect Antecedents of Entitativity

Implications of being a group outside of Facebook.   Our model shows that perceiving respondents to be a group outside of Facebook does *not* directly contribute to entitativity and group identity. Rather, consistent with social presence theory, the relationship between being a group outside of Facebook and entitativity is entirely mediated through interactivity. This means that it is not enough for an individual to know that members of a group interact outside of Facebook, but they must perceive them interacting *in* Facebook to promote entitativity and group identities. This reinforces the affordance of visibility within social media and hints at potential contextual boundaries (e.g., FtF vs. online) of group.

Groups interacting in both FtF and online setting do not necessarily experience an automatic "groupiness spill-over effect." Rather, even preexisting groups must interact through the social media and these interactions must be visible to other members to foster entitativity. Our scale asked whether respondents were a group outside of Facebook — we did not specify offline or through other social media. This paints an unclear picture of the feelings of entitativity in offline groups versus in other social media platforms. On the one hand, perceptions of being a group in one social media platform may enhance entitativity *if* group members also interact on Facebook. From this perspective, it may be beneficial for managers to encourage groups to interact through a variety of social media platforms. On the other hand, since perceptions of interactions of respondents in the medium in question (e.g., status updates) is what allows entitativity to develop, it may be more advantageous to funnel all interactions to one social media platform to garner the entitativity benefits there.

Implications of similarity.   In FtF settings, perceptions of similarity are a strong predictor of entitativity. This is particularly true for noninteracting groups, in which members that do not work together still feel groupy because they share a common demographic characteristic. For example, students that have never worked together may still perceive some level of entitativity due to the perceived shared experiences of being a student. Interestingly, we did not find support for this finding in our model of entitativity in social media. Similarity was, however, related to being a group outside of Facebook.

A further review of the literature shows that other scholars have found similar results. While research consistently finds a relationship between entitativity and similarity of group members, the prevailing thought is that "similarity by itself is not a necessary condition for perceiving entitativity" (Crump et al., 2010, p. 1214). Entitativity and similarity, then, are distinct constructs that differ in their importance depending on group goals. Through experimental manipulation, Crump et al. concluded that similarity is more important "when group goals require the same behaviors or thoughts for different group members, and when interchangeability among members is necessary" (p. 1228), while entitativity is more important when "group goals are at stake, when role differentiation is required, and when there is a high level of interdependence among group members" (p. 1227).

Viewing our model under these findings suggests that groups emerging from status updates place more value on role differentiation and interdependence than homogeneity. Managers should consider this when determining what kind of groups should use social media. While there is no evidence to suggest that similar groups will function worse on social media, there is no evidence to suggest that it helps. Rather, it may be more advantageous for diverse, cross-functional groups to use social media as similarity does not impact their perceived entitativity.

Finally, similarity was related to perceptions of being a group outside of Facebook. Both previous research and the affordances of social media provide insights for why this may be. First, to perceive that people are a group outside of Facebook heavily implies that they have access to information about this group, which allows them to make inferences about the similarity of group members (Crump et al., 2010). Furthermore, the affordances of visibility and association suggest that individuals see group activities occurring outside of Facebook through photos, status updates, and comments on Facebook. These observations would likely lead one to believe that people interacting outside of Facebook are more similar.

Null Relationships

Our model that extends perceptions of entitativity to social media has indicated several significant relationships. However, the model also shows an interesting null relationship that is useful for understanding what may or may not promote group identity.

Activity. This variable refers to the total number of comments, responses, likes, etc. that a status update garnered. We found that the sheer number of such activities on a status update was not associated with entitativity. For a manager, this means that developing group identity is not a matter of a one-off "welcome to the team" message. Nor is it necessarily productive to encourage a mass of group members to respond to a status update. When taken within the context of our model, it reveals that there is no one easy way to promote group identity — it requires that co-workers interact with each other and see the interactions of others.

Conclusions

To the extent that organizations can increase members' perceptions of entitativity through social media, they are likely to increase those members' participation and performance in these groups. Entitativity is a key antecedent to group identity and processes. With the new affordances of interaction that social media provides, managers are challenged to find ways to use these tools to improve organizational functioning. In articulating how these new affordances impact entitativity, we hope to provide managers with guidelines for how to encourage social media practices that reinforce group processes.

References

Abrams, D., & Hogg, M. A. (2008). Collective identity: Group membership and self-conception. In M. A. Hogg & R. S. Tindale (Eds.), *Blackwell handbook of social psychology: Group processes* (pp. 425–460). Oxford, UK: Blackwell Publishers Ltd.

Arazy, O., Gellatly, I., Jang, S., & Patterson, R. (2009). Wiki deployment in corporate settings. *Technology and Society Magazine, IEEE, 28*(2), 57–64.

Ashforth, B. E., Rogers, K. M., & Corley, K. G. (2011). Identity in organizations: Exploring cross-level dynamics. *Organization Science, 22*(5), 1144–1156.

Balkundi, P., & Kilduff, M. (2006). The ties that lead: A social network approach to leadership. *The Leadership Quarterly, 17*(4), 419–439.

Biocca, F., Harms, C., & Burgoon, J. K. (2003). Toward a more robust theory and measure of social presence: Review and suggested criteria. *Presence: Teleoperators & Virtual Environments, 12*(5), 456–480.

Brzozowski, M. J., Sandholm, T., & Hogg, T. (2009). Effects of feedback and peer pressure on contributions to enterprise social media. *Proceedings of the ACM 2009 international conference on supporting group work*, ACM, New York, NY (pp. 61–70).

Campbell, D. T. (1958). Common fate, similarity, and other indices of the status of aggregates of persons as social entities. *Behavioral Science, 3*(1), 14–25.

Castano, E., Yzerbyt, V., & Bourguignon, D. (2003). We are one and I like it: The impact of ingroup entitativity on ingroup identification. *European Journal of Social Psychology, 33*(6), 735–754.

Crump, S. A., Hamilton, D. L., Sherman, S. J., Lickel, B., & Thakkar, V. (2010). Group entitativity and similarity: Their differing patterns in perceptions of groups. *European Journal of Social Psychology, 40*(7), 1212–1230.

Danis, C., & Singer, D. (2008). A wiki instance in the enterprise: Opportunities, concerns and reality. *Proceedings of the 2008 ACM conference on computer supported cooperative work*, ACM, New York, NY (pp. 495–504).

DiMicco, J., Millen, D. R., Geyer, W., Dugan, C., Brownholtz, B., & Muller, M. (2008). Motivations for social networking at work. *Proceedings of the 2008 ACM conference on computer supported cooperative work*, ACM, New York, NY (pp. 711–720).

Ding, X., Danis, C., Erickson, T., & Kellogg, W. A. (2007). Visualizing an enterprise Wiki. *CHI '07 Extended Abstracts on Human Factors in Computing Systems* (pp. 2189–2194). New York, NY: ACM.

Ehrlich, K., & Shami, N. S. (2010). Microblogging inside and outside the workplace. *Proceedings of the 4th international AAAI conference on weblogs and social media*, AAAI Press, Menlo Park, CA (pp. 42–49).

Ellemers, N., De Gilder, D., & Haslam, S. A. (2004). Motivating individuals and groups at work: A social identity perspective on leadership and group performance. *Academy of Management Review, 29*(3), 459–478.

Erickson, T., & Kellogg, W. A. (2000). Social translucence: An approach to designing systems that support social processes. *ACM Transactions on Computer-Human Interaction (TOCHI), 7*(1), 59–83.

Fowler, F. J. (1995). *Improving survey questions: Design and evaluation.* Thousand Oaks, CA: Sage.

Gaertner, L., Iuzzini, J., Witt, M. G., & Oriña, M. M. (2006). Us without them: Evidence for an intragroup origin of positive in-group regard. *Journal of Personality and Social Psychology, 90*(3), 426.

Goodwin, S. A., Williams, K. D., & Carter-Sowell, A. R. (2010). The psychological sting of stigma: The costs of attributing ostracism to racism. *Journal of Experimental Social Psychology*, *46*(4), 612–618.

Grudin, J., & Poole, E. S. (2010). Wikis at work: Success factors and challenges for sustainability of enterprise Wikis. *Proceedings of the 6th international symposium on wikis and open collaboration*, ACM, New York, NY.

Günther, O., Krasnova, H., Riehle, D., & Schöndienst, V. (2009). Modeling microblogging adoption in the enterprise. *Americas Conference on Information Systems (AMCIS) 2009 Proceedings*. Paper 544.

Hamilton, D. L. (2007). Understanding the complexities of group perception: Broadening the domain. *European Journal of Social Psychology*, *37*(6), 1077–1101.

Hamilton, D. L., Sherman, S. J., & Lickel, B. (1998). Perceiving social groups: The importance of the entitativity continuum. In C. Sedikides, J. Schopler & C. A. Insko (Eds.), *Intergroup cognition and intergroup behavior* (pp. 47–74). Mahwah, NJ: Erlbaum.

Hampton, K.N., Goulet, L.S., Rainie L., & Purcell, K. (2011). Social networking sites and our lives: How people's trust, personal relationships, and civic and political involvement are connected to their use of social networking sites and other technologies. Washington, DC: Pew Research. Retrieved from http://www.pewinternet.org/Reports/2011/Technology-and-social-networks.aspx

Hinds, P. J., & Pfeffer, J. (2003). Why organizations don't "know what they know": Cognitive and motivational factors affecting the transfer of expertise. In M. Ackerman, V. Pipek & V. Wulf (Eds.), *Sharing expertise: Beyond knowledge management* (pp. 3–26). Cambridge, MA: MIT Press.

Hogg, M. A., Abrams, D., Otten, S., & Hinkle, S. (2004). The social identity perspective intergroup relations, self-conception, and small groups. *Small Group Research*, *35*(3), 246–276.

Hogg, M. A., & Hains, S. C. (1996). Intergroup relations and group solidarity: Effects of group identification and social beliefs on depersonalized attraction. *Journal of Personality and Social Psychology*, *70*(2), 295.

Hogg, M. A., Sherman, D. K., Dierselhuis, J., Maitner, A. T., & Moffitt, G. (2007). Uncertainty, entitativity, and group identification. *Journal of Experimental Social Psychology*, *43*(1), 135–142.

Igarashi, T., & Kashima, Y. (2011). Perceived entitativity of social networks. *Journal of Experimental Social Psychology*, *47*(6), 1048–1058.

Kaplan, D. (2009). *Structural equation modeling: Foundations and extensions*. Thousand Oaks, CA: Sage.

Kassner, M. P., Wesselmann, E. D., Law, A. T., & Williams, K. D. (2012). Virtually ostracized: Studying ostracism in immersive virtual environments. *Cyberpsychology, Behavior, and Social Networking*, *15*(8), 399–403.

Lickel, B., Hamilton, D. L., & Sherman, S. J. (2001). Elements of a lay theory of groups: Types of groups, relational styles, and the perception of group entitativity. *Personality and Social Psychology Review*, *5*(2), 129–140.

Lickel, B., Hamilton, D. L., Wieczorkowska, G., Lewis, A., Sherman, S. J., & Uhles, A. N. (2000). Varieties of groups and the perception of group entitativity. *Journal of Personality and Social Psychology*, *78*(2), 223–246.

Matschke, C., & Sassenberg, K. (2010). Does rejection lead to disidentification? The role of internal motivation and avoidance strategies. *European Journal of Social Psychology*, *40*(6), 891–900.

Ogungbamila, B., Ogungbamila, A., & Adetula, G. A. (2010). Effects of team size and work team perception on workplace commitment: Evidence from 23 production teams. *Small Group Research, 41*(6), 725–745.

Paroutis, S., & Al Saleh, A. (2009). Determinants of knowledge sharing using Web 2.0 technologies. *Journal of Knowledge Management, 13*(4), 52–63.

Postmes, T., Spears, R., & Lea, M. (1998). Breaching or building social boundaries? SIDE-effects of computer-mediated communication. *Communication Research, 25*(6), 689–715.

Raeth, P., Smolnik, S., Urbach, N., & Zimmer, C. (2009). Towards assessing the success of social software in corporate environments. *Americas Conference on Information Systems (AMCIS) 2009 Proceedings*. Paper 662.

Rutchick, A. M., Hamilton, D. L., & Sack, J. D. (2008). Antecedents of entitativity in categorically and dynamically construed groups. *European Journal of Social Psychology, 38*(6), 905–921.

Schoendienst, V., Krasnova, H., Günther, O., & Riehle, D. (2011). Micro-blogging adoption in the enterprise: An empirical analysis. *Wirtschaftinformatik Proceedings 2011*. Paper 22.

Sherman, S. J., Hamilton, D. L., & Lewis, A. C. (1999). Perceived entitativity and the social identity value of group memberships. In D. Abrams & M. A. Hogg (Eds.), *Social identity and social cognition* (pp. 80–110). Oxford: Blackwell Publishing.

Smart Richman, L., & Leary, M. R. (2009). Reactions to discrimination, stigmatization, ostracism, and other forms of interpersonal rejection: a multimotive model. *Psychological Review, 116*(2), 365.

Spencer-Rodgers, J., Hamilton, D. L., & Sherman, S. J. (2007). The central role of entitativity in stereotypes of social categories and task groups. *Journal of Personality and Social Psychology, 92*(3), 369.

Thom-Santelli, J., Muller, M. J., & Millen, D. R. (2008). Social tagging roles: Publishers, evangelists, leaders. *Proceedings of the twenty-sixth annual SIGCHI conference on human factors in computing systems*, ACM, New York, NY (pp. 1041–1044).

Treem, J., & Leonardi, P. (2012). Social media use in organizations: Exploring the affordances of visibility, editability, persistence, and association. *Communication Yearbook, 36*, 143–189.

Van Dick, R., Van Knippenberg, D., Hägele, S., Guillaume, Y. R. F., & Brodbeck, F. C. (2008). Group diversity and group identification: The moderating role of diversity beliefs. *Human Relations, 61*(10), 1463–1492.

Van Knippenberg, D., De Dreu, C. K. W., & Homan, A. C. (2004). Work group diversity and group performance: an integrative model and research agenda. *Journal of Applied Psychology, 89*(6), 1008–1022.

Warburton, W. A., Williams, K. D., & Cairns, D. R. (2006). When ostracism leads to aggression: The moderating effects of control deprivation. *Journal of Experimental Social Psychology, 42*(2), 213–220.

Williams, K. D. (2007). Ostracism. *Annual Review of Psychology, 58*, 425–452.

Williams, K. D., Cheung, C. K. T., & Choi, W. (2000). Cyberostracism: Effects of being ignored over the Internet. *Journal of Personality and Social Psychology, 79*(5), 748–762.

Williams, K. D., & Jarvis, B. (2006). Cyberball: A program for use in research on interpersonal ostracism and acceptance. *Behavior Research Methods, 38*(1), 174–180.

Williams, K. D., & Sommer, K. L. (1997). Social ostracism by coworkers: Does rejection lead to loafing or compensation? *Personality and Social Psychology Bulletin, 23*(7), 693–706.

Wu, A., DiMicco, J. M., & Millen, D. R. (2010). Detecting professional versus personal closeness using an enterprise social network site. *Proceedings of the SIGCHI conference on human factors in computing systems*, ACM, New York, NY (pp. 1955–1964).

Yardi, S., Golder, S. A., & Brzozowski, M. J. (2009). Blogging at work and the corporate attention economy. *Proceedings of the 27th international conference on human factor in computing systems*, ACM, New York, NY (pp. 2071–2080).

Yzerbyt, V., Castano, E., Leyens, J. P., & Paladino, M. P. (2000). The primacy of the ingroup: The interplay of entitativity and identification. *European Review of Social Psychology, 11*(1), 257–295.

Zellmer-Bruhn, M. E., Maloney, M. M., Bhappu, A. D., & Salvador, R. B. (2008). When and how do differences matter? An exploration of perceived similarity in teams. *Organizational Behavior and Human Decision Processes, 107*(1), 41–59.

Chapter 8

Using Social Media for Job Search: Evidence from Generation Y Job Seekers

Laxmikant Manroop and Julia Richardson

Abstract

Purpose — This study aims to investigate the extent to which Generation Y job seekers use social media to enhance their job search experience.

Design/Methodology/Approach — The chapter draws on an in-depth analysis of qualitative data gathered from 29 interviews with recent university graduates in Human Resource Management (HRM).

Findings — The findings of this study challenge popular stereotypes and anecdotes which seem to suggest that the power of technology come naturally and easily to Generation Y users (The Economist, 2010). It also suggests that young people, particularly graduates are unprepared for the job market. Many of them are stuck in the traditional ways of looking for a job despite the information that is available for them to exploit modern technologies to enhance their job search experience.

Implications — Colleges and universities should include modern job search techniques such as social media into their curricula. In addition, career centers and employers need to play their part in disseminating information about how social media can be used by graduates to search for jobs.

Originality/Value — The study emphasizes the need for individual users to exploit technology such as social media to enhance their professional and career success.

Keywords: Generation Y; job search; qualitative; social media

Social Media in Human Resources Management
Advanced Series in Management, 167–180
ISSN: 1877-6361/doi:10.1108/S1877-6361(2013)0000012012

Introduction

Until recently, social media were predominantly used to connect people — particularly young college and university students — with shared interest. More recently, the use of social media has permeated other spheres of personal and professional life such as job searching and career enhancement (Malita, Badescu, & Dabu, 2010). In particular, it has transformed the ways in which employers, recruiters, individual workers, and job seekers connect and interact with each other (Plummer, Hiltz, & Llotnick, 2011). In this chapter we focus on individual users of social media, particularly Generation Y job seekers. While social media is used more broadly by people to refer to a host of social networking sites, in this study we focus specifically on Facebook, LinkedIn, and Twitter particularly because they are the most popular among employers, job seekers, and individual users.

In a 2011 Jobvite recruitment survey, 89% of the 800 companies surveyed indicated that they intend to recruit through social media this year compared to 83% in 2010 (Jobvite Social Recruiting Survey, 2011). This increase clearly demonstrates the popularity of social media as a recruitment tool among employers. Social media are also becoming increasingly popular among job seekers. For example, in a 2010 poll of college graduates, the National Association of Colleges and Employers (NACE) found that 37% of the respondents use social media as part of their job search compared to only 16% in 2009 (NACE, 2010). These findings coupled with the general assumptions that Generation Y cohort (also referred to as the Millennial generation) is the most connected people in history (Smith & Clark, 2010), suggesting that Generation Y (born between 1980 and 2000) should tend naturally toward and actively use social media to job search (Gerald, 2011).

Despite this commonly accepted wisdom about Generation Y in the popular press (Smith & Clark, 2010), there is virtually little empirical evidence to assess the extent to which Generation Y job seekers actually use social media to job search (Plummer et al., 2011). There is also little evidence to support the commonly held stereotype that a tech-savvy Generation Y cohort should know how to leverage social media to achieve career success. Addressing these issues is important for two reasons. First, using social media can impact job finding success because studies have shown that employers increasingly use social media as a recruitment tool (de Janasz & Forret, 2008; Malita et al., 2010). Thus, in order to expand our understanding of contemporary job search practices, it may be important to examine whether Generation Y job seekers are keeping pace with employers in using this technology. Second, knowing how Generation Y job seekers use social media can provide scholars with insight into how well this group understands the functionality of social media as a job search tool and how this can impact their job finding success.

In the paragraphs that follow, we examine Generation Y and how they use social media. In particular, we highlight how young people are portrayed in the digital age and the common stereotypes associated with such description. We then review the literature on Generation Y job search behaviors as it relates to using social media, particularly Facebook, LinkedIn, and Twitter. Following that review, and using the literature as our theoretical basis, we draw on the findings of a qualitative study examining Generation Y job seekers' use of social media as a job search tool. Although previous research has dealt with young job seekers in much detail, there is still a paucity of empirical studies focusing on how they utilize social media to look for work (Gerard, 2012). Finally, we offer some concluding remarks specific to our findings as they relate to Generation Y job seekers and their use of social media for job searching.

Literature Review

Generation Y and the Social Media Context

It is well established in both the practitioner and academic literature that social media usage (e.g., Facebook, LinkedIn, Twitter, MySpace, YouTube, etc.) is the most prominent characteristic of the Generation Y cohort (Agozzino, 2010; Bracy, Bevill, & Roach, 2010; Gerard, 2012). Widely understood as "Digital Natives," contemporary writers have suggested that Generation Y spend a significant amount of their time on different kinds of networking sites and virtual communities (Bowley, 2010) and less time on other activities such as study and research (Bracy et al., 2010). For example, about 91% of college and university students in the Midwest reported using social media every day to meet new friends, make connections, and upload personal information (Miller, Parsons, & Lifer, 2010). Among Generation Y, the top social media sites as of 2009 include Facebook, MySpace, Twitter, LinkedIn, and Classmates (Nielsen, 2009). Both Facebook and LinkedIn have over 500 million and 30 million active users, respectively, and these figures keep growing every day (Shroeder, 2010). Studies have also suggested that 75% of users on these sites are 35 years and under. It seems hardly surprising, therefore, that the popular and practitioner literature describe Generation Y population as "fast-paced, communication-saturated, well-connected, and tech-savvy" (Aluri, 2009; Holley, 2008). The fact that social media technologies are so widely used by young people in this digital age may create a new set of expectations for Generation Y job seekers to be able to leverage these technologies to access job search information.

Generation Y and Job Search

The academic literature on Generation Y job seekers' use of social media technologies for job search is relatively limited compared to how it has been addressed in the practitioner and popular literature. It is not surprising, therefore, that Richards (2007) laments this deficiency by noting that job seekers who use social media technologies in their search for employment "independent of traditional employment agencies appears, as of yet, not to have stimulated much scholarly interest" (p. 7). Although this observation was made over three years ago, not much has changed since then. For example, a search in scholarly academic journals on this subject reveals three studies, two of which were done in a classroom setting. We review these studies below.

Plummer et al. (2011) developed and tested a preliminary theoretical model, which is part of a larger ongoing study, in which they examined job seekers' intentions to apply for jobs using social media. According to the model, job seekers' use of social media was predicted by four factors, namely, information privacy concerns, perceived justice in the selection process, performance expectancy (i.e., judgment about the value and utility of using social media to find a job), and risk beliefs (i.e., uncertainty and adverse consequences of using social media). The authors found that perceived usefulness and privacy concerns directly predict job seekers' intentions to use social media to apply for jobs, but not risk beliefs and justice in the selection process. These findings suggest that job seekers are more likely to use social media if they believed that these technologies can improve their chances of finding a job. However, the authors also observe that job seekers' chances of finding a job depend, for the most part, on their online networks or "inside connections" and the quality of information they are able to obtain from these connections about the advertised jobs (Plummer et al., 2011). Although concerns about privacy can deter job seekers' use of social media, the authors note that the appeal of social media in job finding success can mitigate the effects of these concerns.

In a similar study, Verhoeven, Mashood, and Chansarkar (2011) explored the use of social media among Generation Y and their views on social media in the recruitment process. Using data drawn from a survey of university students in Dubai, the authors found that social media are regularly used by young job seekers looking for work. The authors write that "forty two percent of job seekers use social network sites very often, 17 percent use it often, and 21 percent use them sometimes" (p. 10). They conclude that social networking sites are regularly used by job seekers which correspond with the belief among Generation Y users that employers actually look at these sites as potential recruitment sources (Verhoeven et al., 2011). In yet another exploratory study designed as part of a classroom assignment, Gerard (2012) explored the possibility of adopting social media as an instructional resource and tool, and to see who was using LinkedIn and for what purposes. Using data gathered from 154 undergraduate students, the author found that while a few students expressed discomfort using the LinkedIn social networking site, the majority felt it was a positive experience. In particular, when asked which LinkedIn job search features they have used or currently use, 90% of the students said they created a profile on LinkedIn, 55% used the job keyword search, and 34% used LinkedIn to research companies (Gerard, 2012). The author notes that "beyond completing the basic assignment ... students were using the LinkedIn tool to create, revisit, and refine their own profiles. They were using job, person, and network searches, which better connected them to their most relevant network resources" (Gerard, 2012, p. 21).

These studies seem to suggest that social media are beginning to play a significant role in job searching, particularly among the younger generation of job seekers. There is also a body of popular literature drawing attention to social media as a job search tool (Challenger, 2009) and advocating for employers to take advantage of this kind of social media services in order to connect with younger job seekers (e.g., Babcock, 2011; Greiner, 2011; Litherland, 2010). This is due, in part, to the widely accepted view that Generation Y individuals are well connected in the digital age, and use social media extensively (Holley, 2008).

Following from the foregoing argument, there is an implicit assumption that because Generation Y use social media in their personal lives they will also do so in their professional lives to build career enhancing networks and connect with potential employers. Contrary to popular belief, however, Loiacono, Djamasbi, and Tulu (2011) ran three experiments with a group of Generation Y students. Study 1 was geared to determine students' familiarity with virtual worlds, namely, Second Life; study 2 examined whether knowledge about job recruitment through Second Life was of interest to participants; and study 3 sought to determine whether job seekers would use Second Life as a job recruitment tool. Overall, the authors found Generation Y users to be less enthusiastic about virtual online recruitment and many of them were not aware of Second Life. The authors found this surprising given the fact that Generation Y users are quite familiar with many technologies and web-based applications (Loiacono et al., 2011).

That being said, however, it may be that Second Life is not nearly as popular as social media platforms such as Facebook, LinkedIn, or Twitter, and the fact that many Generation Y users already have accounts on one or more of these sites, it would be easier for them to leverage social media to enhance their professional life, such as looking for a job.

This is perhaps why employers and recruiters are expanding their recruitment online using social media technologies such as Facebook, LinkedIn, and Twitter. However, much of this is promoted by the popular literature (e.g., Babcock, 2011; Greiner, 2011; Litherland, 2010; Robins, 2008). For example, Robins (2008) posits that companies should be more creative in their use of social media such as YouTube and Facebook to reach younger workers. Similarly, Challenger (2009) notes that employers are increasingly using social media as a recruiting tool in response to changes in the job search landscape in which more and more young people are now turning to social media in order to stand out from the crowd. Regardless of the arguments advanced in the scholarly or practitioner literature — there seems to be general agreement that social media have grown exponentially within the last five years as more and more people have accounts on Facebook, LinkedIn, and Twitter. In addition, online recruitment is becoming the norm as evidenced by survey studies showing more than 80 percent of companies use social media to fill vacant positions (Jobvite Social Recruiting Survey, 2011). Taken together, social media have the potential to revolutionize job search. Therefore, knowing the extent to which Generation Y job seekers actually use social media is of critical importance. Having reviewed the literature on Generation Y job search using social media, we turn now to discussing our methodology and analysis of the findings.

Methodology

The study was conducted with a group of recent university graduates holding bachelor's degree in Human Resource Management (HRM) who completed their degrees in 2010 and 2011 and were actively looking for a full-time job in the HRM field. Qualitative findings from interviews with 29 HRM graduates relating to their use of social media in job searching are discussed. Specifically, we sought to understand the extent to which Generation Y job seekers use social media in their job search and their perception of the impact of these sites on their ability to find a job. The objective was to obtain "thick description" by capturing the individual thoughts and experiences (Denzin, 2001) of HRM graduates. Thus, in-depth semistructured interviews were used as a means of data collection to understand interviewees' experiences with social media.

Sample

Study participants were drawn from southwestern Ontario in Canada, including the greater Toronto area. The sample was based on purposive snowball sampling (Rossman & Rallis, 2003), where access to participants was gained through direct email contact (gained from the institutional databases) and referrals by other graduates. It is common practice among researchers to use snowball sampling and/or network sampling combined (e.g., Collis & Hussey, 2003; Sommer, Ward, & Scofield, 2010) when conducting field research because of the difficulty associated with reaching individuals from the population who exactly fit the study criteria (Marshall & Rossman, 2011).

Participants were assured that the data was being collected for research purposes only and that their responses would remain completely confidential. To encourage participation, every participant was entered into a drawing to win $200 cash. The demographic characteristics of the sample of interviewees in this study are presented in the appendix. All participants were first-time job seekers looking for a job in HRM following graduation.

Data Collection

Given the objectives of the study, that is, to gain an "emic" understanding of participants' job search experiences, in-depth semistructured interview was the most appropriate method for data collection (Marshall & Rossman, 2011). In addition, in keeping with Holstein and Gubrium's (1997) recommendation, an interview agenda, rather than specific interview questions, was used in order to facilitate consistency while allowing interviewees to select which dimensions of their experiences were most important to them. This approach allowed for a more personalized account into the experiences of job searching as it relates to using Social Networking Sites (SNSs).

Data Analysis

Each interview lasted approximately 45 minutes to an hour. All interviews were tape recorded and transcribed verbatim. The data were analyzed in N-vivo (a qualitative data analysis software) using thematic analysis (King, 2004). In keeping with the conventions of thematic analysis, themes were identified from the interview transcripts and then coded into "nodes." This approach falls somewhere between grounded theory and content analysis, that is, between where some codes are predetermined and others emerge from the data. Our study reflects a similar position, in that some themes were data driven while others were theory driven based on the job search literature. For example, one theme that emerged and was added during analysis was how job seekers were using SNSs to search for jobs reactively. By comparison, social media as a theme was identified a priori. In this study, however, the majority of codes were data driven (e.g., Janesick, 1998).

Findings

The findings of this study are reported below. It is important to mention a few things at the outset. First, all names have been changed in order to maintain the anonymity of study participants. Second, five distinct themes were identified during the data analysis, namely, Skill-set deficit, resisting using social media, incognizant of the job search features in social media, skepticism and privacy concerns, and a passive approach to using social media for job search. We should point out also that there is connectivity among the various themes which relate to job seekers' use of social media and the extent to which that connectivity is nested within job seekers' experiences.

Skill-Set Deficit

A dominant theme for many interviewees in our study was a skill-set deficit or lack of "know-how" in using social media for job search. For example, many interviewees were at a loss when discussing social media functionality and the extent to which they used such functionality in their job search endeavors. Clare described her experience as follows:

> I have a profile on LinkedIn for a few months now but I don't know exactly how to use it; I haven't quite figured it out yet. I plan to spend some time and explore the different features and how they might help my job search. (Clare)

Although many Generation Y job seekers knew how to use social media to connect socially with friends and family, they did not seem to understand the potential of these technologies to connect them with prospective employers. They adopt a somewhat passive approach, and in some ways, feel lost as they try to navigate their way through different social media sites. Thus, they only use the functionalities they feel most comfortable with which further highlight a skill-set deficit and the inability of job seekers to capitalize on the potential of social media for job searching.

> I use LinkedIn and Facebook to connect with people but I am very passive when it comes to job search because I don't know how to use it to my benefit. I just post my information but I don't search for jobs. People tell me that they can find a job through LinkedIn and I'm just not sure how you're supposed to do that except looking at the job search positions or writing to someone saying: 'I'm looking for a job, if you know anything please contact me'. That's the only two things I can think of to do on LinkedIn. Other than that I don't know. (Ashley)

This skill-set deficit or lack of "know-how" in using social media for job search limits the extent to which participants could connect with prospective employers and recruiters, which ultimately, could affect their job seeking success. Participants' lack of familiarity with how modern technology might enhance their professional lives challenges the argument made by Palfrey and Gasser (2008) in their book: "Born Digital" in which they argue that growing up with the Internet has transformed Generation Y's approach to education and work. Such anecdotes are used to back calls for employers and recruiters to shift recruitment online to attract younger job applicants.

Resisting Using Social Media for Job Search

While some participants knew about the potential of social media to aid in their job search even though they could not quite figure out how the features on social media sites work, eight of the participants disagreed that social media, particularly Facebook, MySpace, and Twitter, could be used for anything other than connecting with friends and family.

> I don't see Facebook or Twitter as places where you can look for jobs. To me they are more suited to stay in touch and connect with friends and family. I don't see much value in using them for job searching. (Andrew)

> MySpace — I don't even look at that. It just seems too unprofessional. And Facebook is the same things — it's not a job search tool in my mind. (Steve)

These findings clearly reflect participants' resistance to using social media in their personal lives and using social media in their professional lives, that is, to start their career journey. Although it is argued that digital natives (Generation Y) grow up with the Internet (Prensky, 2001), this finding suggests that some individuals may be either unwilling or unable to harness the technologies around them to look for jobs. Their struggles with applying the technologies in another context (e.g., job searching) suggest not only that they do not understand how social media work, but also show resistance to the job search potentialities of social media.

Incognizant of the Job Search Features on Social Media Sites

Interviewees also talked about being completely unaware of the job search features on social media and many of them were surprised to learn that social media could be used for much more than merely connecting socially with people, such as building professional ties and obtaining useful job search information.

> The thing is, I was on LinkedIn for the longest while and didn't know there was a job tab that you could actually use to search for jobs. I didn't know it was there. I just made my profile and that was it. I added people but I didn't think of LinkedIn originally as a place to search for jobs. I thought that by putting up my profile and leaving it there, someone was going to come to me — like a recruiter. I didn't actually think you could find or look for jobs through LinkedIn. (Mark)

> I started using LinkedIn only after a recruiter advised me to go on it. She told me her niece got employed by learning about an opening from one of her contacts. I had known about LinkedIn before, but I thought it was another social media sites to connect with people. I had no idea that employers also go there as well. (Jason)

These accounts illustrate the level of unawareness among Generation Y users when it comes to using social media for job search. The unfamiliarity with social media functionality and features as it relates to job searching is one of the huge struggles Generation Y users have despite the hype in the popular press about their "digital awareness." This finding is consistent with Loiacono et al. (2011) observation that Generation Y users have very little knowledge about recruitment in the virtual world.

Skepticism and Privacy Concerns of Social Media

Some Generation Y job seekers also expressed a great deal of skepticism and privacy concerns about using social media for job search. This theme flows directly from the others we have discussed above and has a direct impact on the extent to which Generation Y job seekers use social media. Monica, for example, preferred not to use social media to job search because she felt very uncomfortable connecting with people who might have access to her personal information. Likewise, Mickey openly expressed reluctance creating a profile or posting a resume on social media sites for fear that her privacy might be compromised.

> I have my LinkedIn account but I don't use it to job search because I feel there should be a separation between SNSs and job search. I don't want my whole history to be known by employers out there. Even though my account is perfectly fine I want to maintain a level of privacy in my personal life. (Monica)

> For me one of the reasons why I'm not using SNSs yet is that I feel it is a huge risk. For example, there is always the issue of privacy and identity theft — you post your profile out there for companies to see but other people are out there too who see the same information and use it for other purposes. People don't really know about it but it's a huge risk. (Mickey)

This is quite interesting because it runs counter to popular belief that young people care less about engaging in risky behaviors that often compromise their privacy and reputation (IT Business Edge, 2011). In a recent survey of Internet experts, conducted by the Pew Research Center's Internet and American Life Project and Elon University, it was projected that Generation Y would continue to disclose personal information in order to stay connected. Contrary to popular opinion, however, Plummer et al. (2011), in an experimental study, found that privacy concerns predicted young people's intentions to apply for jobs using social media.

Passive Approach to Using Social Media for Job Search

In recounting how they used social media to job search, many Generation Y job seekers described a rather passive and laid back approach that include no more than creating a profile and hoping that employers and recruiters would seek them out. Others talked about posting a resume and networking only with friends and fellow classmates, and sharing job-related information among themselves.

> I opened a LinkedIn account, created a profile and I've been adding my friends and tracking their job opportunities too. I also use it to send posting to my friends about entry level jobs and internships. I think it's a great place for recruiters to get to know you. (Mark)

> I'm trying to broaden my network on LinkedIn by making connection with people I know, but I don't think I've been proactive enough in tapping into the right people to get me a job. (Vicky)

> I have a basic account on LinkedIn which I use to apply for jobs. I don't go on it always, but whenever I have time I would update my connection and see what new jobs are there and I apply for them. (Miss M)

The accounts above provide evidence that although many Generation Y job seekers knew the value of social media in improving their job search outcome, they did not know how to proactively go about their job search. It exposes a lack of understanding among Generation Y job seekers of exactly what job searching entails and what it would take to stand out from the crowd.

Discussion and Concluding Remarks

The findings presented here suggest several factors that can determine the extent to which Generation Y job seekers use social media to job search, namely, a skill-set deficit, resistance to using social media, incognizant of the job search features on social media sites, skepticism and privacy concerns, and a passive approach to social media. Many Generation Y job seekers fall into one or more of these categories, which certainly impact their job finding success. From a social media job search perspective, Generation Y job seekers can also be easily divided into two groups. First, there are those who know about the power and significance of social media in helping them find jobs, but they lack the know-how or skill-set to harness the technologies. These are passive job seekers that look for jobs by posting a resume and/or creating a profile to connect with the people they know. Second, there are those who do not think social media can be of any value other than to connect socially with friends and family and those who fear their privacy can be compromised.

The people in this category do not use social media to job search but rely solely on traditional job search methods.

The above, notwithstanding, there is still a group of Generation Y job seekers who know about the power of social media and actively use them to job search. However, the evidence presented in this empirical study suggests that the majority of Generation Y job seekers are at a loss when it comes to applying modern technologies to enhance their professional life. The findings of this study challenge popular stereotypes and anecdotes which seem to suggest that the power of technology come naturally and easily to Generation Y users (The Economist, 2010). It also suggests that young people, particularly graduates are unprepared for the job market. Many of them are stuck in the traditional ways of looking for a job despite the information that is available for them to exploit modern technologies to enhance their job search experience.

The onus, therefore, is upon colleges and universities to include modern job search techniques into their curricula. In addition, career centers and employers need to play their part in disseminating information about how social media can be used to look for jobs.

References

Agozzino, A. L. (2010). *Millennial students relationship with 2008 top 10 social media brands via social media tools.* OhioLINK/Bowling Green State University. Retrieved from http://rave.ohiolink.edu/etdc/view?acc_num. Accessed on September 15, 2011.

Aluri, A. (2009). To investigate the usage of social networking sites as a career enhancement tool among Generation Y: An empirical research. ScholarWorks@UMass Amherst. Retrieved from http://scholarworks.umass.edu/isenberg/. Accessed on April 27, 2011.

Babcock, P. (2011). Recruiting strategies for social media. Retrieved from http://www.shrmindia.org/recruiting-strategies-social-media. Accessed on September 13, 2011.

Bowley, G. (2010). A fear that academics are distracted directors. *The New York Times.* Retrieved from http://www.nytimes.com/2010/08/01/business/01prez.html?hpw=&pagewanted=print. Accessed on September 15, 2011.

Bracy, C., Bevill, S., & Roach, T. D. (2010). The millennial generation: Recommendations for overcoming teaching challenges. *In Academy of Educational Leadership, 15*(21).

Challenger (2009). *Social networking explodes as job search tool.* Retrieved from http://iwsdocumentednewsdaily.blogspot.com/2009/11/iws-challenger-social-networking.html. Accessed on September 16, 2011.

Collis, J., & Hussey, R. (2003). *Business research: A practical guide for undergraduate and postgraduate students.* Basingstoke: Palgrave Macmillan.

de Janasz, S. C., & Forret, M. L. (2008). Learning the art of networking: A critical skill for enhancing social capital and career success. *Journal of Management Education, 32,* 629–650.

Denzin, N. K. (2001). *Interpretive interactionism* (2nd ed.). Thousand Oaks, CA: Sage.

Gerard, J. G. (2012). Linking in with LinkedIn: Three exercises that enhance professional social networking and career building. *Journal of Management Education, 36*(6), 866–897.

Greiner, L. (2011). *How to use social media as a recruiting tool.* Retrieved from http://www.theglobeandmail.com/report-on-business/small-business/digital/web-strategy/article 2048571.ece. Accessed on September 11, 2011.

Holley, J. (2008). Generation Y: Understanding the trend and planning for the impact. Paper presented at the 32nd Annual IEEE International Computer Software and Applications Conference.

Holstein, J. A., & Gubrium, J. F. (1997). Active interviewing. In D. Silverman (Ed.), *Qualitative research: Theory, method and practice* (pp. 113–129). Thousand Oaks, CA: Sage.

IT Business Edge (2011). *Generation Y employees and privacy.* Retrieved from http://www.itbusinessedge.com/cm/blogs/poremba/generation-y-employees-and-privacy/?cs = 42206. Accessed on September 16, 2011.

Janesick, V. J. (1998). The dance of qualitative research design: Metaphor, methodolatry and meaning. In N. K. Denzin & Y. S. Lincoln (Eds.), *Strategies of qualitative enquiry* (pp. 35–54). Thousand Oaks, CA: Sage.

Jobvite Social Recruiting Survey (2011). *More than 80% of companies plan to recruit through social networks in coming year.* Retrieved from http://recruiting.jobvite.com/news/press-releases/pr/jobvite-social-recruiting-survey-2010.php. Accessed on September 15, 2011.

King, N. (2004). Using interviews in qualitative research. In G. Symon & C. Casell (Eds.), *Essential guide to qualitative methods in organizational research.* London: Sage.

Litherland, D. (2010). Branding and hiring in a "social" world. *Canadian HR Reporter, 23,* 17–18.

Loiacono, E., Djamasbi, S., & Tulu, B. (2011). Why virtual job recruitment is not well accepted by Generation Y? — A case study on second life. In J. A. Jacko (Ed.), *Human computer interaction*, Part 1V, HCII, (pp. 245–254).

Malita, L., Badescu, I., & Dabu, R. (2010). Cultural tips of online job searching. *Procedia Social and Behavioral Sciences, 2,* 3070–3074.

Marshall, C., & Rossman, G. B. (2011). *Designing qualitative research* (5th ed.). Thousand Oaks, CA: Sage.

Miller, R., Parsons, K., & Lifer, D. (2010). Students and social networking sites: The posting paradox. *Behavior and Information Technology, 29,* 377–382.

NACE (2010). *Social networking sites account for little job search activity.* Retrieved from www.naceweb.org/Publications/Spotlight_Online/2010/0609/Social_Networking_Accounts_for_Little_Job-Search_Activity.aspx. Accessed on September 15, 2011.

Nielsen (2009, March). *Led by Facebook, Twitter, Global Time Spent on social media sites up 82% year over year.* Retrieved from http://blog.nielsen.com/nielsenwire/global/led-by-facebook-twitter-global-time-spent-on-social-mediasitesup-82-year-over-year/. Accessed on September 09, 2011.

Palfrey, J., & Gasser, U. (2008). *Born digital: Understanding the first generation of digital natives.* New York, NY: Basic Books.

Plummer, M., Hiltz, S. R., & Llotnick, L. (2011). Predicting intentions to apply for jobs using social networking sites: An exploratory study. *HICSS 11, Proceedings of the 2011 44th Hawaii international conference on system sciences* (pp. 1–10).

Prensky, M. (2001). Digital natives, digital immigrants. *On the Horizon, 9,* 1–6.

Richards, J. (2007). Workers are doing it for themselves: Examining creative employee application of Web 2.0 communication technology. Paper presented at the Work, Employment and Society (WES) 2007, September 12–14, 2007, University of Aberdeen, Aberdeen Scotland. Retrieved from http://www.scribd.com/doc/6873217/JRichards WES2007. Accessed on December 23, 2008.

Robbins, M. (2008). Recruiting and retaining the best of Gen Y. *Employee Benefits News,* February, pp. 20–22.

Rossman, G, & Rallis, S. (2003). *Learning in the field: An introduction to qualitative research* (2nd ed.). Thousand Oaks, CA: Sage.

Shroeder, S. (2010). *Web users now on Facebook longer than Google*. CNN Tech. Retrieved from http://articles.cnn.com/2010-09-10/tech/facebook.google.time_1_mark-zuckerberg-facebook-web-users?_s = PM:TECH. Accessed on September 16, 2011.

Smith, J., & Clark, G. (2010). New games, different rules – Millennials are in town. *Journal of Diversity Management*, *5*, 1–11.

Sommer, C. A., Ward, J. E., & Scofield, T. (2010). Metaphorical stories in supervision of internship: A qualitative study. *Journal of Counseling and Development*, *88*, 500–508.

The Economist (2010). *The net generation, unplugged*. Retrieved from http://www.economist.com/node/15582279. Accessed on September 16, 2011.

Verhoeven, H., Mashood, N., & Chansarkar, B. (2011). *Recruitment and Generation Y: Web 2.0 the way to go?* Retrieved from http://www.wbiconpro.com/8.Neelofar.pdf. Accessed on September 16, 2011.

Appendix: Demographic Information of HRM Graduates

	Number of individuals Time 1	$(N = 29)\%$ Time 1
Sex		
Male	9	31%
Female	20	69%
Total	29	100%
Education		
Bachelor's Degree	29	100%
Age		
20–25	22	76%
26–30	4	14%
30–35	3	10%

Chapter 9

The Integration of Online Face-to-Face Social Networking: The Need for Managerial Reconfiguration

Barbara Imperatori and Dino Ruta

Abstract

Purpose — The chapter explores if and how online and face-to-face organizational environments can interact, and if and how this interaction could foster managerial practices to sustain personal growth, organizational development, and employee–organization relationships.

Methodology — Research project is based on an emblematic case study: Fubles.com is a social sport sharing platform with one of the most active sport communities in Europe. This case is representative of a novel initiative, useful in understanding how social media drive organizational results.

Findings — Social media activities do not always substitute face-to-face relationships; online connections can enhance relationships, in terms of quantity, quality, and fairness, generating comprehensive reconfiguration of people practices, before and after the game. Thanks to social networks, organizations can support interpersonal contacts, enabling people to organize collective activities both virtually and physically.

Practical implications — The case advocates three levels of possible organizational reconfigurations through social media (individual, collective, and organizational) that can foster the quality of the employee–organization relationship.

Originality/value — Results suggest that social media are sources of new and innovative ways to interact within and across organizations, reinforcing not only the

Social Media in Human Resources Management
Advanced Series in Management, 181–200
ISSN: 1877-6361/doi:10.1108/S1877-6361(2013)0000012013

online interactions, but especially traditional face-to-face connections through a process of reconfiguration of people practices.

Keywords: Managerial reconfiguration; employee–organization relationship; sport organization; social organization; social media

Introduction

Most of the studies on social media activities are focused on how social networking web applications can be considered an autonomous virtual space (Mangold & Faulds, 2009). Social media can create a parallel way to the traditional one of experiencing services and social ties, one that could *substitute* the offline connections (Matei & Ball-Rokeach, 2001).

Research indicates that there is a relationship between being social media users and the likelihood of being involved in the real world, even if the direction of this relationship is not consolidated (Howard, Raine, & Jones, 2001). Evidence suggests that the more we are online, the more we will abandon our neighbors and families, preferring online relationships for their greater degree of freedom (Kraut et al., 1998). On the other hand, empirical studies have provided substantial evidence that people who connect to the Internet are more likely to use it for cultivating their social and cultural proclivities (Katz & Aspden, 1997). However, updated evidence is still scarce, and no study addresses the core question of how to design and manage effective organizational solutions where social relationships in either space (online and face-to-face) could interact. Our study seeks to fill this gap, considering social media as potential sources of new and innovative ways to interact within and across organizations, reinforcing the traditional face-to-face connections through a process of reconfiguration of people practices.

We present a descriptive case study on Fubles. Fubles.com (www.fubles.com) is a successful social networking website that brings football enthusiasts together to play games and pursue their passion for the beautiful game, combining face-to-face and online spaces. Fubles has a peer-to-peer rating system; after every game, players rate each other's performance out of 10 in the same way that newspapers routinely rate professional players. Then Fubles players receive a message inviting them to go to the website to see how their performance was evaluated by the other players. These ratings are also tracked on their Fubles playing card profile for other players to see. The ratings naturally give rise to post-match analysis, banter, and punditry; it is this social networking element that is the key to Fubles' success. People are encouraged to "real" participation for their "virtual" status and reward system.

Our findings indicate that social media can generate value only if there is a link between online and face-to-face interactions. Social media have the potential to enhance people behaviors through the reconfiguration of people practices. The case advocates three levels of possible organizational reconfigurations (individual, collective, and organizational) which can foster the quality of the employee–organization relationship. This happens through three online key processes of *sharing feedback*, *status building*, and *reward system* that are able to reinforce the traditional functioning of organizations and the quality of relations among people. Our conclusions and theoretical arguments can be transferred to different contexts, inside and outside organizations.

Information Communication Technologies and Organization: Substitution and Reconfiguration Effects

The diffusion of Internet-based networking technologies has accelerated the emergence of novel forms of organization that shape, and are shaped by, available Information and Communication Technologies (ICT). New forms of organization are neither vertically organized hierarchies like their bureaucratic predecessors, nor are they unorganized marketplaces governed by supply and demand (Powell, 1990; Williamson, 1975). These new organizational forms include relational and social forms of organizations that link people and knowledge in all parts of the organization to one another, while simultaneously tying them to multiple external contacts (Miles & Snow, 1995; Monge & Fulk, 1999).

A strategic and mature adoption of ICT implies the development of knowledge flows and networks at different levels: individuals, teams, and organizations (Monge & Contractor, 2003). It is possible to identify three stages of the use of ICTs: *substitution*, using technologies to do old things in new ways; *enlargement*, providing more individual and corporate feedback to more employees and users; *reconfiguration*, changing the organizational processes that sustain and work with the ICT in question (Ruta, 2005, 2009). Reconfiguration is the most advanced approach that organizations can implement in order to create value. The goal is to leverage technology to shift from efficiency to effectiveness, from cost reduction to productivity.

Organizational reconfiguration through ICT gives employees and users the possibility to link and integrate the various components of information and knowledge together. Technology increases access to information and transactions for the employees. Moreover, it promotes change both at organizational and at behavioral levels, encouraging people to adopt a self-reliance approach through ICT. Employees can update personnel records, perform tasks just in time, reply to on-demand organizational needs, and so on. Following this approach, ICT gave birth to Web 2.0 and more recently to social media, including many relatively inexpensive and widely accessible electronic tools that enable anyone to publish and access information, collaborate on a collective project, or build relationships.

Social Media and Social Interactions

Social media technologies give people access to highly interactive platforms they can use to share, create, discuss, collaborate, and modify user-generated content

(Bradley & McDonald, 2011). These two-way solutions — the so-called Web 2.0 activities — encourage users to participate in various communities, sharing and building knowledge (Kietzmann, Hermkens, McCarthy, & Silvestre, 2011).

Web 2.0 activities are numerous and rapidly proliferating, offering more and more sophisticated possibilities that can be classified according to various taxonomies in light of underlying technologies (such as social networking technology for Facebook or wiki technology for Wikipedia); media richness (from low for blogs, to very high for virtual social worlds); accessibility (public, private, and membership communities); purpose (such as content generation, community building, decision support, entertainment); targets (external to the organization such as customers, or internal such as employees) (Bradley & McDonald, 2011; Lockwood & Dennis, 2008).

Also in the managerial domain growing attention is being focused on the Web 2.0 phenomenon considering its possible impact on communication, knowledge sharing, and creation. The affects of Web 2.0 could potentially be felt not only across organizational boundaries, as a means to interact with the external environment and actors such as customers, prospect employees, communities of practice, but also within the organizational context offering managerial tools to enhance cooperation and coordination among employees (cf. Kaplan & Haenlein, 2012; Kietzmann et al., 2011; Lockwood & Dennis, 2008). Within organizations, in fact, social media could allow employees to collaborate and to actively cocreate organizational results and environments, codifying and managing knowledge, sharing practices, communicating and coordinating activities (Chui, Miller, & Roberts, 2009). There is a wide variety of possible internal Web 2.0 solutions. For example:

- *Collaborative internal projects* that enable the joint and simultaneous creation of content by many employees. Applications include, for instance, online wiki environments to update employees on project status and to exchange ideas.
- *Corporate blogs* that are equivalent to personal web pages, usually managed by a single person but providing the possibility of interaction with others. Internal applications include blogs for learning purposes or also blogs that encourage employees to share ideas and comments about company products or procedures, to increase internal transparency, and to exchange opinions.
- *Social networking site*s that enable employees to connect by creating personal information profiles and sending e-mails and instant messages to one another. Social network company sites are virtual spaces where, for instance, current and prospective employees could share employment information.
- *Communities of practices*, the main purpose of these internal communities is to develop and share knowledge about specific domains or professional topics.
- *Virtual games world* are platforms that replicate a three-dimensional environment in which users can appear in the form of personalized avatars and interact with each other as they would in the real world. These media are developed for learning and recruiting purposes, among other possible applications.

These Web 2.0 solutions are not only enabling new communication channels within organizations; they are new ways of acting and interacting that impact behaviors, work practices, and spatial relations within the company as well (Jahnke & Koch, 2009).

In particular, the new Web 2.0 technologies are the harbinger of what is known as the "social organization" (Bradley & McDonald, 2011), where a large part of the relations are mediated and enacted by technology. There is evidence that this transition can foster several positive outcomes for the organization, such as the possibility to relocate production and business units, trim labor costs, enhance organizational and workforce flexibility, coordinate geographically remote operations, and improve the use of organizational space, working hours, and collaboration.

Yet there are cues that also suggest potential negative outcomes relating to the social capital of organizations. Research on social media confirms that they can create a parallel way to the traditional one of experiencing services and social ties that could substitute offline connections (Matei & Ball-Rokeach, 2001). This is precisely the main concern: that online social spaces would replace offline ties entirely. The more employees are online, the more they will abandon their rich personal ties, preferring online relationships thanks to the greater degree of freedom they afford. The risky result could be a change, not from offline relationships to online ties, but from people to technology (Nie & Erbring, 2000).

Despite these positive and negative views of social media, these considerations suggest that there is a relationship between being a social media user and an employee involved in the real world and in an organization.

Social Media and Employee–Organization Relationship

Research on employee–organization relationships suggests that labor contracts are idiosyncratically perceived and understood by individuals (Rousseau, 1989; Schein, 1980). The subjective interpretation of the contract has been called a "psychological contract" to underscore its emotional as opposed to its legal nature. Originally employed by Argiris (1960) and Levinson (1962) to underscore the subjective nature of the employment relationship, the present use of the term centers on the individual's belief in and interpretation of a promissory contract. Employee–organization exchanges are promissory contracts in which commitment of future behaviors is offered in exchange for payment (Rousseau & Mclean Parks, 1993). Employees develop some expectations about the organization's context and adapt their behaviors according to their perception of the reciprocal obligation (Gouldner, 1960; Levinson, 1962). Empirical evidence has confirmed that employees look for reciprocity in a labor relationship and that their motivation to work is heavily influenced by their perceptions. In fact, the more the relationship is perceived as balanced, the more employees are disposed to contribute and perform, even beyond the duties called for by their role (Coyle-Shapiro & Shore, 2007; Tsui, Ashford, Clair, & Xin, 1995; Van Dyne, Cummings, & McLean Parks, 1995).

Previous literature supports the relevance of design and implementation of organizational solutions that can sustain employee–organization relationships. Examples of such solutions are the so-called high involvement and high performance work systems (HPWS) (Becker & Huselid, 1998), where managerial practices such as team work, pay for performance, and development systems, together sustain organizational performances. Among others, Guzzo and Noonan (1994) argue that employees systematically analyze human resource (HR) practices to make sense of their psychological contract; Sims (1994) supports the HR management system's role in clarifying new psychological contracts; Sels, Janssens, and Van Den Brande (2004) prove the significance both of formal contract characteristics and HR practices as two antecedents which shape the nature of psychological contracts.

The changes brought about by new technologies allow organizations to gradually abandon old work rationale because for many types of employees sharing space is no longer required. Indeed, not only does the organization transfer certain types of knowledge through electronic channels to the workforce, but the people working inside and outside the company exchange information and knowledge electronically also (Imperatori & De Marco, 2009). These factors are making the traditional concept of work space obsolete, forming the basis for the virtual worker. In this new scenario, technology is a mediator of the relationship between the employee and the company, and the means that allows work to be moved from inside to outside the organization.

Extending these results to innovative web-based practices, we argue that Web 2.0 could offer many possibilities to reconfigure organizations and their employment relationships as new effective tools and novel resourceful management solutions. These innovations would not merely substitute traditional practices or enlarge them, but could actually play a role in supporting employees' expectations.

Organizations are still looking for ways to effectively implement social media as managerial tools. There are various solutions that partially confirm their relevance as online communication tools across organizational boundaries, for instance with customers for marketing purposes, or with potential employees for recruitment (Bradley & McDonald, 2011; Jue, Marr, & Kassotaks, 2010). Despite this evidence, there are no practical guidelines on if and how social media could support the quality of relationships in face-to-face interactions.

Methods

In keeping with the aim of exploring and describing if and how social media could lead to organizational reconfiguration, this research project is based on the analysis of an emblematic case of a successful organization which intensively uses social media as resourceful managerial solutions. Fubles.com is a social sport sharing platform with one of the most active sport communities in Europe. It efficiently helps people to organize sport matches of all types while saving time and money, bringing together players, games, and sports centers in a local area. Fubles allows anyone to sign up for free and organize games with friends or participate in already-scheduled matches. This case represents a novel and remarkable initiative that can be useful in understanding the role of social media in face-to-face and online relationships, and how they drive organizational results. Data was gathered through document analysis, semi-structured interviews with the principal actors, and participative observation.

Data collection was conducted through document analysis (i.e., Fubles website, public data, press clippings), direct observation and semi-structured interviews with 24 stakeholders representing different interests and perspectives (i.e., players, organizers, team leaders, owners of sports centers, exponents of organized leagues, as detailed below). The case study followed a standard protocol (Yin, 1993). All the interviews adopted a common structure, consisting of an open-ended format that enabled us to collect both factual data and personal impressions. We first asked our respondents to reconstruct their personal experience to distinguish facts from individual observations. We taped and transcribed all the interviews. Some inform-ation we collected required further probing or clarification of minor discrepancies at a later stage; this meant that we interviewed some respondents more than once. Multiple interviews helped us to reconstruct a "story" for each process. Although, our reconstruction was based on our respondents' recall, by combining multiple perspectives we were able to move beyond individual perceptual biases and alleviate potential recall problems.

The multiple data sources enabled us to compare the perceived, declared, and subjective viewpoints of the actors involved, and to describe the organizational practices which were actually implemented along with users' behaviors and experiences. We used an iterative process of cycling between data, emerging theory, and relevant literature. We developed initial categories related to online and face-to-face experiences based on all the interview transcripts. Then we related these categories to literature and to other data gathered, controlling for internal consis-tency. When consistency was confirmed, we retained the topic; otherwise, when evidence contradicted an emerging theme, we abandoned it, returning to the theory to investigate and refine the framework (Hargadon & Bechky, 2006).

The Case Study: Fubles.com

Background Information

Fubles.com is a Social Sport Sharing Platform that has the goal of helping football players organize pick-up matches. Football is the Italian national sport; crowds of people watch professional football and play on a recreational basis with friends. However, organizing games at a certain time or on a certain day is not always an easy job. Most of the time, volunteers among friends face a real quest consisting of phone calls, text messages, and e-mails, persuading and even pestering people to find enough players; and there is always the fear of last minute no-shows. For these reasons, organizing a simple game with friends is always a time-consuming ordeal, and not always successful at that. Fubles.com is an online tool that is meant to solve these problems.

Fubles provides the features of a social network with specific functionalities customized for sport, such as handling rosters, game results, feedback, and statistics.

Players see a list of geolocalized matches they can join. Organizers stop chasing people, and participants follow their matches. After each match Fubles prompts participants to rate one another. Fubles aims at replicating real-world matches online, supporting them with services such as: a ranking system, virtual currency, awards, virtual goods, odds, and a player transfer market.

Today Fubles is one of the most active sport communities in Europe. It was started in 2007, and became a company in 2009. Now Fubles boasts over 25,000 users and more than 7000 matches already played. In a few months, Fubles went from 1000 players in Milan to 25,000 users, 7000 matches around Italy (Milan, Bologna, Florence, Bari, Rome, Torino, Taranto, etc.) and has more than 1500 football fields in the database.

Fubles achieves constant positive results. While increasing the size of the community (500% per year) the website won national and international awards for web innovation. Fubles was invited to the "Summit Web 2.0 2010," one of the world's most important conferences around the web, attended by all the major players. The company was also a finalist at the "Mind The Bridge Competition 2010" which rewards the best Italian initiatives and business plans with a tour of Silicon Valley. Fubles was also considered one of the top 10 business ideas at the "Talento delle idee"[1] contest, organized by UniCredit Group to support the creation and growth of new business ideas in Italy.

Beyond the technology itself, Fubles is widely studied because of its processes. The website is continuously improving and the Fubles team is carrying out multiple projects in an effort to build one of the most interesting entrepreneurial successes in Italy. Fubles is now working to expand internationally and increase the number of services it offers to amateurs and friends who love to play football on the field and online.

The Game of Football at an Amateur Level

Football is played by two teams of 11 players with a round ball which may not be handled during play except by the goalkeepers. The aim of the game is to score points by kicking or heading the ball into the opponents' goal. The international game is administered by the International Football Federation (FIFA), which is also responsible for the World Cup. Football is played by over 250 million people in more than 200 countries, making it the most popular sport in the world (Dunning, 1999). At the amateur level, in part due to the difficulties involved in organizing games with 22 players, over the years five-a-side football has become popular (also called Futsal) and more recently a seven-a-side version of the sport has emerged. Futsal is played between two teams of five players each, one of whom is the goalkeeper. Unlimited substitutions are permitted and it is typically played on hard court surface and indoors, so adverse weather conditions do not prevent play.

---

[1]In English: "The talent of ideas."

How Online Games of Football and Fubles Work

Football has inspired a number of electronic and online games and social networks over the years. Particularly popular games include PES (pesgame.org) and FIFA (ea.com/fifa) which today offer innovative versions with high-quality graphics and functionalities, with the aim of offering a more and more realistic experience. Users train their players, and position and move them on the pitch. Other football-related games center on team management, for example, Football Manager (footballmanager.com). The web has transformed these games from competitions for one or two players into online platforms where multiple users can interact, and organize matches and tournaments.

Another online football game is Fantasy Football, which has always had a strong social connotation. This is a popular fantasy game that consists of organizing and managing virtual teams made up of real footballers, picked from players who actually participate in any given championship. The results of the chosen team depend on the actual on-the-field performances of the real players. The winner is the person who picks and buys the fittest players, the highest scorers, and the top performers, week by week. The aim of all these games is to simulate reality, leveraging the fact that football is fun, and that football fans are passionate about their sport, which stimulates the social dimension. Within this context, Fubles has succeeded in building something truly innovative.

Fubles.com is a Social Sport Sharing Platform that helps organize pick-up sport games of all types more efficiently. Players see a list of geolocalized games they can join. After the game Fubles prompts participants to rate one another. With Fubles people can: find/book the closest pitch to their home, find matches to play in local communities, find players to fill out their teams' rosters, know who is coming and who is not, avoid cheating and no-shows, and make matches more exciting with ratings, posts, and teases.

Game Mechanics

Using virtual rewards and status, also known as game mechanics (or funware), is one of the strategies that Fubles is pursuing for engaging players. Fubles' core functionality is something that can be done (and people do) with many other means (e-mails, phone calls, instant messaging) or platforms (Facebook, Google Calendar, Evite). What Fubles provides in reality is a whole set of functionalities and experiences that players perceive as value adding. In sport, people like to win and to track statistics. Fubles has designed a set of game mechanics providing incentives for its players in order to increase value and satisfaction for users, generating the following effects: increasing traffic and active users, increasing Website Activity and Stickiness, offering a loyalty program that is cheaper than a traditional one, improving user satisfaction. The following sections describe the main game mechanics experiences that Fubles provides.

Feedback: peer ratings of performance after a game.   After the game, Fubles asks players to indicate who won and to rate their teammates and opponents on a scale of 4–10. Each player gets a scorecard with the result of the ratings from every game. The final rating is the average of the ratings received by excluding the highest and the lowest (to reduce the effect of individual likes or dislikes). The rating may reflect not only the player's performance but also a more general judgment about sporting qualities and behaviors. If players want to see the ratings they have received, they have to rate the others players first. When the rating process is over all the ratings become public and everyone can view them.

If a player does not take part in a match, a "no-show" is reported during the rating process. Players are allowed only one no-show in a season (it can happen to anyone). If they have more than one no-show they lose access to the site and can no longer play through Fubles.

Loyalty program: Fubles currency.   Fubles introduced a virtual currency reward system to encourage behaviors that would stimulate viral growth and active participation. Fublis are virtual currency that Fubles gives its users in recognition of their contribution to the growth and improvement of the community. Earning Fubli will show others that you are an active player in the Fubles community both on and off the pitch. Users can spend their Fubli on profile enhancements or on prizes provided by Fubles sponsors and partners.

Earning Fubli: RULES

Here are the actions that help you earn Fublis:

- Play in a private match[a]   1 F
- Play in a public match[a]   3 F
- Join a match less than four hours before kick-off[a]   20 F
- Play a match in a Fubles Sports Center[a]   50 F
- Withdraw from a match 16 to 8 hours before kick-off   −25 F
- Withdraw from a match 8 to 4 hours before kick-off   −50 F
- Commit a No-show   −10,000 F
- Organize a private match[a]   10 F
- Organize a public match[a]   50 F
- Organize an open challenge match[a]   50 F
- Organize a match in a Fubles Sports Center[a]   1000 F
- Invite a friend who is within the range of 30 km   800 F
- Invite a friend from beyond a range of over 30 km   1000 F
- Add a new sports center[b]   200 F
- Add a field to an existing structure[b]   50 F
- Install the app Facebook (link) (for every notification)[c]   1 F
- Commit an action judged fraudulent or harmful by the Fubles staff[b]   −100,000 F

[a]At least three players per side; Fubli credited after the release of final ratings.
[b]After review and approval by staff.
[c]Monthly final balance.

Ranking: build a career on Fubles with Rango. Rango is a ranking system in Fubles, something similar to Elo Rating in chess. Rango is a method for calculating the relative skill levels of players in two-player games. Each player has a numerical rating. A higher number indicates a better player, based on results against other rated players. The winner of a contest between two players gains a certain number of points in his or her rating and the losing player loses the same amount. The number of points won or lost in a contest depends on the difference in the ratings of the players, so a player will gain more points by beating a higher-rated player than by beating a lower-rated player.

In Fubles Rango takes into account who participated to the game, the final score of the game, and the ratings given and received. Everyone starts with 1500 Rango points. Before every game, every team can win or lose Rango points according to the level of the teams. If the stronger team wins it will earn fewer points than if the weaker team wins. After the game the points are distributed to the individual players of the winning team and taken from the individual players of the losing team according to the result and to the scores. The players with better scores will earn more points if they win and lose fewer points if they lose.

Rango works like a sort of complementary rating system to the match rating that goes beyond the performance on the field and tries to describe the career of a player in Fubles. Rango has inspired great enthusiasm in the community and enhanced the level of the games. All users are taking this ranking system seriously (on occasion too much so). Players with Rango over 1950 points earn the title of GODs of Fubles, players over 1750 are labeled as PROs.

Competition: the global rankings at Fubles. Fubles has launched new global rankings. This consists of a page that shows the rankings in Fubles according to Fublis, Rango points, games played, games organized, No shows, or Man of the Match designations collected. Users can also view "All Time" rankings or the variations in the last three months. It is also possible to check only the rankings for the people a player follows. These rankings allow everyone to identify top players by Rango and top influencers by Fublis. Fubles is planning on using these rankings to identify new stars or elect local community managers (Mayors).

Fubles has partnered with Adidas in a marketing initiative based on these rankings. In fact, for Adidas the Fubles Community represents the perfect target of early adopters for launching a new tech product. The GODs of Fubles will be asked to play a special match with videomakers, journalists, and Adidas testimonials.

Stakeholders' Experience

The following are the typologies of Fubles stakeholders. We have collected comments and insights about the Fubles experience from people representing different stakeholders.

- **Casual Players**: People who like playing team sports and look for more playing opportunities in a safe environment, minimizing the time and money spent to arrange matches.

    Comment: I just got transferred to Torino for my work and I don't know many people. Thanks to Fubles I can play futsal and get to know new people.

    Comment: I only play every once in a while, and that's a problem because I'm not part of a central or organized group. So they don't call me very often anymore, or they forget to put me on the mailing list. Fubles is a good way to keep up to date on everything, even if I only want to play three times a year.

    Comment: I have a schedule that's hard to plan. This system allows me to call at the last minute to find out if anyone's cancelled, without being pushy or out of line. Now with Fubles I'm actually useful! I like to be ready to get out on the field at a moment's notice. That way everyone's happy, and I earn Fubli!

    Comment: It's great to play and then rate the other players, and see how they rate my performance too. The great thing about Fubles is that it's turned a weekly event into a daily game — first you talk about the last match, and then you go right on to talk about the next one, and so on. It's more fun to play now that Fubles is around.

- **Casual Organizers**: The ones that generally organize groups to play matches by booking the field, calling together the players, and managing the roster of participants.

    Comment: Fubles is a true innovation that everyone likes, because it's simple, and everyone has wished there was something like it at least once: I used to use the bulletin board at the bath house at the sea to organize friendly matches on the beach. Now it's more fun because I'm kind of like the editor of the Gazzetta (a national sport newspaper) who reports on what happened.

    Comment: With Fubles there's a sense of accountability. If you want to play, you take the initiative, you don't wait to be called. Even the best players have to participate actively.

    Comment: I can organize a match even while I'm working. Essentially I'm honing my desire to become the president of a real team, and I consult Fubles a lot, especially before the match to see how the teams are shaping up.

- **Team Leaders**: Those who manage a team, organizing challenges against other teams or enrolling the team in competitions and leagues.

    Comment: Five-a-side soccer is something that fills up our days. Not only is it great to play, but even better is getting ready to play, figuring out who's playing, what shape we're in physically, who we're playing against and how, and so on.

    Comment: I don't like social networks where people tell all sorts of personal things about themselves. This is great because you use social networks for something real!

    Comment: We're a really good team, because some of us are actually real ex-footballers. Playing in tournaments is great because there's always something to win, a trophy, a trip, or something like that. With Fubles we have everything under control, but before it was more complicated to figure out who was organizing tournaments and where.

- **Sports Centers**: The owners of sports centers manage facilities and handle scheduling. They try to increase their offer value while minimizing the number of unsold time slots.

   Comment: Fubles has changed our work somewhat. We can fill a lot more slots for our pitches. For us that's essential.

   Comment: With Fubles, more tournaments are organized, but above all more people come to play at this center. Often I notice that individuals or even entire teams come in from out of town. Thanks to Fubles.

   Comment: Seeing teams play with only nine players (instead of ten) was always really hard for us, because players are looking for competition, and that's tough with nine players. Setting up an open system lets the people here see if they can fill in for any missing players in matches that are about to start. So they're happier, and so are we.

- **Organized Leagues**: People who organize sports competitions or leagues want visibility, and look for the channels to collect subscriptions and memberships.

   Comment: I've always loved organizing tournaments, to make a little money by collecting sign-up fees from the players and sponsorship fees from local businesses. Fubles simplifies my work and lets me be a real manager!

   Comment: I manage to sign up teams from towns nowhere near here, before with my contacts I couldn't reach them.

   Comment: A company team signed up for the last tournament through Fubles, and that led to my finding my current job. It's hard to imagine, but in a way it happened thanks to Fubles.

Lesson Learned

Fubles has made it possible for countless players to do online what they used to do face-to-face (or via e-mail or by phone): to get a team together to play a football/ futsal match or tournament, to give feedback on personal performance, and teammates' performance on the field, to create a social reputation (e.g., punctual, reliable, available, unselfish, loyal, etc.) or a reputation as a player (e.g., skilled technically, physically, etc.), to build the ideal team and challenge better teams, and so on.

Fubles serves as an accelerator for these processes. Unlike other games based on football (FIFA, PES, Fantasy Football), Fubles does not create a separate world that is disconnected from reality. Fubles sets up game mechanisms that encourage people to play, to organize, and to participate. The online dimension facilitates the real dimension, but does not replace it.

From a business perspective, however, Fubles' strength becomes a limitation. The organizational structure of Fubles is based on covering a given territory, the number of games played, the sports facilities involved. This is very different from online gaming, which counts the number of players and games played as growth indicators. In the professional context, this means that online activities must be gauged in proportion to face-to-face time. It is not always positive when online activities become abundant compared to face-to-face interactions, especially if there is physical proximity.

Fubles has won several awards precisely because it reinforces the face-to-face dimension through online mechanisms that encourage socialization and participation. Real sport is a vehicle for growing social capital. In other words, people who already know one another can build stronger relationships. Also, they can meet new people and gain new information, and as a result, create new ties and social networks.

Comment: It was great playing with you! Next time I'll tell some other friends of mine too and we'll organize a match.

Answer: Sounds good, but in the meantime, do you want to sign up with us in this new tournament that's just come out on Fubles? You're a good goalkeeper, but more than that you're punctual!

Discussion

The evidence presented in this case study suggests certain considerations as to how social media impacts people practices, with critical implications for both theory and practice. The Fubles case is an archetypal success story that confirms the potential relevance of social media in determining and reshaping social relationships, both online and face-to-face. Moreover, this case underscores the role of Web 2.0 solutions as managerial tools that can enable organizations to activate people, driving their behaviors and performances, through new e-practices. The actual interaction between "real" and "online" behavior also implies some possible considerations about human resources management (HRM) theory and future directions for the role of social media within management literature.

Social Media and Social Capital: Linking Online Interaction to Real Events

The first, and in some ways unexpected, major finding from our analysis of the Fubles case pertains to the virtuous relationship between online interactions and face-to-face relationships. The case study demonstrates that, thanks to social network activities, organizations can support interpersonal contacts, enabling people to better organize themselves and their collective activities both virtually and physically. In addition, social media can help people meet, and directly interact and communicate with better results, considering efficiency, effectiveness, and fairness of collective behaviors.

Literature and practice always highlight the risk of depersonalization of web-based relationships that could decrease and even substitute real-world interactions and personal relationships (Matei & Ball-Rokeach, 2001). There is evidence that people who spend more and more time online could exchange face-to-face interactions with virtual ones, and in doing so impoverish themselves and their social capital, to the point where they pathologically lose contact with real life (Nie & Erbring, 2000).

The case we present here tells a different story. Online activities do not always substitute face-to-face relationships; on the contrary, online connections can improve these relationships. The key element is that most of the online interactions in question are based on real incidents and actions. In a sense, online activities can capture and record memories from the real world. Evidence also confirms the relevance of properly designing the mechanisms that can allow these positive effects, while avoiding possible negative ones, such as depersonalization and virtualization.

Fubles is not an online or an electronic game. Its focus is to make the face-to-face interactions (games) more interesting and fun. This happens, before and after the game, through the sharing of information and the development of social data such as: reputation, rankings, and rewards. This case study suggests some useful guidelines for reconfiguring — not substituting — people practices, to drive organizational behaviors and to develop people performance through Web 2.0 technology, always linking information and knowledge to real facts.

Social Media and People Practices: The Challenge of Reconfiguration

The Fubles experience confirms that social media has the potential to enhance people behaviors in face-to-face interactions. Furthermore, the Fubles case suggests that online mechanisms have to be designed to reconfigure people practices toward face-to-face interactions. This could be possible, as the case study confirms, using technology to manage real interactions, behaviors, and performances.

The case suggests *three levels of possible reconfigurations* of management practices that could be designed and implemented through social media to sustain organizational affiliations at individual, collective, and organizational levels respectively.

The *basic configuration* can be designed with the aim of helping people exchange a great deal of accurate information, sustaining the processes of knowledge creation at a *personal level*. Social media could be implemented as efficient mechanisms that allow quick, widespread, and low-cost information sharing. Moreover, social media do not replace face-to-face meetings, but can serve to rapidly organize these meetings in a more resourceful way. This basic configuration confirms the relevance of social media for real-life behaviors, suggesting that Web 2.0 tools can be implemented to develop real individual behaviors; as such they can be seen as development tools. The evidence also implies that to be effective, online mechanisms have to reinforce real-life activities, to avoid the risk of a change, not from offline relationships to online ties, but from people to technology (Nie & Erbring, 2000). In keeping with this solution, social networking could be adopted to enlarge the quantity and enhance the accuracy of information available to people, information which they can use for actual behaviors, such as real-life decision making and work activities.

An *advanced configuration* can be designed to help people improve the quality of *shared behaviors and social relationships,* offering more and more effective opportunities for personal interactions and multisource feedback (Ruta, 2005; Ruta, 2009). Previous research has confirmed that the possibility to collect information before interactions and to give and receive feedback after, could sustain positive relationships and better collective performances considering team climate (Hargadon & Bechky, 2006), creative solutions (Bissola & Imperatori, 2011), and overall participant satisfaction. Again, this solution has to factor in the risks of depersonalization. Social media could, in fact, give rise to pathological situations, where online relationships prevail over face-to-face relationships, eroding rather than enhancing social capital. To avoid this risk, social media managerial solutions have to integrate, prepare, and reinforce real collective activities, not to substitute them. In terms of quality, Web 2.0 solutions could make it possible for users to expand their knowledge sharing and collective decision making. In fact, because these solutions are inherently two-way and participative, users are able to collect multisource data, give and receive feedback, reduce negative cognitive biases, motivate, and prepare for face-to-face processes. All this develops the quality of the relationships among users as well.

Finally, at the organizational level, a *comprehensive reconfiguration* could help organizations to foster the quality of their relationships with participants and stakeholders. Social media drive real behaviors and performances, allowing people to quickly share information in an open, transparent, and "neutral" environment where it is easier to give and to receive feedback. This type of environment also promotes fairness and developmental relationships. The end result of this would be to intensify the personal satisfaction of people involved. Web 2.0 solutions make this possible by enabling organizations to design and implement more sophisticated, shared, and transparent Web 2.0 managerial practices such as online performance evaluation systems, rewarding practices, and development mechanisms referred to real events. Fubles has online mechanisms which increase and leverage the link between online and face-to-face interactions (e.g., sharing feedback, reputation building, and reward systems). These are typical people management practices based on the concept of peer feedbacks, where social media are able to collect and store multiple data and contributions always linked to real actions. We like to see social media as a way to reconfigure the traditional people interactions, exactly like Fubles did with the management and organization of football games.

Adopting the employee–organization relationship framework, the new Web 2.0 technological opportunities are a bridge that connects two different scenarios, allowing organizations to sustain labor relationships. From the organizational perspective, social media could be a way to support flexibility, knowledge sharing, and development. From the employees' perspective, instead, these media could be seen as a new approach to enhance their ways of interacting, participating, deciding and, consequently, their work satisfaction and motivation. Social media technologies make work solutions possible that move work from inside to outside the organization. This can have various positive outcomes on the employees' perception of the organization's determination to meet their needs. In a word, Web 2.0 solutions could have a positive impact in shaping psychological contracts as a form of employer signaling. However this approach has to be designed and integrated with traditional people management processes.

Managerial and Theoretical Implications

Organizations are based on people. People need to establish human contacts. Social media must be designed not to create a parallel environment, but to improve the real one by fostering the quality of the employee–organization relationship. Organizations must design "game mechanisms" in order to reconfigure their people practices through social media, like Fubles did with football players and amateurs through Web 2.0-based practices.

From the HRM perspective, our evidence sustains the relevance of social media in designing effective HRM practices as new tools for managing employee relationships. Our findings also contribute to the growing e-HRM literature. E-HRM practices are a way of implementing HR policies and practices in organizations through the direct support of web technology-based channels (Bondarouk, Oiry, & Guiderdoni-Jourdain, 2009; Ruta, 2005; Strohmeier, 2007).

Empirical results on the strategic impact of e-HRM practices are controversial. Some studies suggest that e-HRM can assist the HR department in becoming more strategic (Haines & Lafleur, 2008; Olivas-Lujan, Raminez, & Zapata-Cantu, 2007; Parry & Tyson, 2011). However, the primary justification of implementing e-HR technology is cost reduction, with very little evidence of the strategic role of HR (Marler, 2009; Shrivastava & Shaw, 2003).

Our results confirm that appraisal (peer feedback among players in Fubles), rewards (Fublis in Fubles), and career (rankings and Rango in Fubles) can be communicated, shared, and reinforced by Web 2.0 solutions that contribute to a wider intelligibility within organizations. Moreover, e-HRM practices can also enhance knowledge sharing and knowledge development, defining new ways of working. Our evidence supports not only the operational meaning of e-HRM practices, but also the relational and above all the transformational meaning (Ruel, Bondarouk, & Looise, 2004). Moreover, our findings suggest that these practices do not replace traditional face-to-face ones, but they offer an opportunity to reshape the employee–organization bond, also making a new HRM department role possible which is more directly related to employees.

Another interesting line of research that our results suggest pertains to the intersection between social media and HPWS (Becker & Huselid, 1998). Social media could be used to further evolve HPWS and to create a more contemporary HR system. Employees must be considered as users of Web 2.0 initiatives outside the professional contexts. In this perspective, employees will have more and more expectations as far as the integration of social media and daily working activities and behaviors. The HR department can reinforce the link between the organization and the employees, the so-called psychological contract, giving the employees modern ways of interacting. The challenge of management is to interpret social media as one of the main tools of a comprehensive reconfiguration of HRM systems and therefore of people management, always focusing on the human element of the organization.

References

Argiris, C. P. (1960). *Understanding organisational behaviour*. Homewood, IL: Dorsey Press.

Becker, B. E., & Huselid, M. A. (1998). High performance work systems and firm performance: A synthesis of research and managerial implications. *Personnel and Human Resources Management, 16*, 53–101.

Bissola, R., & Imperatori, B. (2011). Organizing individual and collective creativity: Flying in the face of creativity clichés. *Creativity and Innovation Management, 20*(2), 77–89.

Bondarouk, T., Oiry, E., & Guiderdoni-Jourdain, K. (Eds.). (2009). *Handbook of research on e-transformations and human resources management technologies: Organizational outcomes and challenges*. Hershey, PA: IGI Global.

Bradley, A. J., & McDonald, M. P. (2011). *The social organisation: How to use social media to tap the collective genius of your customers and employee*. Boston, MA: Harvard Business Review Press.

Chui, M., Miller, A., & Roberts, R. P. (2009). Six ways to make Web 2.0 work. *The McKinsey Quarterly*, February.

Coyle-Shapiro, J. A. M., & Shore, L. M. (2007). The employee-organization relationship: Where do we go from here? *Human Resource Management Review, 17*(2), 166–179.

Dunning, E. (1999). *The development of soccer as a world game* (p. 103). *Sport matters: Sociological studies of sport, violence and civilisation*. London: Routledge. .

Gouldner, A. W. (1960). The norm of reciprocity: A preliminary statement. *American Sociology Review, 25*(2), 161–178.

Guzzo, R., & Noonan, K (1994). Human resource practices as communications and the psychological contract. *Human Resource Management, 33*(39), 447–462.

Haines, V. Y., III., & Lafleur, G. (2008). Information technology usage and human resource roles and effectiveness. *Human Resource Management, 47*(3), 525–540.

Hargadon, A., & Bechky, B. (2006). When collections of creatives become creative collective — A field study of problem solving at work. *Organization Science, 17*(4), 484–500.

Howard, P. E. N., Raine, L., & Jones, S. (2001). Days and nights on the Internet: The impact of a diffusing technology. *American Behavioral Scientist, 45*(3), 283–404.

Imperatori, B., & De Marco, M. (2009). Labour processes transformation. In T. Bondarouk, E. Oiry & K. Guiderdoni-Jourdain (Eds.), *Handbook of research on e-transformations and human resources management technologies: Organizational outcomes and challenges* (pp. 34–54). Hershey, PA: IGI Global: Information Science Reference.

Jahnke, I., & Koch, M. (2009). Web 2.0 goes academia: Does Web 2.0 make a difference? *International Journal of Web Based Communities, 5*(4), 484–500.

Jue, A., Marr, J., & Kassotaks, M. (2010). *Social media at work: How networking tools propel organizational performance*. San Francisco, CA: Jossey-Bass.

Kaplan, A. M., & Haenlein, M. (2012). The Britney Spears universe: Social media and viral marketing at its best. *Business Horizons, 55*(1), 27–31.

Katz, J., & Aspden, P. (1997). A nation of strangers. *Communications of the ACM, 40*(12), 81–86.

Kietzmann, J. H., Hermkens, K., McCarthy, I. P., & Silvestre, B. S. (2011). Social media? Get serious! Understanding the functional building blocks of social media. *Business Horizons*, *54*(3), 241–251.

Kraut, R., Lundmark, V., Patterson, M., Kielser, S., Mukopadhyay, T., & Scherlis, W. (1998). Internet paradox: A social technology that produces social involvement and psychological well-being? *American Psychologist*, *53*(9), 1017–1031.

Levinson, H. (1962). *Men, management and mental health.* Cambridge, MA: Harvard University Press.

Lockwood, N., & Dennis, A. L. (2008). Exploring the corporate blogosphere: A taxonomy for research and practice. *Proceedings of the 41st Hawaii international conference on system sciences.* Waikoloa, HI.

Mangold, W. G., & Faulds, D. J. (2009). Social media: The new hybrid element of the promotion mix. *Business Horizons*, *52*(4), 357–365.

Marler, J. H. (2009). Making human resources strategic by going to the Net: Reality or myth? *The International Journal of Human Resource Management*, *20*(3), 515–527.

Matei, S., & Ball-Rokeach, S. (2001). Real and virtual social ties: Connections in the everyday lives of seven ethnic neighborhoods. *American Behavioral Scientist*, *45*(3), 550–563.

Miles, R. E., & Snow, C. C. (1995). The new network firm: A spherical structure built on a human investment philosophy. *Organizational Dynamics*, *22*, 5–18.

Monge, P. R., & Contractor, N. (2003). *Theories of communication networks.* New York, NY: Oxford University Press.

Monge, P., & Fulk, J. (1999). Communication technology for global network organizations. In G. DeSanctis & J. Fulk (Eds.), *Shaping organizational form: Communication, connection, and community.* Thousand Oaks, CA: Sage.

Nie, N. H., & Erbring, L. (2000). *Internet and society: A preliminary report.* Stanford, CA: Stanford Institute Quantitative Study Society.

Olivas-Lujan, M. R., Raminez, J., & Zapata-Cantu, L. (2007). E-HRM in Mexico: Adapting innovations for global competitiveness. *International Journal of Manpower*, *28*(5), 418–434.

Parry, E., & Tyson, S. (2011). Desired goals and actual outcomes of e-HRM. *Human Resource Management Journal*, *21*, 335–354.

Powell, W. W. (1990). Neither market nor hierarchy: Network forms of organization. In B. M. Staw & L. L. Cummings (Eds.), *Research in organizational behavior* (pp. 295–336). Greenwich, CT: JAI.

Rousseau, D. M. (1989). Psychological and implied contracts in organizations. *Employee Responsibilities and Rights Journal*, *2*(2), 121–139.

Rousseau, D. M., & Mclean Parks, J. (1993). The contract of individuals and organisations. In B. M. Staw & L. L. Cummings (Eds.), *Research in organisational behaviour* (Vol. 15, pp. 1–43). Greenwich, CT: JAI Press.

Ruel, H., Bondarouk, T., & Looise, J. K. (2004). E-ERM: Innovation or irritation. An explorative empirical study in five large companies on web-based HRM. *Management Revue*, *15*(3), 364–380.

Ruta, C. D. (2005). The application of change management theory to HR portal implementation in subsidiaries of multinational corporations. *Human Resource Management*, *44*(1), 35–53.

Ruta, C. D. (2009). The HR portal alignment for intellectual capital development. *International Journal of Human Resource Management*, Special Issue Electronic HRM: Challenges in the Digital Era, *20*(3), 562–577.

Schein, E. H. (1980). *Organizational psychology* (3rd ed.). Englewood Cliffs, NJ: Prentice Hall.

Sels, L., Janssens, M., & Van den Brande, I. (2004). Assessing the nature of psychological contracts: A validation of six dimensions. *Journal of Organizational Behaviour, 25,* 461–488.

Shrivastava, S., & Shaw, J. (2003). Liberating HR through technology. *Human Resource Management, 42,* 201–222.

Sims, R. R. (1994). Human resource management's role in clarifying the new psychological contract. *Human Resource Management, 33*(3), 373–382.

Strohmeier, S. (2007). Research in e-HRM: Review and implications. *Human Resource Management Review, 17,* 19–37.

Tsui, A. S., Ashford, S. J., St., Clair, L., & Xin, C. (1995). Dealing with discrepant expectations: Response strategies and managerial effectiveness. *Academy of Management Journal, 38,* 1515–1540.

Van Dyne, L., Cummings, L. L., & McLean Parks, J. (1995). Extra-role behaviors: In pursuit of construct and definitional clarity. In L. L. Cummings & B. M. Staw (Eds.), *Research in organizational behavior* (Vol. 17, pp. 215–285). Greenwich, CT: JAI Press.

Williamson, O. E. (1975). *Markets and hierarchies: Analysis and antitrust implications.* New York, NY: Free Press.

www.fubles.com Accessed on December 15, 2012.

Yin, R. (1993). *Applications of case study research.* Newbury Park, CA: Sage.

Chapter 10

Personae of Interest — Managers' Identities and the Online Mirror

Giulia Ranzini and Christian Fieseler

Abstract

Purpose — In this chapter we discuss the implications social media have for the self-representation and identity formulation of professionals within organizations. Under the assumption that new, technology-mediated networking possibilities call for a reformulation of the boundaries between the professional and the private, we propose several avenues of investigation. The concept of "online personae" is also introduced in order to describe how managers may strive for equilibrium while balancing on and offline identities with impression management efforts.

Approach — Proceeding conceptually, we review the existing literature and practice of managerial social media use and delineate the challenges, or "tensions" professionals have to mitigate while expressing themselves online. This allows for a full exploration of digital interaction as a quest for equilibrium, between one's professional and personal self-expression, but also between the management of one's impression, and the emotional attachment to a social media profile.

Findings — We argue that social media may challenge current conceptions of managerial identity and work practices to a degree. Social media may demand different forms of representation both to inside and outside audiences, which can lead to the mediatization of both the professional and the organization, and call for a more conscious formulation of identity and management of impressions. We argue in particular that, within this context, online personae may serve as entities (through single or multiple accounts) delineating boundaries between the various roles managers are asked to perform within their professional and personal lives.

Implications — Managerial awareness toward a tool such as online personae may help in critically reflecting the embeddedness of managerial practice within social networks. A critical management of personae can also help in formulating

Social Media in Human Resources Management
Advanced Series in Management, 201–213
ISSN: 1877-6361/doi:10.1108/S1877-6361(2013)0000012014

identity-based strategies for gaining access and improving the quality of connections and interactions. Ultimately, as social media become a tool for workplace collaboration, the strategic thinking behind online personae might take a progressively larger importance for the success of individuals, and for organizations at large.

Originality/value — The chapter introduces a managerial point-of-view to the field of digital identities, widely analyzed on samples of adolescents and young adults. This allows to investigate matters proper of a professional life, such as the management of work/life boundaries, which become increasingly blurry in the online world. The chapter also introduces the concept of "online personae," which aims at describing with more specificities the message and audience consequences behind the choice of one single social media profile, or several coexisting ones.

Keywords: Identity theory; impression management; privacy management; self-conceptualization

Introduction

Social media has proven to be more than a mere communication tool since its very beginning: in particular, the potential for user identity exploration and experimentation has been widely studied (Strano, 2008; Zhao, Grasmuck, & Martin, 2008). For professionals in particular, online self-expression allows for a more direct and unmediated rendition of who they are, in relation to the stakeholders which characterize their online and offline working practices (Waters, Burnett, Lamm, & Lucas, 2009). However, engaging in social media also gives rise to tensions: between private and professional spheres (Karlson, Meyers, Jacobs, Johns, & Kane, 2009), and between the different motives driving online self-representation (Ellison, Hancock, & Toma, 2011). In the next sections, we derive a concept of "online personae," that is, the digital selves of individuals, and explore why they can be useful for managers in order to find equilibrium among the tensions rising in computer-mediated interactions.

On Social Media and the Identities of Managers

Digital communication, that is, the exchange of messages mediated by computers, was not always "about the individuals." At the beginning of the internet, and especially through IRC chat rooms (Bechar-Israeli, 1995), conversations were taking place behind usernames, and, independently from their frequency, carried only moderate identity meaning (Subrahmanyam, Smahel, & Greenfield, 2006). The progressive democratization and individualization of online presence brought by the emergence of social media has introduced new practices of self-communication online, allowing individuals to have a profile (whether potentially anonymous, such as in MySpace, or explicit on names and details, such as on Facebook), a set of chosen contacts, and sometimes even a virtual body (as in the case of Second Life).

Only with the emergence of "nonymous" Social Network Websites, those requiring the user to register under a real name, online interaction has gone from being a mere conversation, to becoming an opportunity for self-expression (Zhao et al., 2008), information collection (Puckett & Hargittai, 2012; Ramirez, Walther, Burgoon, & Sunnafrank, 2002), and even job seeking (Cahuc & Fontaine, 2009). As a consequence, participants in social media today can no longer be ascribed to one particular demographic category: each group of users can find specific advantages in being on the network, different in nature from those of the others (Karavidas, Lim, & Katsikas, 2005; Lenhart, 2009).

For professionals, social media has taken an even more peculiar identity-defining role: in its pervasiveness, it has influenced work practices and conditions, triggering changes in how professions are portrayed (cf. Ibarra, 1999). For managers in particular, the selection and involvement in digital media has become, in the predictive words of Lengel and Daft, a true "executive skill" (1989). As corporate identities are, in fact, constructed and communicated to the outside, individual actors within organizations must interact and engage stakeholders (Waters et al., 2009) while thinking, at the same time, about the image they project to the digital world (Strano, 2008). This involves processes of identity negotiation even for managers who used to only be involved in IT to a limited extent (Walsham, 1998). In the words of Pallas and Fredriksson (2011), we are currently witnessing a process of "mediatization" of organizations, and of society as a whole. The role of managers consists therefore not only in the circulation of digital knowledge within the institution, but also in the influence of the "one voice" of the corporation composed of personal characteristics, opinions, and leadership (Pallas & Fredriksson, 2011).

Social media becomes therefore a space where managerial identity can be established, challenged, and reshaped through processes of experimentation (DiMicco & Millen, 2007; Zhao et al., 2008). In the relationship with networks of stakeholders related to the many sides of managerial and personal life, individuals can enrich their self-representation, creating meaningful relationships at the same time (Waters et al., 2009).

In the upcoming sections, we will explore how managers express their identities through social media. Through a review of the existing literature, we will conceptualize a tool (i.e., "online personae") that can be used by executives in order to be present in the digital world in a manner which they deem fitting with their offline selves. In the following sections, we will derive from the literature two main "tensions" ("Professional vs. Private" and "Impression Management vs. Emotional Attachment") which managers must manage while representing themselves online. Through the employment of online personae, we intend to explore how equilibrium can be found, in order to obtain a successful, coherent, and healthy dimension to digital self-expression.

Introducing Online Personae

Considering, in a parallel, the social life of individuals on and offline, some elements remain common: the audience to a message can be carefully chosen, and, thanks to mobile technology, communications are delivered in real-time, resembling, at least in a distant manner, face-to-face conversations. What remains however remarkably unique of social media-based communication is the potential for representation: different social networks do not exclude membership from other websites, allowing a person to be present online through a multitude of different channels. Through social media, individuals can, factually, be in multiple places at the same time, and as the same person. Or as different persons?

In the words of Zhao et al. (2008), social network sites provide an incentive to interact under a real name leaving, at the same time, a space for "highly socially desirable identities (which) individuals aspire to have offline but have not yet been able to embody for one reason or another." The participation to several social networks and the sharing of private and personal elements, such as images or phone numbers, can therefore be thought of as triggering identity experimentation processes (DiMicco & Millen, 2007; Zhao et al., 2008).

This resonates well with the theoretical description of the self as composed by multiple hierarchical roles (Stets & Burke, 2003); a vision which sees the individual permanently confronting her different selves (e.g., professional, mother, sister ...) and choosing the one that is most "salient" with the outside setting (Stryker, 1980; Stryker & Burke, 2000). Social media help this process by providing a space for both "possible" (Brewer, 2003; Ibarra, 1999) and "desired selves" (Ellison et al., 2006; Zhao et al., 2008); this applies to personal and professional identities alike.

Considering the experience of managers with social media, one thing seems evident: the ease in the creation and maintenance of connections allows them to be significantly closer to a wide amount of stakeholders (Waters et al., 2009). In identity terms, however, this means adding complexity to the process of identity negotiation (cf. Stryker & Serpe, 1994), as multiple constituencies of reference are constructed. For this reason, it seems particularly interesting to explore the meanings of online self-representation for those called to make decisions.

In order to ascribe to one concept not only the mere ownership of a profile on social media, but also all the choices related to audiences and personal messages, we define *online personae* (in Jungian psychology: the personality reflections one decides to project to others, cf. Progoff, 1953) as the social media representations of the overall identity of a person. Through different personae, based on different social networks and communicating to different audiences, individuals can decide what to share about themselves, setting the same limits and boundaries they would put in place "in real life."

For managers in particular, online personae represent the different entities (through single, or multiple accounts) which may serve as the boundary, if any, taking place between the various roles they are asked to perform within their professional and personal lives. Choosing if and where to draw the line, allows managers to preserve identity stability while still portraying the various roles they perform on a daily basis (Goffman, 1959). Involvement in digital life for a manager, when aware of personae, becomes therefore more complex, but also a more fitting representation of the individual behind the computer.

Considering professional roles, the most recurrent theme to managers is the duality taking place in everyday practices between professional and private identities, and the difficulty to strike a balance between the two (Lyness & Judiesch, 2008; McCarthy, Darcy, & Grady, 2010). Within the online world, this conflict takes different dimensions, as it concerns both the audiences to which messages are directed (cf. Kaplan & Haenlein, 2010) and the (hyper)presence of media within private and professional lives (Karlson et al., 2009). Through a conscious use of personae, the duality of private and professional online spaces can be consciously explored, as managers can engage in different conversations with specific audiences, setting walls in between, or rather building bridges, as they deem adequate.

The concept of online personae is, however, not only useful for the exploration of borders between private and professional roles. Another tension we would like to explore concerns the drives to managerial online interaction. Self-presentation, in fact, appears to be a strategized process, which engages the rational self-monitoring skills of a person (Leary & Kowalski, 1990; Swann, 1987), as well as her capability of understanding the outside perception of her message (Turnley & Bolino, 2001). However, this is only just part of the picture: self-exposure entails also emotional reactions unmediated by strategic thought. While "attachment," in fact, can certainly exist between individual and avatar (Wolfendale, 2007), also in social media profiles we have expressions of concerns and fears (Bollen, Pepe, & Mao, 2009), especially when it comes to the exposure of personal worlds. Whether as part of the overall corporate strategy, or emerging from an individual need for self-expression (Kaplan & Haenlein, 2010), managers should be aware of the mechanisms leading to the choice of specific messages about themselves.

Taking conscience over online personae, and defining their boundaries, allows managers to make sense and mediate between the tensions, which emerge in social media-based interaction. In the next sections, we will explore the literature defining each tension, and consider how the management of online personae can help finding equilibrium.

The Private and the Professional

Managerial identities, and the self-narratives supporting them, are hardly constructed in a vacuum (Sveningsson & Alvesson, 2003): the coexistence with people, the application of new strategies or working practices, as well as self-images contribute greatly to the roles which managers assign to themselves and to others. Technology has determined a specific, if slightly ambiguous, influence in the definition of public and private spaces within a person's life: on the one hand, the speed and reach of communications have shown to increase managerial productivity (Yun, Kettinger, & Lee, 2012), on the other, problems of over-exposure and techno-stress tend to rise (Karlson et al., 2009). It seems to become harder and harder for managers to identify clearly their professional audiences, contacts, and roles, from their personal spaces and their private connections. According to Korica and Molloy (2010), technology helps workers in redefining boundaries and collectively improving work practices, but does that also apply to the borders between "private" and "professional"?

In the words of Stryker and Serpe, individuals are composed of "multiple selves into an organized structure" (1994): personal identities are, in fact, seen as the combination of the social categories in which individuals classify themselves (Ashforth & Mael, 1989; Petriglieri, 2011). This perspective seems to apply perfectly in the world of social media: the social network site becomes in fact a tool for the establishment of a hierarchy of salience within everyone's possible selves (McCall & Simmons, 1978; Stets & Burke, 2003); through the customization of profiles, and the separation of audiences, individuals can portray different sides of themselves simultaneously. Furthermore, if we consider coexistence to be triggering mutual identity negotiation processes among groups of people (Ellemers, Spears, & Doosje, 2002; Stets & Burke, 2000), sporting multiple social media profiles allows for the representation of complex and meaningful identities.

The complexity that such an opportunity entails for managers, however, stands in their necessity to broker between different networks (Walker, Kogut, & Shan, 1997), and therefore constantly question the order in which they rank the different roles they cover. This requires a continuous choice of what information to share with whom, which does not only separate professional from private contexts, but also makes it necessary to differentiate among stakeholders, proactively thinking about the self-messages sent out. Social media, in this sense, other than encouraging the creation of new connections and the rediscovery of old ones, can truly provide a space for the catalyzation of identity negotiation processes (Toma, 2010), whether professional, private, or anywhere in between.

Considering the use of social media as a tool for the maintenance of personal and professional contacts, it becomes difficult to establish whether a complete separation of the two worlds might be advantageous, or even feasible. A separation of profiles can be necessary in order to stress opinions which are not shared by the organization, or driven by concerns over the lack of control on private information (Dinev & Hart, 2003): setting precise boundaries through different accounts can provide control over unwanted exposure. On the other hand, however, a "conservative" use of social media can hinder some of the advantages that a bridge between professional and personal contacts could guarantee, certainly in terms of social capital (Ellison et al., 2006), but also coming to the accurateness of the image managers send out about themselves (Ellison et al., 2011; Lampe, Ellison, & Steinfield, 2007).

The tension between private and professional dimensions of online interaction becomes even more substantial if we consider the self-presentational value of social media (Strano, 2008): the way individuals decide to present themselves on a social network profile has ramifications on both how they perceive themselves (Zhao et al., 2008), and how they want to be seen by others (Pempek, Yermolayeva, & Calvert, 2009). Furthermore, thoroughly established professional selves are thought to be a necessity for achieving social approval, well-being, and even the recognition leading to power (Baumeister, 1982; Ibarra, 1999; Leary & Kowalski, 1990), but the maintenance of personal traits and narratives is necessary for an overall well-being of the person. Additionally, given the importance that personality and personal traits play in leadership emergence (Hoffman, Woehr, Maldagen-Youngjohn, & Lyons, 2010; Judge, Bono, Ilies, & Gerhardt, 2002), their inclusion within a digitally mediated self-discourse could account for a more honest, and more coherent message.

The translation of an offline message into a digital medium requires, however, a set of technical skills (Hargittai, 2010) which are equitable to the knowledge, and application of another language. Online personae help in the disentangling of the self-representational issue by focusing not only on which message is sent across, but also of the audiences allowed to receive it. Through a strategic choice over the boundaries of personae, whether technical (i.e., who can access the profile, what information is circulated, who is related to this account), or personal (i.e., how the owner wants to be seen by which audience) managers have the option to reinforce their self-concepts, and achieve self-affirmation (Toma, 2010). The online world, through the multiplicity of both self-expression possibilities, and different constituencies, seems to offer a valuable playground for image experimentation (cf. Giacalone & Rosenfeld, 1991; Ibarra, 1999): through personae, managers can be present as needed in private and professional contexts, acquiring and sending out differentiated information depending on the role they cover. A conscious exploration of what the concept of personae entails for a manager, as well as a proactive experimentation of how it can be used for the best self-representation can lead to an equilibrium between personal and professional dimensions, allowing individuals to find a solution which best fits their requirements.

Impression Management and Emotional Attachment

Another tension characterizing social media-based interaction, especially for managers, stands in the mediating drivers between their offline and online existences. In fact, the type of processes connecting the person behind the computer to her social network profiles can entirely differentiate an individual's experience, leading to significant changes in the advantages of being online at all. Considering processes of self-representation as a spectrum, rather than as alternative measures, we identified two possible extremes: Impression Management and Emotional Attachment.

Impression Management, in itself, existed long before social media, and consists in those tactics, as put in place by individuals, which allow them to influence the perception of others (Roberts, 2005) by projecting to the outside an adaptable image corresponding to a person's desired self, while also taking into account the "audience feedback" (cf. Goffman, 1959), that is, the likes and dislikes of a person's reference group of peers (Rosenfeld, Giacalone, & Riordan, 2001).

Within managerial identities, Impression Management takes a specifically important role, as an individual's professional self is thought of as stemming from the process of shaping of others' impressions through the enactment of attitudes and roles representing desirable qualities (e.g., intelligence, confidence, initiative, trustworthiness, gracefulness, and seriousness about one's work) (Rosenfeld et al., 2001).

The complexity of interaction with different stakeholders provides a multitude of overlapping different audiences, toward whom managers communicate with the objective to elicit approval and recognition from key constituents, gradually constructing their identity at the same time (Goffman, 1959; Ibarra, 1999; Rafaeli, Dutton, Harquail, & Mackie-Lewis, 1997; Rafaeli & Pratt, 1993).

In the online world, Impression Management finds a particularly good fit: given the limited space, the asynchronicity of the communication (interaction hardly happens real-time) and the malleability of the communication (which can normally be drafted and modified), self-representation is substantially selective, and leaves significant space for the construction of a desired self (Ellison et al., 2011). Furthermore, the direct contact to an audience (boyd & Ellison, 2010; Pempek et al., 2009) allows for an unmediated reception of feedback, which works its way into the projected image much faster than offline (Leary & Allen, 2011).

Impression Management, as a construct, advocates for a strategic manner of being online: by planning and adapting one's self-projections, managers can monitor the perceptions of others, motivate the need for a change, and modify existing identities (Roberts, 2005), thereby exerting full control over their online being. Whether such a dimension of full control might be possible online, is an entirely different matter: aside from the concerns related to personal data circulation and misuse (Dinev & Hart, 2003), it seems like focusing on entirely rational drives of online self-presentation might signify settling for just one side of the picture.

The literature on identity formulation, outside of the digital world, puts in fact a strong emphasis on aspects of self-confidence and self-worth (Gecas, 1982), stressing the fact that, aside from relational and strategic/cognitive skills, there might still be a significant role played by emotions. Shifting the focus to social media, it appears that the nature of individuals (Ellison et al., 2011) might have an influence into how they decide to appear online and, even more importantly, on the way they feel about technology (Eastin & LaRose, 2000). This requires an exploration of emotional states, as connected with online interaction: elements of anxiety (Zung, 1971) applied to technology, as well as anger, excitement, and happiness (Beaudry & Pinsonneault, 2010) play a role in a person's online well-being, and therefore also in the way she chooses to characterize her digital identity.

There is however, another layer of analysis, which more closely concerns self-presentation, and is the element of Emotional Attachment. Investigated within collective online gaming platforms, and on "avatar-based" social network sites such as Second Life, a dimension of deep identification between player and representation exists (Wolfendale, 2007), which leads individuals to establish an emphatic, emotional bond with their online representation (Bessiere, Seay, & Kiesler, 2007). The "physical" dimension with Emotional Attachment is quite obvious: the time, and resources, spent in the choice, adaption, and customization of an avatar trigger the identification process (Ducheneaut, Wen, Yee, & Wadley, 2009). However, any online interaction with a purpose, from online dating (Ellison et al., 2011; Toma, Hancock, & Ellison, 2008) to mere networking (Ellison et al., 2006), brings about emotional drivers to self-representation. For managers, who are most often purposeful in their self-communications online, this can apply with even more strength: identification with one's work leads to the creation of affordances (i.e., personal influences; Bolino & Turnley, 1999) which are constructed on personal bonds (such as friendship, companionship, empathy) which are sometimes difficult, or impossible, to rationalize.

Between the extremes of purely rational Impression Management, and entirely Emotional Attachment stands the online experience of most professionals. The concept of online personae can help in establishing an equilibrium, as it allows professionals to explore the cues and signals indicating how others perceive them (cf. Higgins, 1996). Online personae can therefore be used as a reflection instrument of self-monitoring (cf. Snyder & Gangestad, 1986), raising managers' awareness over their multiple online representations. Since self-monitoring, on and off the web, is considered to be an antecedent to a good management of self-representational outcomes (Gangestad & Snyder, 2000), online personae can help in the mediation between fine-tuned, rational self-communication, and the less strategized, and more emotional cues which emerge when personal profiles are used on social media.

Conclusions

The different dimensions behind the self-communication of managers have increased in size and complexity since the emergence of social media. Such a consequence is to be attributed mainly to the mere existence of large, variegated networks of contacts capable, at the same time, of blurring the boundaries between public and private realms (cf. Schlenker, 1986), among groups of stakeholders (Waters et al., 2009), and between strategized images (cf. Bolino & Turnley, 1999; Ellison et al., 2011) and unmediated self-expression (Wolfendale, 2007). Such many tensions behind personal communication can contribute to a much more complex picture, but also give rise to a deliberate depiction of a manager's many relationships and skills.

The management of online personae may help managers find their personal balance both in how they express themselves (through a proactive understanding of the "tensions" they face while interacting online), and in how they manage their networks, representing the stakeholders to different parts of their lives. Viewed as an organizational practice, conscious personae management may help improve the quality of connections and interactions promoting group work cohesion (Leana & Van Buren, 1999), and foster personal well-being by putting managers in the condition to critically consider the information they share about themselves, as professionals and as private persons. If, quoting Goffman, managers are called to "perform the roles" within their work environments (1959), through online personae they are given a choice over the stage (i.e., what social networks to use), the play (i.e., the type of self-message), and the audiences (i.e., who is capable of seeing their information).

The online self-presentation of managers has consequences which extend well into their offline realms: personae management can be thought of as entering in the consistency-seeking processes of managers and stakeholders in general (cf. Scott & Lane, 2000), and could therefore play a role in strategy making, especially when aspects of organizational image and stakeholder communication are concerned. Furthermore, given the mediatization of organizations, the importance of social media-based self-expression will grow also for managers currently not involved in technology. In fact, as social media becomes a tool for workplace collaboration, the strategic thinking behind online personae might take a progressively larger importance for the well-being of individuals, and for organizations at large. For this reason, we feel that more research should be conducted on the use of social media within management studies: if the social media-bound self-representation of individuals can be integrated within a manager's processes of image creation, then it could help bridge between organizational and corporate identity, giving individuals a path to a coherent expression of who they are.

In terms of social identity theory, the conceptualization of online personae is only a first step in the exploration of the online exposure of professionals, and on its meaning for the identity formation of individuals, as the usage patterns of social media seem to be covering a growing role in the self-definition processes of those who employ them. In a historical moment when professional roles are, at the same time, enriched and challenged by technology, empirical research on impression and image management online could be helpful in grounding the meaning of social media for professional identities at the current time. Given how embedded individuals are in relationships, independently from their nature, empirical research on personae-based self-expression could help in sketching the digital image of the networked executive.

References

Ashforth, B. E., & Mael, F. (1989). Social identity theory and the organization. *Academy of Management Review*, *14*, 20–39.

Baumeister, R. F. (1982). A self-presentational view of social phenomena. *Psychological Bulletin*, *91*(1), 3.

Beaudry, A., & Pinsonneault, A. (2010). The other side of acceptance: Studying the direct and indirect effects of emotions on information technology use. *MIS Quarterly*, 689–710.

Bechar-Israeli, H. (1995). From < Bonehead > to < cLoNehEAd >: Nicknames, play, and identity on internet relay chat. *Journal of Computer-Mediated Communication*, *1*(2). Retrieved from http://jcmc.indiana.edu/vol1/issue2/bechar.html. Accessed on June 25, 2013.

Bessiere, K., Seay, A., & Kiesler, S. (2007). The ideal Elf: Identity exploration in world of warcraft. *Cyberpsychology & Behavior*, *10*(4), 530–535.

Bolino, M., & Turnley, W. (1999). Measuring impression management in organizations: A scale development based on the Jones and Pittman taxonomy. *Organizational Research Methods*, *2*, 187–206.

Bollen, J., Pepe, A., & Mao, H. (2009). Modeling public mood and emotion: Twitter sentiment and socioeconomic phenomena. *arXiv.org*. arXiv:0911.1583v0911 [cs.CY] 0919: Nov 2009.

boyd, d. m., & Ellison, N. B. (2010). Social network sites: Definition, history, and scholarship. *Engineering Management Review, IEEE*, *38*(3), 16–31.

Brewer, M. B. (2003). Optimal distinctiveness, social identity, and the self. In M. R. Leary & J. Tangney (Eds.), *Handbook of self and identity* (pp. 480–491). New York, NY: Guilford Press.

Cahuc, P., & Fontaine, F. (2009). On the efficiency of job search with social networks. *Journal of Public Economic Theory, 11*(3), 411–439.

DiMicco, J., & Millen, D. (2007). Identity management: Multiple presentations of self in Facebook. *ACM group conference*. New York, NY, USA.

Dinev, T., & Hart, P. (2003). Privacy concerns and internet use. *Best paper proceedings of annual academy of management meeting*, Seattle (pp. 131–137).

Ducheneaut, N., Wen, M.-H., Yee, N., & Wadley, G. (2009). Body and mind: A study of avatar personalization in three virtual worlds. *Proceedings of CHI*, Boston, MA (pp. 1152–1160).

Eastin, M. S., & LaRose, R. (2000). Internet self-efficacy and the psychology of the digital divide. *Journal of Computer-Mediated Communication*, 6.1. Retrieved from http://jcmc.indiana.edu/vol6/issue1/eastin.html. Accessed on June 25, 2013.

Ellemers, N., Spears, R., & Doosje, B. (2002). Self and social identity. *Annual Review of Psychology, 53*, 161–186.

Ellison, N., Hancock, J., & Toma, C. (2011). Profile as a promise: A framework for conceptualizing veracity in online dating self-presentation. *New Media & Society*, 1–18.

Gangestad, S. W., & Snyder, M. (2000). Self-monitoring: Appraisal and reappraisal. *Psychological Bulletin, 126*(4), 530–555.

Gecas, V. (1982). The self-concept. *Annual Review of Sociology, 8*, 1–33.

Giacalone, R. A., & Rosenfeld, P. (1991). *Applied impression management: How image-making affects managerial decisions*. Newbury Park, CA: Sage.

Goffman, E. (1959). *The presentation of self in everyday life*. New York, NY: Anchor Books Doubleday.

Hargittai, E. (2010). Digital natives? Variation in internet skills and uses among members of the net generation. *Sociological Inquiry, 80*(1), 92–113.

Higgins, E. (1996). The "self digest": Self-knowledge serving selfregulatory functions. *Journal of Personality and Social Psychology, 71*, 1062–1083.

Hoffman, B., Woehr, D., Maldagen-Youngjohn, R., & Lyons, B. (2010). Great man or great myth? A quantitative review of the relationship between individual differences and leader effectiveness. *Journal of Occupational and Organizational Psychology, 84*, 347–381.

Ibarra, H. (1999). Provisional selves: Experimenting with image and identity in professional adaptation. *Administrative Science Quarterly, 44*, 764–791.

Judge, T., Bono, J., Ilies, R., & Gerhardt, M. (2002). Personality and leadership: A qualitative and quantitative review. *Journal of Applied Psychology, 87*(4), 765–780.

Kaplan, A., & Haenlein, M. (2010). Users of the world, unite! The challenges and opportunities of social media. *Business Horizons, 53*, 59–68.

Karavidas, M., Lim, N., & Katsikas, S. (2005). The effects of computers on older adult users. *Computers in Human Behavior, 21*(5), 687–711.

Karlson, A. K., Meyers, B. R., Jacobs, A., Johns, P., & Kane, S. K. (2009). Working overtime: Patterns of smartphone and PC usage in the day of an information worker. In *Pervasive computing* (pp. 398–405). Heidelberg, Berlin: Springer.

Korica, M., & Molloy, E. (2010). Making sense of professional identities: Stories of medical professionals and new technologies. *Human Relations, 63*(12), 1879–1901.

Lampe, C., Ellison, N., & Steinfeld, C. (2007). A familiar Face(book): Profile elements as signals in an online social network. *Proceedings of conference on human factors in computing systems*, ACM Press, New York, NY (pp. 435–444).

Leana, C., & Buren, H. (1999). Organizational social capital and employment practices. *Academy of Management Review, 24*(3), 538–556.

Leary, M., & Allen, A. (2011). Self presentational persona: Simultaneous management of multiple impressions. *Journal of Personality and Social Psychology, 101*(5), 1033–1049.

Leary, M. R., & Kowalski, R. (1990b). Impression management: A literature review and two-component model. *Psychological Bulletin, 107*, 34–47.

Lengel, R., & Daft, R. L. (1989). The selection of communication media as an executive skill. *The Academy of Management Executive, 2*(3), 225–232.

Lenhart, A. (2009). *Adults and social network websites* (Retrieved from http://www.pewinternet. org/Reports/2009/Adults-and-Social-Network-Websites.aspx. Accessed on June 25, 2013). Washington, DC: Pew Internet and American Life Project.

Lyness, K. S., & Judiesch, M. K. (2008). Can a manager have a life and a career? International and multisource perspectives on work-life balance and career advancement potential. *Journal of Applied Psychology, 93*(4), 789.

McCall, G., & Simmons, J. (1978). *Identities and interactions*. New York, NY: Free Press.

McCarthy, A., Darcy, C., & Grady, G. (2010). Work–life balance policy and practice: Understanding line attitudes and behaviors. *Human Resource Management Review, 20*, 158–167.

Pallas, J., & Fredriksson, M. (2011). Providing, promoting and co-opting: Corporate media work in a mediatized society. *Journal of Communication Management, 15*(2), 165–178.

Pempek, T., Yermolayeva, Y., & Calvert, S. (2009). College students' social networking experiences on Facebook. *Journal of Applied Developmental Psychology, 30*, 227–238.

Petriglieri, J. L. (2011). Under threat: Responses to and the consequences of threats to individuals' identities. *Academy of Management Review, 36*(4), 641–662.

Progoff, I. (1953). *Jung's psychology and its social meaning*. New York, NY: Dialogue House Library.

Puckett, C., & Hargittai, E. (2012). From dot-edu to dot-com: Predictors of college students' job and career information seeking online. *Sociological Focus, 45*, 85–102.

Rafaeli, A., Dutton, J., Harquail, C. V., & Mackie-Lewis, S. (1997). Navigating by attire: The use of dress by female administrative employees. *Academy of Management Journal, 40*, 9–45.

Rafaeli, A., & Pratt, M. G. (1993). Tailored meanings: On the meaning and impact of organizational dress. *Academy of Management Review, 18*, 32–55.

Ramirez, A. J., Walther, J. B., Burgoon, J. K., & Sunnafrank, M. (2002). Information seeking strategies, uncertainty and computer-mediated communication: Toward a conceptual model. *Human Communication Research, 28*, 213–228.

Roberts, L. M. (2005). Changing faces: Professional image construction in diverse organizational settings. *The Academy of Management Review, 30*(4), 685–711.

Rosenfeld, P., Giacalone, R., & Riordan, C. (2001). *Impression management: Building and enhancing reputations at work*. New York, NY: International Thompson Business Press.

Schlenker, B. R. (1986). Self-identification: Toward an integration of the private and public self. In R. Baumeister (Ed.), *Public self and private self* (pp. 21–62). New York, NY: Springer Verlag.

Scott, S., & Lane, V. (2000). A stakeholder approach to organizational identity. *Academy of Management Review, 25*, 43–62.

Snyder, M., & Gangestad, S. (1986). On the nature of self-monitoring: Matters of assessment, matters of validity. *Journal of Personality and Social Psychology, 51*, 125–139.

Stets, J., & Burke, P. (2000). Identity theory and social identity theory. *Social Psychology Quarterly, 63*, 224–237.

Stets, J., & Burke, P. (2003). A sociological approach to self and identity. In M. Leary & J. Tangley (Eds.), *Handbook of self and identity* (pp. 128–152). New York, NY: The Guilford Press.

Strano, M. M. (2008). User descriptions and interpretations of self-presentation through Facebook profile images. *Cyberpsychology: Journal of Psychosocial Research on Cyberspace*, 2(2). Retrieved from http://cyberpsychology.eu/view.php?cisloclanku = 2008110402& article = 1. Accessed on June 25, 2013.

Stryker, S. (1980). Identity salience and role performance. *Journal of Marriage and the Family*, 4, 558–564.

Stryker, S., & Burke, P. J. (2000). The past, present, and future of identity theory. *Social Psychology Quarterly*, 63(4), 284–295.

Stryker, S., & Serpe, R. (1994). Identity salience and psychological centrality: Equivalent, overlapping, or complementary concepts? *Social Psychology Quarterly*, 57(1), 16–35.

Subrahmanyam, K., Smahel, D., & Greenfield, P. (2006). Connecting developmental constructions to the internet: Identity presentation and sexual exploration in online teen chat rooms. *Developmental Psychology*, 42(3), 395–406.

Sveningsson, S., & Alvesson, M. (2003). Managing managerial identities: Organizational fragmentation, discourse and identity struggle. *Human Relations*, 56(10), 1163–1193.

Swann, W. B. (1987). Identity negotiation: Where two roads meet. *Journal of Personality and Social Psychology*, 53, 1038–1051.

Toma, C. (2010). Affirming the self through online profiles: Beneficial effects of social networking sites. *Proceedings of CHI 2010* (pp. 1749–1752). doi: 10.1145/1753326.1753588

Toma, C., Hancock, J., & Ellison, N. (2008). Separating fact from fiction: An examination of deceptive self-presentation in online dating profiles. *Personality and Social Psychology Bulletin*, 34, 1023–1036.

Turnley, W. H., & Bolino, M. C. (2001). Achieving desired images while avoiding undesired images: Exploring the role of self-monitoring in impression management. *Journal of Applied Psychology*, 86, 351–360.

Walker, G., Kogut, B., & Shan, W. (1997). Social capital, structural holes and the formation of an industry network. *Organization Science*, 8, 109–125.

Walsham, G. (1998). IT and changing professional identity: Micro studies and macro theory. *Journal of the American Society for Information Science*, 49(12), 1081–1089.

Waters, R., Burnett, E., Lamm, A., & Lucas, J. (2009). Engaging stakeholders through social networking: How nonprofit organizations are using Facebook. *Public Relations Review*, 35(2), 102–106.

Wolfendale, J. (2007). My avatar, my self: Virtual harm and attachment. *Ethics and Information Technology*, 9, 111–119.

Yun, H., Kettinger, W., & Lee, C. (2012). A new open door: The smartphone's impact on work-to-life conflict, stress, and resistance. *International Journal of Electronic Commerce*, 16(4), 121–152.

Zhao, S., Grasmuck, S., & Martin, J. (2008). Identity construction on Facebook: Digital empowerment in anchored relationships. *Computers in Human Behavior*, 24, 1816–1836.

Zung, W. (1971). A rating instrument for anxiety disorders. *Psychosomatics*, 12, 271–279.

Chapter 11

Toward the Development of a Social Information System Research Model

Opal Donaldson and Evan W. Duggan

Abstract

Purpose — The purpose of this research is to develop a Social Information System research model that uses the core constructs intrinsic motivation, extrinsic motivation, and amotivation to explain social networking adoption among tweens, teens and young adults.

Methodology — In developing the research model, we triangulated theories to examine the different orientations of motivation. The data collection process included a stratified sample size of 270 respondents. Following data collection we analyzed the results using structural equation modeling in the Partial Least Square software package.

Findings — The constructs amotivation, intrinsic and extrinsic motivations were all statistically significant in explaining continuance intention to use social networking services (SNS).

Practical implications — Researchers and practitioners have intimated that although there has been a rise in the number of persons accessing and becoming members of SNS, several subscribers who join subsequently leave after a minimal period. The practical implication of this study lies in providing a preliminary understanding of what determines or inhibits continuance intention of SNS membership.

Originality/value — Despite efforts, research in IS and technology acceptance literature regarding SNS diffusion is limited in scope. The theoretical implication of this study lies in the model that has been developed and validated to provide a more effective tool for the scholarly evaluation of SNS adoption. Existing adoption models are insufficient to explain voluntary technology usage of this nature.

Keywords: Social information system; intrinsic motivation; extrinsic motivation; amotivation; social networking services

Social Media in Human Resources Management
Advanced Series in Management, 215–242
Copyright © 2013 by Emerald Group Publishing Limited
All rights of reproduction in any form reserved
ISSN: 1877-6361/doi:10.1108/S1877-6361(2013)0000012015

Introduction

In this chapter we propose a Social Information System research model that seeks to explain continuance intention to use social networking services (SNS). Theotokis and Doukidis (2009) defined a Social Information System as one that enables users to perform socially-related activities and in order to provide social value to the user. The characteristics of the acceptance of a Social Information System set it apart from other types of information systems (IS) (Theotokis & Doukidis, 2009). One of the main differences is that motivations related to the individuals' social life and activities usually lead them to adopt and use these systems, instead of utilitarian or hedonic motivations that have been found to affect users' adoption of other types of IS (Theotokis & Doukidis, 2009; Venkatesh, 2000; Venkatesh, Morris, Davis, & Davis, 2003). Most importantly, users of Social Information Systems expect mainly to gratify social-emotional rather than informational or utilitarian needs, and they are connected in a person-to-person manner which is more direct and interpersonal (Theotokis & Doukidis, 2009).

Social media research is beginning to accumulate; however, mostly in the areas of communication and social psychology where such studies are typically concerned with how SNS settings can be used to build and maintain social capital (Wudd, 2009). In this chapter, we depart from this focus and seek to make a contribution to the adoption process of Social Information Systems as recommended by Hu and Kettinger (2008), who pointed out that while many people spend an increasing amount of time on SNS, others use them minimally or discontinue use after a short period of time. This led them to suggest an urgent need to assess factors related to the adoption and usage of this emerging phenomenon. Although research exists on IS continuance and post adoption, existing models are insufficient to explain the SNS phenomena as its usage tends to be more voluntary, more socially bound, and more evolutionary in use attributes and levels of involvement (Hu & Kettinger, 2008) than is the case with other technologies.

One of the most widely applied adoption model in information systems is the Technology Acceptance Model (TAM) (Lee, Kozar, & Larsen, 2003). Wudd (2009) explained that despite the successful reputation of TAM, researchers have found that its task-related nature underplays the effect of possible intrinsic factors. Schwarz, Gallego, Sorial, and Aborg (2008) corroborated this view and suggested that adoption research has relied traditionally upon a relatively narrow set of users' perceptions of the technology to explain adoption decisions. According to Schwarz, Wiley-Patton, Schwarzz, Perez-Mira, and Jungyy (2009), adoption research has been examined from a "proxy view," that is, making a determination of and explaining adoption intention on the basis of the individual's perception of the technology. An evaluation of the adoption literature seem to support the position of Wudd (2009) and Schwarz et al. (2009) regarding the limitations of existing models used to evaluate technology adoption. Specifically, it is noted that technology adoption models have rarely focused on a combination of the different aspects of motivation (intrinsic, extrinsic and amotivation) in explaining behavior. We therefore seek to answer the following question:

- How do intrinsic motivation, extrinsic motivation and amotivation explain usage continuance behavior of SNS among tweens, teens and young adults?

  In the remainder of the chapter, we first outline the reason for selecting the demographic of users to investigate (tweens, teens and young adults). Then we discuss the constructs that are involved in the research model, which is followed by the development and presentation of the model. In the penultimate section we describe the methodology and discuss our findings. The chapter ends with an in-depth discussion of our conclusion and recommendation.

Why Tweens, Teens and Young Adults?

The social interactions of an individual age 40 or over will differ from those of a teenager or young adult (Adams, 2011). Based on this premise, Adams (2011) contended that the nature of social networking usage and adoption will vary among age groups. Evidence in the literature suggested that the preponderance of SNS membership consist of young people (Acquisti et al., 2008; Bonneau & Preibusch, 2009; Boyd, 2007). Bonneau and Preibusch (2009) reported that the popularity of SNS among the younger generation is high with studies finding that more than 80% of American university students were active SNS users who commonly spent at least 30 minutes every day on social networks. The presence of social networking in youth culture has been compared to that of an addiction (Bonneau & Preibusch, 2009). Young people particularly are quick to use the new technology in ways which increasingly blur the boundaries between their online and offline activities.

  Acquisti et al. (2008) pointed out that several mainstream SNS are aimed at teenagers and young adults. Most services have a minimum membership age of 13 or 14, and many explicitly state that they are designed for over 18s. Acquisti et al. (2008) further explained that there may be safety restrictions on the accounts of 14- to 17-year-olds; for example, regarding whether their profiles appear in public or off-site searches. Some sites are specifically designed for young people, for example, both Teen Second Life and Habbo Hotel are aimed at teens while Imbee.com is primarily a blogging service for tweens (children aged 9–13), requiring a parent's permission to sign up. According to Ahonen (2007) the growth of Mobile SNS among younger users has been surprising and Khan (2008) argued that the primary Mobile SNS consumers are Generation Y or younger Generation X. These user groups have mobile phones, text frequently, use mobile data and are active with social networking. It was also noted that Generation Y seem more active with Mobile SNS like Facebook Mobile or MocoSpace, while the younger Generation X also use social mapping and tagging as a way to stay connected to their friends and local information (Khan, 2008).

Motivation

In order to explain behavior, it is important to understand the motives behind the behavior (Amabile, Hill, Hennessey, & Tighe, 1994). Motives are reasons people initiate and perform voluntary activities, and can affect a person's perception, cognition, emotion and actions (Reiss, 2004). Amabile et al. (1994) argued that the investigation of individual differences in motivational orientation is potentially important for both personality and social psychology. One of the important points illustrated by these authors is that an individuals' temporary motivational orientation toward activities can differ as a function of the social contexts in which they have engaged in those activities. McCullagh (2005) defined motivation as the intensity and direction of effort. Intensity is the quality of effort while direction speaks to what an individual is drawn to. Similarly, Ryan and Deci (2000a) asserted that to be motivated means to be moved to do something and further argued (Ryan & Deci, 2000b) that most studies of motivation view the phenomena from a unary perspective one that varies from little to great motivation to act. The authors cautioned that motivation should not be viewed as a unary phenomenon as persons not only have different levels of motivation but there may be differences in the orientation of motivation.

Ryan and Deci (2000b) presented a classification of human motivation in their formulation of the self-determination theory (see Figure 1). The authors expressed the view that there are three types of motivation (intrinsic, extrinsic, and amotivation) and they are organized in the taxonomy to reflect their differing degrees of autonomy or self-determination.

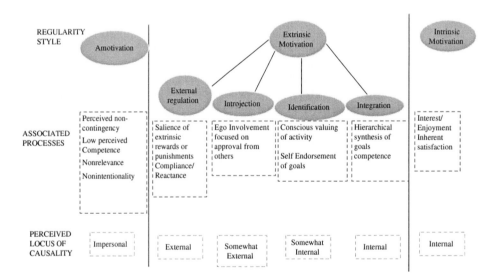

Figure 1: The self-determination continuum illustrating types of motivation adapted from Ryan and Deci (2000a).

According to Carton (1996), social-cognitive theorists distinguish between intrinsic and extrinsic motivation; intrinsic motivation is associated with relatively high-valued constructs such as competence, personal causation and self-determination, while extrinsic motivation describes the performance of an activity to obtain an external consequence. Carton (1996) claimed that of the two forms of motivation, intrinsic motivation is considered to be superior. Intrinsic motivation is considered a pervasive and important activity because from birth onwards humans in their healthiest state are active, inquisitive, and curious, displaying a readiness to explore without the need for extraneous incentives to do so (Ryan & Deci, 2000b). This natural motivational tendency is critical because it is through acting on ones inherent interest that one grows in knowledge and skills (Ryan & Deci, 2000b). Intrinsic motivation residing within a person or derived from an activity itself will positively affect behavior, performance and well-being (Ryan & Deci, 2000b). Lepper and Greene's (1978) initially proposed that as extrinsic motivation increases in individuals, their intrinsic motivation will decrease. In fact intrinsic motivation has been defined by researchers as the absence of extrinsic motivation (Amabile et al., 1994). However, there are a few theorists (e.g., Deci & Ryan, 1985 and Lepper, Corpus, & Iyenger, 2005) who have suggested that, under some circumstances, intrinsic and extrinsic motivation need not work in opposition.

Amotivation

Beyond intrinsic and extrinsic motivation is the concept of amotivation (Ryan & Deci, 2000b). According to Ryan and Deci (2000a) whenever a person encourages certain behaviors in others it may result in amotivation Deci and Ryan (1985) explicated that in order to fully understand human behavior amotivation must be considered. Amotivation describes the absence of intentionality and a sense of causation in a person's behavior (Ryan & Deci, 2000b). This results when an individual does not value an activity, feels incompetent to perform it or does not believe the action will yield the desired outcome (Ryan & Deci, 2000b). Consequently, Ryan and Deci (2000c) argued that environments that also block satisfaction of the needs for competence and relatedness tend to promote amotivation, and that the controlled and amotivational orientations, relative to the autonomous orientation, have negative effects on performance and well-being. Deci and Ryan (2000c) outlined that their findings coincided with those of other researchers who found that people's general sense of amotivation with respect to engaging in activities such as recycling and other environmentally friendly behaviors resulted from believing that they are not really capable of carrying out the necessary behaviors and that the behaviors do not make a difference to the environment anyway.

Vallerand and Bissonnette (1992) explained that amotivated persons are non-motivated and because of this they see no rewards whether intrinsically or extrinsically and as a result participation in the activity eventually ceases. Both (Thibert & Karsenti, 1998) and (Vallerand & Bissonnette, 1992) compares amotivation to a concept known as learned helplessness since the individuals experience feelings of incompetence and expectancies of uncontrollability. In their study Vallerand and Bissonnette (1992) found amotivation to be an important predictor of behavior and negatively related to a person's actions. This negative association was also identified by Deci and Ryan (2000c). The authors clarified that a distinction was made between amotivation and motivation in several motivational theories sometimes under different labels; however, in all cases amotivation seemed to be associated with a range of negative outcomes.

Intrinsic Motivation

According to Deci, Koestner, and Ryan (1999) the concept of intrinsic motivation was brought to the forefront by Deci (1971), who argued that some tasks provide their own inherit rewards and do not require external rewards. In their meta-analysis, Deci, et al. (1999) spoke about the controversy that Deci's (1971) initial findings sparked. The debate was centered on arguments related to the obscure existence of intrinsic motivation and its presence in inhibiting scientific progress as there was no acceptable evidence of an undermining effect. On the other hand, many behavioral and cognitive theorists expressed the view that there was indeed a need to look at the phenomena and assess their possible undermining effects (Deci et al., 1999). Consequently numerous explanations were given to assess the effect of reward on intrinsic motivation. One such explanation was outlined in the Cognitive Evaluation Theory (CET) by Deci and Ryan (1985).

Ryan and Deci (2000b) explained that CET was created by Deci and Ryan (1985) to identify the factors in social contexts that produce variability in intrinsic motivation. According to Deci et al. (1999) CET asserts that underlining intrinsic motivation are the psychological needs for autonomy and competence. Therefore assessing the effect of reward depends on how it affects perceived self-determination and perceived competence. CET characterizes social contexts as either being autonomy supportive (informational), controlling, or amotivating (Ryan & Deci, 2000c). According to Wiechman (2005) CET proposes that the needs for competence and autonomy are undermined when people are offered rewards for engaging in intrinsically motivated behaviors. Individuals' perceived locus of causality (PLOC) greatly impacts their degree of felt autonomy and competence. CET asserts that rewards affect intrinsic motivation by bringing about changes in people's perceived competence and PLOC (Wiechman, 2005). When given reward, people do not feel fully in control of their actions and rather they sense a shift of their PLOC from internal to external, as their behavior is moderated by the rewards (Wiechman, 2005).

Although CET typically focuses on negative effects of rewards there are events where CET points to positive impact of rewards (Cameron, Pierce, Banko, & Gear, 2005). CET further posits that interpersonal events and structures (e.g., rewards, communications, feedback), which results in feelings of competence during an action, can enhance intrinsic motivation for that action because they allow satisfaction of the basic psychological need for competence (Deci & Ryan, 2000a). In addition, optimal challenges, effectance promoting feedback, and freedom from demeaning evaluations are all predicted to facilitate intrinsic motivation.

With all the conflict surrounding the effect of rewards on intrinsic motivation, Deci et al. (1999) provided a structure to understand the phenomena. According to the authors in making predictions about the effect of tangible rewards on intrinsic motivation, rewards are assessed against the criterion of whether the reward is expected while a person is doing a task and, if so, on what behaviors the rewards are depend. Ryan, Mims, and Koestner (1983) provided the following topology of reward contingencies, for expected rewards while a person is doing a particular task:

- *Task- noncontingent reward:* These rewards are offered for reasons other than engaging in the task activity: for example, simply participating in a study. This class of reward is not considered to have an effect on intrinsic motivation since these rewards do not require, doing the task, completing the task or doing well at the task.
- *Performance-contingent reward:* these rewards are given specifically for performing an activity well, matching some standard of excellence or surpassing some criterion. This type of reward results in strong control so there is a strong tendency for these rewards to undermine intrinsic motivation.
- *Completion-contingent reward:* This is a form of task contingent reward that is dependent on the completion of the task. Persons have to complete the activity so there is a level of control however the receipt of the reward requires some level of competence which is thought to offset the controlling effect.
- *Engagement-Contingent Reward:* Task-contingent activity that requires engagement in the activity but do not require completing it. With this type of reward people do not work on a task to get the reward so the effect is likely to be controlling. That this type of task carries little or no affirmation of competence and therefore engagement-contingent rewards are predicted to undermine intrinsic interest.

Extrinsic Motivation

Deci et al. (1999) explained in their seminal article that, by 1971, hundreds of studies had established that extrinsic reward can control behavior. Bateman and Crant (2003) argued that extrinsically motivated behavior is just as important as behavior driven by intrinsic interest. Unlike theorists such as Carton (1996), Bandura and Schunk (1981), and Reiss (2004) who all present extrinsic motivation from a unary perspective, Ryan and Deci (2000b) outlined, in the self-determination theory, that extrinsic motivation exist across a spectrum (see Figure 1). The following were identified along the continuum for extrinsic motivation:

- *External regulation* behavior is performed to satisfy an external demand or obtain an externally imposed reward contingency. Individuals typically experience externally regulated behavior as controlled or alienated, and their actions have an external PLOC.

- *Introjection* describes a type of internal regulation that is still quite controlling because people perform such actions with the feeling of pressure in order to avoid guilt or anxiety or to attain ego-enhancements or pride. For example a person performs an act in order to enhance or maintain self-esteem and feeling of worth.
- *Identification* is considered a more autonomous, or self-determined, form of extrinsic motivation. In this instance the person has identified with the personal importance of a behavior and has thus accepted its regulation as his or her own. For example a boy who memorizes spelling lists because he sees it as relevant to writing, which he values as a life goal, has identified with the value of this learning activity.
- *Integrated regulation* is considered the most autonomous form of extrinsic motivation. It occurs when identified regulations have been fully assimilated to the self. This occurs through self-examination and bringing new regulations in line with one's other values and needs. The more a person internalizes the reasons for an action and assimilates them to the self, the more one's extrinsically motivated actions become self-determined. Integrated forms of motivation share many qualities with intrinsic motivation, being both autonomous and unconflicted. However, they are still extrinsic because behavior motivated by integrated regulation is exhibited for its presumed instrumental value with respect to some outcome that is separate from the behavior, even though it is valued by the self.

Extrinsically motivated behaviors are driven by the expectation of the attainment of externally registered reward which includes pay, material possession, prestige and positive evaluation from others (Amabile, 1985; Bateman & Crant, 2003). This research focuses on the positive evaluation from others which falls under the extrinsic motivation category of introjection. According to Bandura (1989) peers are sources of much social learning. One of the most consistent determinants of an individual's behavior is the influence of others (Wen, Tang, & Chang, 2009). According to Lopez and Manson (1997) social influences play an important role in the prediction of IT usage. Pedersen (2001) noted that subjective norms are determined by external and interpersonal influence and added that they capture the individual's perceptions of the influence of significant others such as family, peers, authority figures, and media. Khalifa and Shen (2006) highlighted that subjective norms have been identified as a major predictor of perceived usefulness and suggested that the direct effect of subjective norms on perceived usefulness is realized through the internalization process, whereby people incorporate the important referents' opinions into their own belief structure, especially when usage is voluntary.The effects of extrinsically motivated behavior were observed in Boyd's (2007) research. According to Boyd (2007) the results showed that there are two types of nonparticipants in SNS: disenfranchised teens and conscientious objectors. Disenfranchised teens are those without Internet access, whose parents succeed in banning them from participation, or online teens who primarily access the Internet through school and other public venues where SNS are banned. On the other hand conscientious objectors include politically minded teens who are protesting against Murdoch's News Corp. (the corporate owner of MySpace) and obedient teens that respect or agree with their parents' moral or safety concerns.

Continuance Intention

The dependent construct in the proposed model is continuance intention. Usage continuance is also known in the literature as Post-Adoptive IS Usage (Kefi, Mlaiki, & Kalika, 2010) and it refers to "all forms of behavior that reflect continued use of an IS [*or*] ending with the final decision of the user to stop this use" (Limayem, Hirt, & Cheung, 2007, p. 707). One of the critical success factors for SNS that researchers highlighted is the retention of existing customer base and participation (Nov & Ye, 2008; Schwarz et al., 2009; Wudd, 2009). Hu and Kettinger (2008) argued that although there has been an increase in the number of persons accessing and becoming members of SNS. Many subscribers join and leave after a minimal period of engagement. It has been observed that a user may become a member of several SNS; but the reasons he or she remains faithful to a given SNS while others do not is unclear (Kefi et al., 2010). Kefi et al. (2010) stated that with these discrepancies in usage patterns it is important to capture the process of SNS continuance intention since long-term viability of these platforms is more critical than their initial acceptance to evaluate their success.

To understand the differences in usage and membership, the adoption process must be evaluated. Theotokis and Doukidis (2009) explained that innovation diffusion research can be broken down into two categories**: adoption-diffusion (AD) paradigm and use-diffusion (UD) processes. They further asserted that AD is the process by which an innovation reaches a critical mass of adopters, the diffusion is accelerated, and innovation is considered successful. On the other hand, the UD model examines the evolving nature of use (rate and variety), sustained continuous use (or disadoption), and technology outcome considerations. Theotokis and Doukidis concluded that, in the case of Social Information Systems, the UD approach could better model the varying levels of user adoption and usage of technology.

The Research Model

The research model (see Figure 2) depicts the relationships between the constructs previously discussed in the review of the literature. The dependent construct in the model is *continuance intention* and it is predicted by the core constructs *intrinsic motivation* and *extrinsic motivation* and *amotivation*. It is proposed that *continuance intention* has a positive relationship with both *intrinsic* and *extrinsic motivation* but a negative relationship with *amotivation*. *Perceived self-determination* and *perceived competence* are both considered predictors of *intrinsic motivation* and in return *engagement-contingent reward* is considered a predictor of both *perceived*

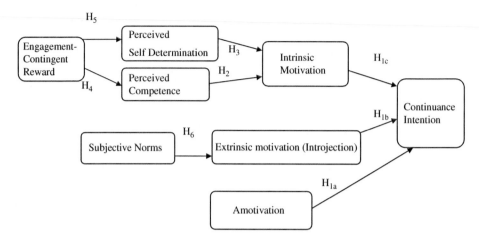

Figure 2: Social information system research model.

self-determination and *perceived competence*. It is also proposed that *subject norm* will positively predict *extrinsic motivation*.

The following hypotheses are posited:

H_1: There is a difference in the relationships among the three categories of motivation and continuance intention to use SNS.

H_{1a}: Amotivation will have a negative impact on continuance intention to use SNS.
H_{1b}: Extrinsic motivation will have a positive impact on continuance intention to use SNS.
H_{1c}: Intrinsic motivation will have a positive impact on continuance intention to use SNS.

H_2: Perceived Competence will have a positive impact on intrinsic motivation in SNS.
H_3: Self-determination will have a positive impact on intrinsic motivation in SNS.
H_4: Engagement-contingent rewards will have a positive impact on SNS users' perceived competence in social networking activities.
H_5: Engagement-contingent rewards will have a positive impact on SNS users' self-determination.
H_6: Subjective norms will have a positive impact on extrinsic motivation to use SNS.

Methodology

A positivist approach was used in the conduct of the research and the evaluation of the proposed research model. The data were collected using a questionnaire instrument adopted from several sources based on previous research conducted in

Table 1: Constructs and sources.

Theory	Construct	Source
Self-Determination Theory	Amotivation, Extrinsic Motivation (Introjected Regulation)	Noels, Pelletier, Clément, and Vallerand (2000)
Self-Determination Theory	Perceived Competence, Self-Determination and Intrinsic Motivation	Shroff and Vogle (2009)
Theory of Reasoned Action	Subjective Norm	Malhotra and Galletta (1999)
Theory of Reasoned Action	Continuance Intention	Agarwal and Karahanna (2000)
Cognitive Evaluation Theory	Engagement-Contingent Reward	Developed from Literature

the field (see Table 1). Using Denzin's (1978) notion of theory triangulation, several constructs were adopted from the field of behavioral psychology and IS. This approach to creating the instrument helps to enhance face validity, which according to Hair, Black, Babin, Anderson, and Tatham (2006) is the assessment of the degree of correspondence between the items selected to constitute a summative scale and its conceptual definitions; a critical requirement prior to theoretical testing. The authors cautioned that without an understanding of each item's content or meaning, it is impossible to express and correctly specify a measurement theory.

The data used to test the research model were drawn from a sample size of 270 participants. There is little consensus on the recommended sample size for SEM however a proposed 'critical sample size' of 200 is recommended (Hoe, 2008). Heidt and Scott (2007) also offered another rule of thumb for using ten subjects per item in scale development. In this research, each of the constructs to be measured had three to four indicators. Applying this 10:1 heuristic a sample size of 30–40 would have been sufficient. Therefore the sample size of 270 respondents selected is considered adequate.

The sample was stratified based on the age groups: teens, tweens and young adults who are current or previous users of SNS. The specific demographic stratification was created using Facebook demographic reports published by Ignite Social Media (2011). The most recent report was used as at the point of data collection. The sample was stratified using educational level as a proxy for the age groups (teens, tweens and young adults) (see Figure 3). It was necessary to use education level as a proxy, as the representation of age groups in the Ignite report and other publications were not consistent with the age groupings of this research. The sample was also stratified based on the gender distribution of Facebook in the Ignite social media (2011), which indicated that there was 62% female and 38% male membership. See Table 2 for the stratification structure of the sample.

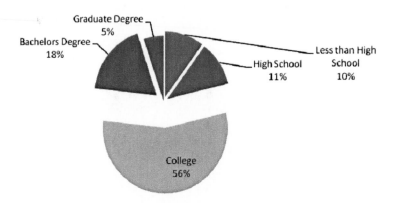

Figure 3: Educational level by facebook membership (adopted from Ignite Social Media, 2011).

Table 2: Sample stratification.

Facebook structure	Sample stratification by age	Portion of the sample	Male	Female
Primary school (10%)	9–12 (tweens)	27	10	17
High school (11%)	13–17 (teens)	30	11	19
College (56%)	18–19 (teens)\young adults (20–29)	151	57	94
Bachelors degree (18%)	18–19 (teens)\young adults (20–29)\older than 29	48	18	30
Graduate level (5%)	Young adults (20–29)\older than 29	14	4	14
Total		270	100	170

Following the development of the sampling framework the instrument was pretested by a small group of participants (15) to ensure its clarity and plausibility. Next, educational institutions at the primary, secondary and tertiary level were contacted to request the participation of students. Once permission was given to collect data an appointment was made with the institution and the site visited. On each visit, students were assembled in room on the compound and the survey instruments were distributed within the mass gathering. Respondents were given an introduction to the instrument and then allowed to complete it. Once instruments were completed they were collected on spot. This was done to facilitate a high response rate. Following data collection the model was evaluated using SEM in the Partial Least Square Software Package.

Findings

The findings of the results are presented in two segments: (1) the confirmatory factor analysis which represents the measurement model and (2) the structural model which provides the results for the path analysis. The measurement model is defined below (see Table 3).

Construct Validity

Convergent validity is established when the items that are indicators of a specific construct converge or share a high portion of variance in common (Hair et al., 2006). They further explained that a good rule of thumb is that the standardized loadings estimates should be 0.5 or higher and ideally 0.7 or higher. The data revealed that the standardized loadings for all manifest variables were greater than 0.5 — except for selfdet4 and subjective norm1 with values 0.3892 and 0.432 respectively. Both were removed from the analysis and the construct validity reassessed (see Table 4). The majority of the latent variables had loadings larger than 0.7 which suggest good reliability. Another indicator of convergence is the average variance extracted (AVE). The results in Table 4 indicate that the AVE values for each latent variable are within the acceptable range with all values larger than .5.

Construct Reliability

Reliability is an indicator of convergent validity where values of 0.7 or higher indicate adequate convergence or internal consistency (Hair et al., 2006). The results revealed that all constructs included in the model surpassed the internal consistency threshold with only Subjective Norm having a composite reliability value (0.772) less than 0.800 (see Table 5).

Discriminant Validity

Discriminant validity is the extent to which a construct is truly different from other constructs. High discriminant validity therefore provides evidence that a construct is unique and captures some dimensions that other measures do not (Hair et al., 2006). According to Hair et al. (2006) the assessment discriminate validity requires a comparison of the AVE values for any two constructs with the variance estimate between the two constructs; discriminate validity is assured when the AVE is greater than the variance estimate. Our results suggest that the constructs display good discriminant validity with the AVE values for each latent variable greater than the variance shared between constructs (see Table 6).

Table 3: Measurement model definition.

Manifest variable	Description	Latent variable
Continuance Intention	I plan to use the social networking in the future.	Continuance1
	I intend to continue using the social networking in the future.	Continuance2
	I expect my use of the social networking to increase in the future.	Continuance3
	I would like to spend more time learning about social networking.	Continuance4
Amotivation	I cannot see why I should engage in social networking, and frankly, I don't give a damn.	Amot1
	Honestly, I truly have the impression of wasting my time in engaging in social networking	Amot2
	I can't come to understand what I am doing engaging in social networking	Amot3
Intrinsic Motivation	I would say social networking is very interesting.	Intrinsic Motivation 1
	I enjoyed social networking.	Intrinsic Motivation 2
	I feel as if social networking holds my attention.	Intrinsic Motivation 3
	I feel as if social networking is a fun activity.	Intrinsic Motivation 4
Extrinsic Motivation	I would feel ashamed if I couldn't communicate with my friends using this medium.	Introjection1
	I would feel guilty if I didn't have a social networking account.	Introjection2
	I want to show myself that I am keeping up with the trend because I have a social networking account.	Introjection3
Self-Determination	I believe I had some choice in becoming a member of social networking.	SelfDet1
	I feel as if it was my own choice as to how often I participated in the social networking activities.	SelfDet2
	I contribute to photo commenting and other social networking activities because I want to.	SelfDet3

Table 3: Continued.

Manifest variable	Description	Latent variable
	I had different selections in determining which social networking to join.	SelfDet4
Perceived Competence	I feel I am competent in engaging in social networking activities.	Perceived Competence1
	I feel that my engagement in the social networking activities have increase my competence in using the technology.	Perceived Competence2
	I feel I am skilled in the social networking activities such as posting comments, sending messages etc.	Perceived Competence3
	I feel I am capable to teach someone else to use a social networking service.	Perceived Competence4
Subjective Norm	I use social networking services because my friends and family uses it.	Subnorm1
	I use social networking services because it was recommended by someone whose opinion I value.	Subnorm2
	I use Social networking services because if it helps me to fit in with friends.	Subnorm3
Reward	I appreciate positive photo comments from friends.	Reward1
	I like positive feedback on my profile from friends and family.	Reward2
	I look forward to wall postings that commend me on my appearance and my profile page.	Reward3

Structural Model

The results of the structural model are displayed below (see Figure 4). The p-values are in parenthesis with the path coefficients above them. The significance level is 0.05.

Model Results

The overall outcome of the model illustrated that 29.48% of the variance in the dependent construct, continuance intention was explained by the independent

Table 4: Confirmatory factor analysis- standardize loadings.

Constructs/Latent variables	Manifest variables	Original sample estimate	Mean of subsamples	Standard error	T-statistic
Continuance Intention (η_1)					AVE = 0.625
	Continuance1	0.8877	0.8853	0.0208	42.7177
	Continuance2	0.9001	0.8986	0.0233	38.6218
	Continuance3	0.7397	0.738	0.0528	13.9978
	Continuance4	0.5946	0.5945	0.0615	9.6642
Amotivation (η_2)					AVE = 0.671
	Amot1	0.8181	0.8069	0.0621	13.1656
	Amot2	0.9182	0.9197	0.0477	19.2652
	Amot3	0.7083	0.6825	0.1039	6.8182
Intrinsic Motivation (η_3)					AVE = 0.733
	Intrinsic Motivation1	0.8948	0.89	0.0236	37.8979
	Intrinsic Motivation2	0.9143	0.9122	0.0142	64.2663
	Intrinsic Motivation3	0.7126	0.6999	0.0539	13.2199
	Intrinsic Motivation4	0.8877	0.8821	0.0232	38.1811
Extrinsic Motivation (η_4)					AVE = 0.653
	Introjection1	0.7946	0.791	0.0409	19.4297
	Introjection2	0.849	0.8474	0.0294	28.8597
	Introjection3	0.7796	0.7755	0.0399	19.56

Self-Determination (η_5)	SelfDet1	0.6662	0.6619	0.1006	6.6246
	SelfDet2	0.7195	0.7156	0.0854	8.426
	SelfDet3	0.8834	0.882	0.0417	21.162
Removed	SelfDet4				AVE = 0.581
Perceived Competence (η_6)	Perceived Competence1	0.8237	0.8236	0.0263	31.3477
	Perceived Competence2	0.8641	0.8632	0.0227	38.1115
	Perceived Competence3	0.8069	0.7987	0.0396	20.3619
	Perceived Competence4	0.6516	0.6434	0.0617	10.5586
					AVE = 0.625
Subjective Norm (ξ_1)	Subnorm1				
Removed	Subnorm2	0.6324	0.6389	0.0888	7.12
	Subnorm3	0.9348	0.9281	0.0309	30.2155
					AVE = 0.637
Reward (ξ_2)	Reward1	0.9211	0.9187	0.0184	50.1849
	Reward2	0.9306	0.9293	0.0164	56.6448
	Reward3	0.8074	0.8067	0.0329	24.5192
					AVE = 0.789

Table 5: Construct validity measure.

Construct	Composite reliability	Variable type
Continuance Intention (η_1)	0.867	Endogenous
Amotivation (η_2)	0.858	Exogenous
Intrinsic Motivation (η_3)	0.916	Endogenous
Extrinsic Motivation (η_4)	0.850	Endogenous
Self-Determination (η_5	0.804	Endogenous
Perceived Competence (η_6)	0.868	Endogenous
Subjective Norm (ξ_1)	0.772	Exogenous
Reward (ξ_2)	0.918	Exogenous

constructs. The research model depicted that the findings provided support to reject the null hypothesis and accept the alternate H_1 based on the testing of three sub-hypothesis (H_{1a}, H_{1b} and H_{1c}) and the following structural equation:

$$\text{Continuance Intention} = 0.442 \,(\text{Intrinsic Motivation})$$
$$+ 0.140 \,(\text{Extrinsic Motivation}) - 0.1270 \,(\text{Amotivation}) + \zeta$$

- H_{1a}: *Amotivation will have a negative impact on continuance intention to use SNS.*
  The results provide support to reject the null hypothesis. Based on the path coefficient, the findings indicate that there is a negative relationship between amotivation and continuance intention with a *p*-value of 0.046 (see Figure 4).
- H_{1b}: *Extrinsic motivation will have an impact on continuance intention to use SNS.*
  The results provide support to reject the null hypothesis. Based on the path coefficient, the findings confirm that there is a positive relationship between extrinsic motivation and continuance intention with a p-value of .014 (see Figure 4).
- H_{1c}: *Intrinsic motivation will have a positive impact on continuance intention to use SNS.*
  The results provide support to reject the null hypothesis. Based on the path coefficient, the findings signify a positive relationship between intrinsic motivation and continuance intention with a *p*-value of 0.000 (see Figure 4). Intrinsic motivation also had the greatest direct impact on continuance intention to use SNS in the model with the largest path coefficient of 0.443.
- H_2: *Perceived competence will have an impact on intrinsic motivation in SNS.*
  The results provide support to reject the null hypothesis. Based on the path coefficient, the findings indicate a positive relationship between intrinsic motivation and Perceived competence with a *p*-value of 0.000. The results also show that perceived competence had the greatest direct impact on intrinsic motivation with a path coefficient of 0.3030.

$$\text{Intrinsic Motivation} = 0.2460 \,(\text{Self} - \text{Determination})$$
$$+ 0.3030 \,(\text{Perceived Competence}) + \zeta$$

Table 6: Discriminant validity.

Variables	Continuance intention	Intrinsic motivation	Extrinsic motivation	Amotivation	Self-determination	Competence	Reward	Subjective norm
Continuance Intention	**0.625**							
Intrinsic Motivation	0.265	**0.733**						
Extrinsic Motivation	0.060	0.057	**0.653**					
Amotivation	0.068	0.093	0.000	**0.671**				
Self-Determination	0.120	0.171	0.018	0.020	**0.581**			
Competence	0.228	0.196	0.078	0.053	0.314	**0.625**		
Reward	0.127	0.281	0.047	0.043	0.156	0.141	**0.789**	
Subjective Norm	0.056	0.045	0.176	0.001	0.025	0.058	0.071	**0.637**

Note: Bold values along the diagonal represent the average variance extracted for each construct.

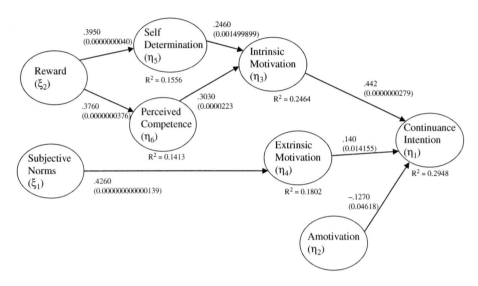

Figure 4: Structural model results.

- H_3: *Self-determination will have an impact on intrinsic motivation in SNS.*

  The results provide support to reject the null hypothesis. Based on the path coefficient, the findings indicate that here is a positive relationship between intrinsic motivation and self determination with a *p*-value of 0.001. When combined, both perceived competence and self determination explain 24.64% of the variance in intrinsic motivation.

- H_4: *Engagement-contingent rewards will have an impact on SNS user's perceived competence in social networking activities.*

  The results provide support to reject the null hypothesis. Based on the path coefficient, the findings indicate that a positive relationship between engagement-contingent rewards and perceived competence with a *p*-value of 0.000. See structural equation below:

$$\text{Perceived Competence} = 0.376(\text{Reward}) + \zeta$$

- H_5: *Engagement-contingent rewards will have an impact on SNS's user's self-determination.*

  The results provide support to reject the null hypothesis. Based on the path coefficient, the findings indicate a positive relationship between engagement-contingent rewards and self determination with a *p*-value of 0.000. See structural equation below:

$$\text{Self Determination} = 0.395(\text{Reward}) + \zeta$$

- H_6: *Subjective norms will have a positive impact on extrinsic motivation to use SNS.*

  The results provide support to reject the null hypothesis. Based on the path coefficient, the findings indicate a positive relationship between subjective norms and extrinsic motivation with a *p*-value of 0.000. See structural equation below:

$$\text{Extrinsic Motivation} = 0.4260(\text{subjective norms}) + \zeta$$

Goodness-of-Fit

PLS has no proper single goodness-of-fit (GOF) measure (Schepers, Wetzels, & Ruyter, 2005). However, the authors assert that the R^2 values of the endogenous constructs indicate whether a particular PLS model accomplishes the objective of maximizing the variance explained (Schepers, et al., 2005). Schepers et al. (2005) and Gefen, Straub, and Boudreau, (2000) corroborated this statement and added that, in PLS, good model fit is established by significant path coefficients, acceptably high R^2 and internal consistency. In this study the R^2 for Continuance Intention, Intrinsic Motivation, Extrinsic Motivation, Perceived Self-Determination and Perceived Competence were 0.2948, 0.2464, 0.1802, 0.1556, and 0.1413, respectively (see Table 7). In accordance with the categorization of R^2 effect sizes by Cohen (1988) (small: 0.02; medium: 0.13; large: 0.26) the results suggest the following effect sizes on the endogenous constructs:

- *Large effect*: Continuance Intention
- *Medium effect*: Intrinsic Motivation, Extrinsic Motivation, Amotivation, Perceived Self-Determination, Perceived Competence

Vinzi, Trinchera, and Amato (2010) supported Schepers et al. (2005) view that there is no overall GOF measure in PLS Path Modeling. However Vinzi et al. (2010) reported on a global GoF index that was proposed by Tenenhaus, Amato, and Esposito (2004). This index was created to provide a single measure for the overall prediction performance of both the measurement and the structural models

Table 7: Inner model.

Constructs	Mult. R^2	AvResVar	AvCommun	AvRedund
Continuance Intention	0.2948	0.3753	0.6247	0.1842
Intrinsic Motivation	0.2464	0.2669	0.7331	0.1806
Extrinsic motivation	0.1802	0.3467	0.6533	0.1177
Amotivation		0.3286	0.6714	
Perceived Self-Determination	0.1556	0.4194	0.5806	0.0904
Perceived Competence	0.1413	0.3748	0.6252	0.0883
Reward		0.2112	0.7888	
Subjective Norm		0.3631	0.6369	
Average	0.20366	0.3358	0.6643	0.1322

(Vinzi et al., 2010) and is obtained from the geometric mean of the *average communality* index and the average R^2 value:

$$\text{GoF} = \sqrt{\overline{\text{Com}} + \overline{R^2}}$$

Based on this formula, the GoF value for the model is 0.3678. The GoF criteria for small, medium, and large effect sizes are 0.1, 0.25, and 0.36 respectively (Schepers et al., 2005). According to this classification, the GoF index for our model has a large effect size.

Discussion

The results suggest that the constructs: intrinsic motivation, extrinsic motivation and amotivation all have an impact on SNS usage continuance behavior among tweens, teens and young adults. The findings reveal that the three orientations of motivation have very distinct roles in explaining continuance intention to use SNS. The results further indicate that intrinsic motivation, extrinsic motivation and amotivation together explain 29.48% of the variance in continuance intention to use SNS. Based on the effect size categorization of variance by Cohen (1988) this is considered a large effect.

The performance of all three orientations of motivation in the model is in keeping with the findings of Hassandra, Goudas, and Chroni (2002), sport and exercise theorists. They postulated that participants are not categorically intrinsically or extrinsically motivated, or amotivated; all three may play a role in relation to a single task. More interestingly, this study demonstrates that intrinsic motivation is the most influential construct within the model, having the largest impact on continuance intention, with a path coefficient of 0.442. This corroborates with findings of Liao, Liu, and Pi (2010) in an evaluation of user's blogging intention and conducts. Liao et al. (2010) reported that intrinsic motivation was a more important indicator of blogging intention than extrinsic motivation. Additional support for the performance of intrinsic motivation within the model is found in the work of Ryan and Deci (2000a) which highlighted that:

> In classic literature, extrinsic motivation has typically been characterized as a pale and impoverished (even if powerful) form of motivation that contrasts with intrinsic motivation.

Our analysis further suggests that intrinsic motivation has a positive effect on behavioral intention to continue using SNS. This finding suggests that as a user's intrinsic motivation increases so will his or her intention to continue to use SNS. This positive influence of intrinsic motivation on behavior has been indentified in other studies which have found that intrinsic motivation enhances psychological engagement and builds energy for sustaining effort (Grant & Berry, 2011).

The assessment of the relationship between intrinsic motivation and perceived competence and perceived self-determination revealed that both constructs combined, explains 24.64% of the variance in intrinsic motivation but that perceived competence had a greater impact on intrinsic motivation than self determination, with path coefficients .3030 and .2460 respectively. These findings are in line with arguments put forward by Vansteenkiste, Lens, and Deci (2006) who concluded that the need for competence and personal causation are the energizing bases for intrinsically motivated behavior.

Earlier research conducted by Deci (1971) suggested that reward had an undermining effect on intrinsic motivation, particularly because of the use of extrinsic rewards as instruments of social control. However, further research in the area suggested that the effect of reward is not limited to control (Cameron et al., 2005). Deci et al. (1999) then intimated that the effect of reward on intrinsic motivation depended on how it affects perceived self determination and perceived competence. The results of our study depicts that reward has a positive effect on both competence and self-determination, explaining 15.56% and 14.13% variance in each respectively. This finding contradicts the position taken by Ryan et al. (1983) which implied that engagement-contingent reward will have an undermining effect on intrinsic motivation; however, this result is supported by Eisenberger, Pierce, and Cameron (1999), who found that a reward can decrease, have no effect or increase intrinsic interest depending on its method of presentation.

The effect of reward in the research model was measured by feedback from fellow social networking members. Scholars generally agree on the effect of peer feedback in encouraging social networking engagement. According to Burke, Marlow, and Lento (2009), feedback from fellow social networking members could lead to future participatory behavior by a newcomer. They pointed out that theories of reciprocity and reinforcement both suggest that feedback from other users should predict long-term participation on the part of the newcomer. It was noted that comments receiving positive numeric ratings on a social networking site resulted in participants returning significantly faster to post a second comment, and when their first comment received a reply they also tended to return more quickly.

Ryan and Deci (2000a) related that over three decades of research had shown that the quality of experience and performance can be very different when one's behavior is influenced by intrinsic versus extrinsic triggers. In our study, extrinsic motivation was found to be statistically significant in explaining continuance intention, with a path coefficient of 140; although not as strong as intrinsic motivation. This finding resonates with Shapira, Kantor, and Melamed's (2001) claim that contrary to the assumptions in the literature that extrinsic and intrinsic motivation influence behavior in different circumstances, they can be combined in an additive fashion to produce overall influence in the same situation. Chang and Ching (2011) obtained similar results when they investigated the use of social networking games. The implication of this finding is that an increase in the extrinsic motivation of users of SNS will produce a corresponding increase in their desire to continue such usage, which also corroborates results obtained by Shapira et al. (2001). Our evaluation of the effect of subjective norm on extrinsic motivation also produced statistically significant results (path coefficient of 0.426); the former accounting for 18% of the latter's variance. The findings imply that a positive increase in subjective norm will have a positive impact on extrinsic motivation. The importance of social influences in explaining SNS member-ship was first captured in work presented by Boyd (2009), who found that, in addition to their own feelings of being left out if they do not join; there was strong peer pressure on American teenagers to participate in social networks.

As did Miyake and Rodgers (2008), in their evaluation of the effect of motivation on senior citizens' participation in physical activities, we found that Amotivation, with a path coefficient of –12.07, was least impactful on the intention to continue to use SNS. The former concluded from their study that, in comparison to intrinsic and extrinsic motivation, amotivation was a less powerful indicator of behavior and that it was significantly but inversely correlated to participation. There is consensus among researchers in this domain that amotivation is associated with negative consequences of behavior. Our results, which indicate that amotivation is negatively correlated with usage continuance behavior, bear out this thinking and suggest that an increase in the level of amotivation of potential users will result in a decrease in their intention to persist.

Conclusion

Social media are very important channels for networking and youngsters, more so than others, use these websites increasingly to stay connected with their friends and family (D'Silva, Bhuptani, Menon, & D'Silva, 2011). The participation of tweens, teens and young adults in the social networking process is noteworthy and requires extensive research to provide insights into its various dimensions, including the potential for marketing, commerce, and information dissemination generally. The findings of this study suggest that the most significant determinant of continued usage of social networking among this demographic is intrinsic motivation. Based on these results, rewards in the form of feedback from peers can have a positive impact on intrinsic motivation (via mediators' perceived competence and self determination). This presents an opportunity for SNS providers to ensure that intrinsically motivated participants are provided with appropriate content and options to encourage and indulge their inherent interest.

Extrinsic motivation was also found to be an important determinant of usage continuance of SNS within the specified demographic and subjective norm a significant predictor of extrinsic motivation. These findings give credence to the notion that the roles of peers and influential persons are pivotal for some member's usage continuance in social networking. According to Boyd (2009) peers are very influential in inducing participation in social networks. Providers of services can therefore leverage this theorized relationship among users of SNS to increase participation and, ultimately, earnings by offering appropriate incentives to intrinsically motivated users to mobilize those that are naturally less enthusiastic. According to Hoffman and Fodor (2010), the assessment of consumer motivations for using social media must now be an integral component in managers' prediction of demand and therefore the assessment of ROI.

Although not as influential a determinant as intrinsic and extrinsic motivation, we found that amotivation is significantly but inversely related to usage continuance of SNS. We therefore recommended that those seeking to benefit from increased participation in these services should find ways (although a difficult undertaking) to induce and assist these tentative users (and would-be nonusers by preference) to break out of their shells by providing activities that they can value or some means to boost their confidence by helping them overcome feelings of incompetence.

Future Work

We intend to further validate the model outlined in this chapter through replication studies. We also offer it to researchers for refinement and possible extension and use in similar studies in a very interesting and important domain.

References

Acquisti, A., Bryce, J., Collier, A., Farmer, J., Grant, L., Kelly, B., y Robison, A. (2008). Young people and social networking services: A childnet international research report. *Childnet International.* Retrieved from http://www.digizen.org/socialnetworking/downloads/Young_People_and_Social_Networking_Services_full_report.pdf

Adams, C. (2011). Social networking and extending social capacity. *ICIS 2011 Proceedings*, December 6. Shanghai, China.

Agarwal, R., & Karahanna, E. (2000). Time flies when you're having fun: Cognitive absorption and beliefs about information technology usage. *MIS Quarterly*, *24*(4), 665–694.

Ahonen, T. (2007). Mobile social networking — The 3.45 billion dollar surprise. *Asia Pacific Issue.* Retrieved from http://www.docstoc.com/docs/29745138/Mobile-social-networking—the-345-billion-dollar-surprise

Amabile, T. M. (1985). Motivation and creativity: Effects of motivational orientation on creative writers. *Journal of Personality and Social Psychology*, *48*, 393–399.

Amabile, T. M., Hill, K. G., Hennessey, B. A., & Tighe, E. M. (1994). The work preference inventory: Assessing intrinsic and extrinsic motivational orientation. *Journal of Personality and Social Psychology*, *66*(5), 950–967.

Bandura, A. (1989). Social cognitive theory. In R. Vasta (Ed.), *Annals of child development. Vol. 6. Six theories of child development* (pp. 1–60).

Bandura, A., & Schunk, D. (1981). Cultivating competence, self-efficacy and intrinsic interest through proximal self motivation. *Journal of Personality and Social Psychology*, *41*(3), 586–598.

Bateman, T., & Crant, M. (2003). *Extrinsic rewards and intrinsic motivation: Evidence from working adults.* Unpublished data.

Bonneau, J., & Preibusch, P. (2009). The privacy jungle: On the market for data protection in social networks. *The 8th Workshop on the Economics of Information Security.* University College London, UK.

Boyd, D. (2007). Why youth (heart) social network sites: The role of networked publics in teenage social life. In D. Buckingham (Ed.), *MacArthur foundation series on digital learning—Youth, identity, and digital media volume.* Cambridge, MA: MIT Press.

Boyd, D. (2009). *Taken out of context: American teen sociality in networked publics.* Ph.D. dissertation, University of California, Berkeley, CA.

Burke, M., Marlow, C., & Lento, L. (2009). *Feed me: Motivating newcomer contribution in social network sites.* CHI 2009, ACM 978-1-60558-246.

Cameron, J., Pierce, W. D., Banko, K. M., & Gear, A. (2005). Achievement-based rewards and intrinsic motivation: A test of cognitive mediators. *Journal of Educational Psychology, 97*(4), 641–655.

Carton, J. S. (1996). The differential effects of tangible rewards and praise on intrinsic motivation: A comparison of cognitive evaluation theory and operant theory. *The Behavior Analyst, 19,* 237–255.

Chang, C., & Ching, Y. (2011). *Predicting the usage intention of social networking games: An intrinsic-extrinsic motivation theory perspective.* Annual conference on innovations in business management.

Cohen, J. (1988). *Statistical power analysis for the behavioral sciences.* Hillsdale, NJ: Lawrence Erlbaum Associates.

Deci, E. L. (1971). Effects of externally mediated rewards on intrinsic motivation. *Journal of Personality and Social Psychology, 18*(1), 105–115.

Deci, E. L., Koestner, R., & Ryan, R. M. (1999). A meta-analytic review of experiments examining the effects of extrinsic rewards on intrinsic motivation. *Psychological Bulletin, 125,* 627–668.

Deci, E. L., & Ryan, R. M. (1985). *Intrinsic motivation and self-determination in human Behavior.* New York, NY: Plenum.

Denzin, N. K. (1978). *The research act.* New York, NY: McGraw-Hill.

D'Silva, B., Bhuptani, R., Menon, S., & D'Silva, S. (2011). *Influence of social media marketing on brand choice behaviour among youth in India: An empirical study.* International conference on technology and business management. Dubai, UAE.

Eisenberger, R., Pierce, D., & Cameron, J. (1999). Effects of reward on intrinsic motivation — Negative, neutral and positive, comment on Deci, Koestner and Ryan 1999. *Psychological Bulletin, 125*(6), 677–691.

Gefen, D., Straub, D. W., & Boudreau, M. C. (2000). Structural equation modeling and regression: Guidelines for research practice. *Communications of the AIS, 4*(7), 2–77.

Grant, A. M., & Berry, J. W. (2011). The necessity of others is the mother of invention: Intrinsic and prosocial motivations, perspective taking and creativity. *Academy of Management Journal, 54*(1), 76–98.

Hassandra, M., Goudas, M., & Chroni, S. (2002). Examining factors associated with intrinsic motivation in physical education: a qualitative approach. *Elsevier Psychology of Sport and Exercise, 4*(2003), 211–223.

Hair, J. F., Black, B., Babin, B., Anderson, R. E., & Tatham, R. (2006). *Multivariate data analysis* (6th ed.). Upper Saddle River, NJ: Pearson Education.

Heidt, T. and Scott, D. R. (2007) *Partial aggregation for complex structural equation modelling (SEM) and small sample sizes: An illustration using a multi-stakeholder model of cooperative interorganisational relationships (IORs) in product innovation.* Southern Cross University ePublications@SCU.

Hoe, S. L. (2008). Issues and procedures in adopting structural equation modeling technique. *Journal of Applied Quantitative Method, 3*(1), 76–83.

Hoffman, D., & Fodor, M. (2010). *Can you measure the ROI of your social media marketing? MIT Sloan Management Review,* (52).

Hu, T., & Kettinger, W. J. (2008). *Why people continue to use social networking services: Developing a comprehensive model.* International conference on information systems. Paris, France.

Ignite Social Media. (2011). Social media analysis report. *Ignite Social Media.* Retrieved from http://www.ignitesocialmedia.com/social-media-stats/2012-social-network-analysis-report/

Kefi, H., Mlaiki, A., & Kalika, M. (2010). Shy people and facebook continuance of usage: Does gender matter? *AMCIS 2010 Proceedings.*

Khalifa, M., & Shen, K. (2006). *Determinants of M-commerce adoption: An integration approach.* European and Mediterranean conference on Information Systems (EMCIS), July 6–7, Costa Blanca, Alicante, Spain.

Khan, M. A. (2008). Mobile social computing not an extension of desktop: Forrester analyst. *Mobile Marketer's Mobile Outlook 2008,* .

Lee, Y., Kozar, A. K., & Larsen, K. R. T. (2003). Technology acceptance model: Past, present and future. *Communications of the Association for Information Systems, 12*(50), 752–780.

Lepper, M., Corpus, H. J., & Iyenger, S. S. (2005). Intrinsic and extrinsic motivational orientations in the classroom: Age differences and academic correlates. *Journal of Educational Psychology, 97*(2), 184–196. Copyright 2005 by the American Psychological Association 2005.

Lepper, M. R., & Green, D. (1978). Overjustification research and beyond: Toward a meansends analysis of intrinsic and extrinsic motivation. In M. R. Lepper & D. Green (Eds.), *The hidden costs of reward: New perspectives on the psychology of human motivation* (pp. 109–148). Hillsdale, NJ: Lawrence Erlbaum Associates.

Liao, H., Liu, S., & Pi, S. (2010). Expectancy theory predictions of blogging intentions and conducts. *Issues in Information Systems, 11*(1).

Limayem, M., Hirt, S. G., & Cheung, C. M. K. (2007). How habit limits the predictive power of intention: The case of information systems continuance. *MIS Quarterly, 31*(4), 706–738.

Lopez, D., & Manson, D. (1997). A study of individual computer self-efficiency and perceived usefulness of the empowered desktop information system business administration computer information systems. Retrieved from http://www.learningace.com/doc/2322193/aa6dca55 877f115ad0d8976476add6b3/lopez

Malhotra, Y., & Galletta, D. (1999). Extending the technology acceptance model to account for social influence: Theoretical bases and empirical validation. *Proceedings of the 32nd Hawaii international conference on system sciences.*

McCullagh, P. (2005). *Sport and exercise lecture.* Unpublished data. Cal State University East Bay.

Miyake, M., & Rodgers, E. (2008). Interrelationship of motivation for and perceived constraints to physical activity participation and the well-being of senior center participants. *Proceedings of the 2008 Northeastern Recreation Research Symposium.* Newtown Square, PA.

Noels, K. A., Pelletier, L. G., Clément, R., & Vallerand, R. J. (2000). Why are you learning a second language? Motivational orientations and self-determination theory. *Language Learning, 50,* 57–85.

Nov, O., & Ye, C. (2008). *Community photo sharing: Motivational and structural antecedents.* International Conference on Information Systems (ICIS). Paris, France.

Pedersen, P. (2001). Adoption of mobile commerce: An exploratory analysis Teleøkonomiprogrammet and Telenor ASA.

Reiss, S. (2004). Multifaceted nature of intrinsic motivation: The theory of 16 basic desires. *Review of General Psychology, 8*(3), 179–193.

Ryan, R. M., & Deci, E. L. (2000a). Intrinsic interest and extrinsic motivations: Classic definitions and new directions. *Contemporary Educational Psychology, 25,* 5–67.

Ryan, R. M., & Deci, E. L. (2000b). Self-determination theory and the facilitation of intrinsic motivation. *Social Development, and Well-Being American Psychological Association, Inc, 55*(1), 68–78.

Ryan, R. M., & Deci, E. L. (2000c). The "what" and "why" of goal pursuits: Human needs and the self-determination of behavior. *Psychological Inquiry 2000, 11*(4), 227–268.

Ryan, R. M., Mims, V., & Koestner, R. (1983). Relation of reward contingency and interpersonal context to intrinsic motivation: A review and test using cognitive evaluation theory. *Journal of Personality and Social Psychology, 45*, 736–750.

Sánchez, R. M.A., Gallego, C.E., Sorial, S. M., & Åborg, C. (2008). Technoflow among Spanish and Swedish students: A confirmatory factor multigroup analysis. *Anales de Psicología, 24*(1) (junio), 42–48.

Schepers, J., Wetzels, M., & Ruyter, K. (2005). Leadership styles in technology acceptance: Do followers practice what leaders preach? *Managing Service Quality, 15*(6), 496–508. Emerald Group Publishing Limited 0960-4529.

Schwarz, A., Wiley-Patton, S., Schwarzz, C., Perez-Mira, B., & Jungyy, Y. (2009). An investigation in to virtual world adoption. *Proceedings of Mardi Gras conference*. Baton Rouge, Louisiana.

Shapira, B., Kantor, P. B., & Melamed, B. (2001). The effect of extrinsic motivation on user behavior in a collaborative information finding system. *Journal of the American Society for Information Science and Technology, 52*(11), 879–887.

Shroff, R. H., & Vogel, D. R. (2009). Assessing the factors deemed to support individual student intrinsic motivation in technology supported online and face-to-face discussions. *Journal of Information Technology Education, 8*, 59–85.

Tenenhaus, M., Amato, S., & Esposito Vinzi, V. (2004). A global goodness-of-fit index for PLS structural equation modelling. *Proceedings of the XLII SIS Scientific Meeting*, Volume Contributed Papers, CLEUP, Padova (pp. 739–742).

Theotokis, A., & Doukidis, G. (2009). When adoption brings addiction: A use-diffusion model for social information systems. *International Conference on Information Systems (ICIS) Proceedings*. Phoenix, Arizona.

Thibert, G., & Karsenti, T. P. (1998). The relationship between effective teachers and the motivational change of elementary school boys and girls. *Annual conference of the American Educational Research Association*. San Diego, CA.

Vallerand, R. J., & Bissonnette, R. (1992). Intrinsic, extrinsic, and amotivational styles as predictors of behavior: A prospective study. *Journal of Personality, 60*, 599–620.

Vansteenkiste, M., Lens, W., & Deci, E. (2006). Intrinsic versus extrinsic goal contents in self-determination theory: Another look at the quality of academic motivation. *Educational Psychologist, 4*(1), 19–31.

Venkatesh, V. (2000). Determinants of perceived ease of use: Integrating control, intrinsic motivation, and emotion into the technology acceptance model. *Information Systems Research, 11*, 342–365.

Venkatesh, V., Morris, M., Davis, G., & Davis, F. (2003). User acceptance of information technology: Toward a unified view. *MIS Quarterly: Management Information Systems, 27*, 425–478.

Vinzi, V., Trinchera, L., & Amato, S. (2010). Handbook of partial least squares. *Springer Handbooks of Computational Statistics*. doi:10.1007/978-3-540-32827-83.

Wen, C., Tang, B., & Chang, K. (2009). Advertising electiveness on social network sites: An investigation of tie strength, endorser expertise and product type on consumer purchase intention. *13th international conference on information systems*, Phoenix, AZ.

Wiechman, B. (2005). *Assessing the durability of the undermining effect: The impact of extrinsic rewards on college students' intrinsic motivation*. Unpublished.

Wudd, H. (2009). An integrated framework of SNS users' motivations. *Proceedings of the 15th Americas conference on information systems*. Phoenix, Arizona.

Chapter 12

Social Media as Enabler of Crowdsourcing

Ivan Župič

Abstract

Purpose — The purpose of this study is to investigate how social media features enable crowdsourcing and to gain rich understanding of mechanisms that lead from online community design practices to success in crowdsourcing initiatives.

Methodology/approach — Inductive qualitative methods were used for investigating the case of crowdsourcing-based microstock business model. Twenty-three in-depth interviews with stock photography industry insiders were combined with netnography data and documents.

Findings — Two mechanisms influencing participants' motivation and peer-to-peer learning were identified. Both extrinsic and intrinsic motivations are important for participants' engagement.

Research limitations/implications — Findings of this inductive effort should be replicated in other industry settings and used to develop testable propositions of antecedents and outcomes of crowdsourcing implementations.

Practical implications — Companies embarking on crowdsourcing initiatives can enhance participants' motivations through social media and enable learning through online communities. Managers must understand who participates in the crowd and what their motivation is.

Originality/value — This study is investigating under-researched peer-vetted creative production crowdsourcing model. Managers can use presented ideas for developing crowdsourcing online communities.

Keywords: Crowdsourcing; social media; motivation; learning; stock photography

Social Media in Human Resources Management
Advanced Series in Management, 243–255
Copyright © 2013 by Emerald Group Publishing Limited
All rights of reproduction in any form reserved
ISSN: 1877-6361/doi:10.1108/S1877-6361(2013)0000012016

Introduction

The phenomenon called wisdom of crowds (Surowiecki, 2004) is gaining increasing attention from scholars (Afuah & Tucci, 2012; Felin, 2012) and business press (Howe, 2006, 2008; Malone, Laubacher, & Dellarocas, 2010). This line of thinking suggests that under certain circumstances, collective intelligence of wide range of participants (i.e., the crowd) makes better decisions than the best and most knowledgeable of professionals. One specific manifestation of collective intelligence phenomenon is crowdsourcing (Howe, 2006). Crowdsourcing applications harness collective intelligence through the web to produce solutions and products rivaling those of collaborative groups and talented individuals (Brabham, 2010).

Crowdsourcing has been used as full blown business model for T-Shirt design at Threadless (Lakhani & Kanji, 2008), photographic image production at iStockphoto (Brabham, 2008a) and even corporate R&D for pharmaceutical and other industries at Innocentive (Jeppesen & Lakhani, 2010). Other companies use it as strategy for opening up to external ideas. Dell is using its IdeaStorm community to find out about user needs and ways to satisfy those needs (Bayus, 2013). Sony, JetBlue, and Chrysler tapped 'the crowd' for user-generated advertising content while hoping it would spread virally through the web (Brabham, 2008b). Ford based its entire advertising campaign for new Fiesta 2014 car model on crowdsourced user-generated content and pledged to use zero professionally produced ads (Elliot, 2013).

Despite increasing attention by scholars, crowdsourcing research is still in early stages. Little is known about crowdsourcing best practices, challenges and enabling mechanisms (Marjanovic, Fry, & Chataway, 2012). There is further need to understand why people participate in crowdsourcing in order to develop best practices for designing crowdsourcing initiatives (Brabham, 2010) and improve currently scarce guidance entrepreneurs can use in designing online communities for crowdsourcing. While there is general understanding about motivation of participants in open-source software projects, much less research exist about motivation of participants in commercial co-creating projects (Füller, 2010). This study intends to fill this void.

The purpose of this study is to investigate how social media enable crowdsourcing. To gain rich understanding of mechanisms that lead from online community design practices to success in crowdsourcing initiatives. Managers in crowdsourcing ventures lack traditional control mechanisms available in corporate settings over employees. Therefore strategies for influencing "crowd" behavior are of utmost importance. Particular setting is used for this investigation: stock photography industry, which was in recent years irreversibly transformed by microstock business model based on crowdsourcing.

This study aspires to make two contributions to the knowledge base of crowdsourcing. First, it identifies two mechanisms that connect crowdsourcing community design with actions of participants. Second, it provides additional evidence of participants' motivations in one under-researched crowdsourcing model.

Crowdsourcing

Crowdsourcing term was popularized by Howe (2006), who defines crowdsourcing as "the act of taking a job traditionally performed by a designated agent (usually an employee) and outsourcing it to an undefined, generally large group of people in the form of an open call" (2012). Brabham (2008b) refers to crowdsourcing as "an online, distributed problem-solving and production model."

Crowdsourcing as a phenomenon is not new. The concept builds on open innovation paradigm (Chesbrough, 2003) and the success of open-source movement (Lakhani & Von Hippel, 2003). However, looking back in history, even Wild West sheriff's signs for wanted criminals could be regarded as crowdsourcing (Afuah & Tucci, 2012). Adamczyk, Bullinger, and Möslein (2012) describe numerous innovation contests dating as far back as year 1567. The phenomenon is obviously old, but internet platform elevated the quality, amount and speed of cooperation (Brabham, 2012) and thus enabled modern-day crowdsourcing initiatives.

Four different models of crowdsourcing could be distinguished (Brabham, 2012): knowledge discovery and management (e.g., Peer-to-Patent), broadcast search (e.g., Innocentive), peer-vetted creative production (e.g., Threadless) and distributed human intelligence tasking (e.g., Mechanical Turk). In knowledge discovery and management approach, the "crowd" is employed to find and collect information into common location and format. Broadcast search (often also referred to as "innovation contests" (cf. Adamczyk et al., 2012)) is most thoroughly researched type of crowdsourcing. This approach tasks the crowd to solve empirical problems that have empirically provable but yet unknown solutions. Well known example is Innocentive, where pharmaceutical and other corporations post problems unsolved by their R&D departments, which are then attacked by independent and competing participants for announced prize. In peer-vetted creative production, participants propose and select creative ideas (e.g., T-shirt designs in Threadless, photographic images in iStockphoto). Distributed human intelligence tasking uses the 'crowd' for analyzing large amount of information (Brabham, 2012).

Crowdsourcing is in some ways similar to open-source development model, but there are important differences. Both crowdsourcing and open-source innovation are enabled by web. Both involve open participation of individuals on a particular task. Open source is based on peer production where participants collaborate to create (software) products, usually waiving intellectual property rights. Although mostly used for software, it is a general product development philosophy (Brabham, 2008b). It allows access to elements of the product (i.e., the source code) to anyone for the purpose of changing and improving the product. Producers are often also users of the product and there is no clear structure of ownership and control (Marjanovic et al., 2012). In crowdsourcing, the focal company defines the problem and reward, structures the production and defines the conditions. Collaboration is at the forefront of open-source model, while competition is often the norm at crowdsourcing-based models.

Online community is an Internet-connected collective of people who interact over time around a shared purpose, interest or need (Preece, 2000; Ren, Kraut, & Kiesler,

2007). It is difficult for companies to continuously find new participants for crowdsourcing activities (Ebner, Leimeister, & Krcmar, 2009), so it makes sense to leverage online communities as a way to increase production and motivate people to stay. Firms can influence people's interactions through community design — navigation architecture, site features and organization structures and community policies (Ren et al., 2007). Online communities can enhance knowledge sharing through interaction of community members (Wasko & Faraj, 2000).

Customer demands vary widely, so heterogeneous community of producers is necessary to satisfy their needs (Von Hippel, 2005). This fact is leveraged in peer-vetted creative production approach, where the crowd is tasked with both creating and identifying the best ideas, which transforms the process into firm-consumer cocreation (Brabham, 2012). This type of crowdsourcing is thus appropriate for problems involving taste and user preference. Social media is an essential part of peer-vetted creative production model. It is glue that holds community together and enables wide range of contributors to participate in production and distribution of digital artifacts.

In this study I am particularly interested in peer-vetted creative production approach as examined on the case of microstock business model, where participants produce photographic images for sale to commercial customers through web site. Peer-vetted creative production is under-researched even in nascent crowdsourcing literature, where the bulk of attention is concentrated on broadcast search/innovation contests. It is model destined to play important role in transforming creative industries such as photography, video and design and is undergoing large investments as the prospects for growth are bright (Crook, 2012; Pignal, 2012).

Stock Photography Industry and Microstock Business Model

Stock photography agencies provide photographic images for commercial (advertising, promotion) and editorial (newspaper, magazine, online, textbook publishing) purposes. These agencies support online databases, repositories of images that were shot in advance on speculation without specific request from end customer. Majority of images are sourced from independent photographers and production houses, minority is produced by agencies in-house. Up until the 1990s this industry was fragmented with many small agencies in the market.

Digitization of image databases and internet distribution brought scale efficiencies to the industry and during the 1990s the industry consolidated under the umbrella of two well capitalized companies: Getty images (founded in 1995 by Joe Klein and billionaire Mark Getty) and Corbis (founded in 1989 by Bill Gates). Although these traditional stock photo agencies were mostly selling outside contributor's images, new photographers were facing significant entry barriers as agencies took only the best photographers with large portfolios of images.

Microstock business model came along at the beginning of 2000s, when companies like iStockphoto, Shutterstock and Dreamstime started offering radically cheap stock images. First microstock company iStockphoto was started in February 2000 by Bruce Livingstone as a photo-exchange service for web designers, who had pressing needs for images but could not afford traditional stock prices. Regular traditional stock prices for commercial stock images at the time were in the 100s of USD. iStockphoto first offered photos for free and started charging 20 cents per photo in 2003 as a way to cover computer server and network bandwidth costs. The industry grew rapidly ever since and iStockphoto was acquired by Getty images in 2005.

In 2012 microstock was healthy and growing segment of stock photography business. One of the largest microstock companies Shutterstock had $120 million dollars of revenue in 2011 (SEC, 2012). In October 2012 it held first IPO of NY-based tech company in New York Stock Exchange since 2010 and successfully raised 76 million $ in the process (Crook, 2012). Another microstock company Fotolia received 150 million $ investment from US private equity firm KKR (Pignal, 2012) in May 2012.

The microstock business model was based on crowdsourcing and brought several innovations to the industry compared to the traditional stock photography agencies. Most importantly, anybody could get in. In traditional agencies, a lengthy assessment process was required for agency to start representing a photographer, for which a large portfolio of existing images was needed. What is more, when agencies decided they had enough of a certain type of photographers, they limited the acceptance of new contributors, even if their quality was good. Microstock agencies accepted individual images from any photographer as long as they passed the technical assessment. Approval process for submission of new images took days, not weeks or months and contributors could monitor sales in real time.

The most disruptive innovation of microstock was the price of images. First commercial iStockphoto offering sold images for 20 cents and although the prices have risen since then, they are still multiple times lower than with traditional agencies. At the beginning microstock attracted only amateur photographers, as traditional stock professionals were skeptical of the business model and wary to cannibalize their sales with model that radically lowered the selling price of images. With growing success of the model, however, it became increasingly difficult to ignore it. What contributors lost on price they gained on volume as with the proliferation of Internet web sites and low pricing the demand for images exploded. The model opened a whole new market for images (Kim & Mauborgne, 2005) as customers who never before could afford to buy image licenses were suddenly able to use them.

One microstock company — iStockphoto — was one of Howe's (2006) original examples of crowdsourcing. It could be said that traditional stock companies have long used the open innovation model, but with microstock this model transformed into crowdsourcing. Microstock agencies sourced the images from anybody who could provide technically acceptable digital file. Their web sites used social media building blocks (Kietzmann, Hermkens, McCarthy, & Silvestre, 2011) like web forums, social networking features and blogs to form a community of contributors.

Microstock photo agencies crowdsourced not only production of images, but also some functions that were traditionally performed in-house, like quality insurance. By hiring contributors as photo inspectors that were bound only by few simple rules and were required to assess only technical quality of the images and not their esthetic quality or commercial potential, agencies were able to save costs. Another source of cost savings was automation. Microstock agencies were mostly founded by tech people who loved photography and used their tech skills to automate as many functions of the photo agency as possible. Traditional stock agencies worked closely with contributing photographers to guide production of new images. In microstock, this close cooperation was replaced by self-organized online communities.

Data and Methods

Because of limited research in peer-vetted creative production type of crowdsourcing I used inductive qualitative research methods. Case study methods were implemented in this investigation — a research strategy that focuses on understanding the dynamics within single settings (Eisenhardt, 1989). Inductive case studies are appropriate where existing research does not adequately address the topic of interest (Eisenhardt & Graebner, 2007).

To investigate online crowdsourcing communities I used the netnography approach (Kozinets, 2010). Netnography uses internet-mediated communication as a source of data and is thus an extension of ethnographic approach to the online world. It can incorporate various classic methods: participant observation, interviews, archival data collection, etc.

A triangulation of different data sources (Yin, 1994) was employed to enhance validity of the study. I used in-depth interviews with industry insiders, netnographic data from online forums and mailing lists, news articles, published interviews with company founders and company press releases. Information about launch dates and major changes to web sites was found with the help of a web tool, the "Wayback" machine. I analyzed web discussion forum posts on four major microstock companies: iStockphoto, Shutterstock, Dreamstime and Fotolia for the period between 2005 and 2012.

Twenty-three in-depth interviews with microstock photographers, industry analysts, buyers and company employees were conducted between March 2012 and February 2013. Ten interviews were conducted face-to-face, twelve through Skype and one by e-mail. I used purposive and snowball sampling for assembling contacts to interview. Informants were identified through published interviews, articles, blog posts, stock photography mailing lists, company web sites and author's personal contacts. Additionally I asked some of the informants for contacts of other industry insiders that could provide additional insight. This study also draws on my personal experience with stock photography industry as former professional photographer.

Analytic strategy iteratively shifted between data and theory as recommended by grounded theory approach (Glaser & Strauss, 1967). Data from interviews, documents and netnography artifacts was open coded and repeatedly compared with existing literature and previous findings. Early findings were discussed with later interview participants. Finally, two all-encompassing themes emerged — mechanisms that are the main findings of the study.

Findings

I organize the findings under two sets of themes: first examines how social media features on microstock web sites enabled peer-to-peer learning. The second deals with motivation of contributors to participate in crowdsourcing business model.

(Peer-to-Peer) Learning

Most of the early full-time contributors to microstock were amateur photographers. Lots of them were former web designers, who saw from the photos they were buying how much they were selling, made their calculation and decided to get increasingly involved in the production of images. In the beginning of 2000s digital SLR cameras became cheap enough to be available to general public so there were a number of photographers eager to use them and learn. Social media features at microstock web sites enabled contributor communication and learning.

> There is a bunch of us who grew up with iStock. When I applied I didn't know much about photography. I learned through reading the forums, through the critique of other members, through the rejection of photos (inspectors have to specify why it was rejected). I looked at other photos, see how they sell and tried to synthesize ideas …
>
> In first three or four years at iStock I learned more about photography than in fifteen years before … I learned about lighting, working with models … you can always go to the community and ask — hey, can you take a look at this picture, it did not turn out the way I wanted it to be: what did I do wrong, how can I do better …

Social media, not only through microstock sites, but also much wider, enabled whole generation of photographers to learn their craft and transfer from amateur to professional in different way than was the case before. Traditionally, new photographers learned by working for established professionals as assistants in what could be called master-apprentice model. Social media brought a revolution in learning as now nascent professionals could learn from much wider network of peers than previously possible. Here is how one photographer, who learned his craft in the darkroom, recalled the contrast between learning in analog era and learning with online help:

> In the old times photographers were hiding their techniques. You could never get a photographer to reveal how he made a photo in the darkroom … it was very different on iStock, people were helping each other. When you posted a question on forums, you got immediate answers …

Several social networking features were embedded in the web sites. Contributors could become 'friends', communicate with each other through private messages and see each other's new images in separate photo-feed.

> We used those features primarily so we could imitate other photographer's images. Every photo you can think of is already taken, it was 100 years ago …

Additional peer-to-peer learning took place offline, in the 'real world'. Online community at one of the microstock sites lead to sporadic organizing of gatherings of photographers — so called iStockalypses and minilypses, where photographers got together, hired models, props and jointly shot images that were later sold through agencies.

> ... specially the minilypses helped me tremendously improve my photography ... going somewhere for a few days and see twenty other people how they shoot. Everybody is doing something different, but you get something from each one you watch ...

Motivation

Second set of findings reflects the motivation of contributors to produce images and upload them to microstock web sites. Initially, most of the contributors were amateur photographers eager to find out how good their images are.

> It was a thrill to see that you could sell photos all over the world. We checked how our photos were used ... it was great fun to see what my photos were used for.

The feeling of community was pervasive in the early days of microstock, but diminished over time. This is how one contributor described the development:

> It was like a small village. Everybody knew everybody. Then I lost that feeling of community when there was a large influx of new people. And suddenly you would see 50 replies on your forum posts from people you have seen for the first time. I also started to work as an inspector. And then it was not appropriate for me to comment anything. Before I didn't care, I just posted anything that was on my mind. But now we inspectors have a separate forum where there is still that feeling of community.

Some of the contributors saw each sale as a quality vote for their photos. One contributor wrote on web forum to compare sales to grades on a scale 1–10 and was pleased to find out that buyers are valuing his photos more than his peers:

> I'm choosing to interpret each download as a vote of seven or eight — meets the topic with better-than-average quality. So far, I think my average "score" over there is about double my average here :)

Additional gamification features were provided by web site operators so contributors and buyers could have more fun. Gamification refers to the idea of using game design elements in nongame contexts with the aim to increase user activity and retention (Deterding, Dixon, Khaled, & Nacke, 2011). iStockphoto featured 'Steel cage' contests, where designers were invited to produce competing designs from available images and the winner was voted by the site participants. Dreamstime had a game where participants were shown two photos — one with multiple sales and one who never sold — and had to guess which is which. Specific thematic assignments based on real photo needs were given to photographers and prizes (e.g., iPod, iPad) handed out to winners. Some of the contributors organized games for themselves:

> I tried to arrange competition with other members — for instance who will first upload X number of photos, who would first get to X number of sales ... and we tracked it on the forums. This was a great way to keep you shooting photos and uploading them.

Another motivation for contributors was peer recognition and status. On iStockphoto site, photographers are awarded bronze/silver/gold/diamond canister icons as recognition for the level of sales, which appear near their name on their web profile and forum posts. Some contributors enhanced their recognition by answering questions on forums and responding to specific requests for images:

> You could gain a name by responding to designer requests. In early days web designers posted requests for photos on forums. Then everybody would post what they have or even try to shoot it. Lise Gagne did that a lot in early days and got recognized for that. And when designers noticed you, that could boost your sales.

Another new contributor wrote to a web forum delighted when his photos entered the top downloads list:

> All of my files are in the most downloaded list, including positions 1 and 3 !!! I love this site so much I added it as my signature …

Advanced members might be promoted to inspectors (who decide which images are accepted and which not), which is regarded as step-up in prestige. This enables newly promoted members getting privileged insider information and access to inspector web forums not available to general members.

Social Media as Crowdsourcing Enabler

This study identified two mechanisms through which social media enables crowdsourcing.

First is the facilitation of peer-to-peer learning. Two different kinds of learning are happening: learning about image production techniques and learning about commercial opportunities. Learning about production techniques is enabled by online communications among contributors and further enhanced by offline events. Data about sales of individual images is public for anyone to see, thus copying of successful images is relatively easy and widespread. This is also additional transmission mechanism through which information about needs and opportunities is distributed to the community of content providers.

Helping among participants is commonplace, even though they are competitors. Franke and Shah (2003) demonstrated that members of online communities help others to gain recognition, but this behavior is strongly reduced if they believe rivals will outperform them. Because of the nature of microstock, peer recognition can have other beneficial effects beside status: it can lead to higher sales. This duality manifests in members help others freely with photographic skill development, but keep quiet about where they believe specific gaps in image collection exist that would lead to commercial opportunities. Still, members report that with increased competition the amount of helping on forums decreased substantially.

Because of continuous performance feedback, the cycle of learning and improvement is much faster than is without online community support. Wooten and Ulrich (2012) found that directed feedback leads to improved quality with cumulative entries in innovation contests. Additionally, variance in quality also declines as the contest progresses. Content providers continuously receive feedback about their image quality: first with acceptance/rejection by the inspectors, then with real time download and view numbers and ratings from their peers.

Second mechanism influences motivation. In crowdsourcing setting, monetary incentives alone are not enough to sustain long-term content production.

I draw on self-determination theory (Ryan & Deci, 2000) to explain factors that motivate contributors to participate in crowdsourcing. Individuals can be motivated by intrinsic (e.g., enjoyment) or extrinsic (e.g., money, control) factors. For instance, Lakhani and Wolf (2005) found that intrinsic motivation is the strongest driver of programmer's participation in open-source projects. As evidenced by findings of this study, microstock agencies web sites are designed in a way to maximize both intrinsic (e.g., with gamification of experience) and extrinsic (e.g., monetary incentives, status, etc.) levers of contributors' motivation.

Kaufmann, Schulze, and Veit (2011) examined motivation of workers on Amazon's marketplace for online work Mechanical Turk and found that both intrinsic and extrinsic factors are important, but intrinsic types of motivation seem to dominate the extrinsic ones. Brabham (2010) found four main motivations for participation in crowdsourcing: opportunity to make money, developing creative skills, signaling in order to get freelance work and love of community. Brabham (2008a) also investigated the motivation of participants at iStockphoto site and concluded that making money, developing skills and having fun were most important motivators for contributing. This study largely confirms Brabham's findings with one important difference: I found limited evidence of photographers participating in microstock in order to get freelance work. Quite the opposite: some established professional photographers are participating in microstock, but not under their real name, fearing backlash from their peers, who often perceive this low-price model as undercutting their work.

One important distinction in motivations of photographers should be made: long time contributors reported different motivations for their initial engagement with microstock compared with their current motivations or motivations of contributors that are just starting. In early days of microstock, most photographers started contributing for fun, seeking recognition, or were designers turned photographers who were using images from the community and were looking to give back. Now, making money is the main reason for engagement.

The need for social media involvement in contributors' motivation is inversely proportional to monetary reward — in other words: some do it for money, some do it for fun. When one is motivated by intrinsic factors and non-monetary extrinsic rewards (e.g., peer recognition, status), social media elements are much more important part of the process. For more productive members of the community, however, motivation crowding effect (Frey & Jegen, 2001) takes place as monetary incentives crowd out the intrinsic motivation factors.

The importance of social media elements in microstock business model diminished over time as monetary incentives took over. It was vital at the beginning when the microstock business model had no legitimacy among professional photographers and most of the contributors were amateurs. As the model matured the bulk of sales went to professionals. However, to keep the broad image base it is still important for microstock agencies to keep wide range of contributors, for which social media features are crucial for participants' learning and involvement.

Conclusion

This study advances our understanding of mechanisms that enable crowdsourcing to work. I have identified two theoretical mechanisms through which social media features enable the crowdsourcing model. First influences motivations of contributors and provides supplements to monetary incentives. Second enables learning of production techniques and diffusion of knowledge about commercial opportunities. Additional evidence for variety of motivations of people engaged in crowdsourcing was found.

Managers interested in using social media for tapping the wisdom of crowds can use findings of this study for better implementation of crowdsourcing initiatives. Fundamentally enhancing information flows among contributors and providing non-monetary incentives is crucial in orchestrating business models that are based on aggregating the work of numerous outside entities (i.e., the crowd). "Build it and they will come" attitude is not sufficient. Managers must understand who participates in the crowd and what their motivation is. Community features on web sites should be designed in such a way to influence both extrinsic and intrinsic motivations of participants. Managers can use monetary incentives, gamification, status building and other strategies for this purpose. Social media features must enable online learning with enhanced communication and information diffusion.

This study serves as a window into inner workings of one particular crowdsourcing business model. Although this study researches one model of crowdsourcing, findings have implications for other models as well. It is still premature, however, to generalize these findings to other settings. Future research should examine drivers of other crowdsourcing implementations.

Findings of this inductive effort could be used to develop testable propositions and design quantitative tests of antecedents and outcomes of crowdsourcing implementations. For instance, large-scale research should examine which combinations of motivations and attitudes predict successful crowdsourcing participants. It could be tested whether participant success lowers intrinsic motivations for participation and if peer recognition really leads to higher sales. Longitudinal case studies of crowdsourcing initiatives may shed more light on how online community design practices shape the development of the community. Finally, experimental designs (possibly even using crowdsourcing sites like Mechanical Turk) could help explain how participants react to different web design features.

References

Adamczyk, S., Bullinger, A. C., & Möslein, K. M. (2012). Innovation contests: A review, classification and outlook. *Creativity and Innovation Management, 21*(4), 335–360.

Afuah, A., & Tucci, C. (2012). Crowdsourcing as a solution to distant search. *Academy of Management Review*, *37*(3), 355–375.

Bayus, B. L. (2013). Crowdsourcing new product ideas over time: An analysis of dell's ideastorm community. *Management Science*, *59*(1), 226–244.

Brabham, D. C. (2008a). Moving the crowd at iStockphoto: The composition of the crowd and motivations for participation in a crowdsourcing application. *First Monday*, *13*(6). Retrieved from   http://firstmonday.org/htbin/cgiwrap/bin/ojs/index.php/fm/article/viewArticle/2159/ 1969

Brabham, D. C. (2008b). Crowdsourcing as a model for problem solving: An introduction and cases. *Convergence: The International Journal of Research into New Media Technologies*, *14*(1), 75–90.

Brabham, D. C. (2010). Moving the crowd at Threadless. *Information, Communication & Society*, *13*(8), 1122–1145.

Brabham, D. C. (2012). Crowdsourcing: A model for leveraging online communities. In A. Delwiche & J. J. Henderson (Eds.), *The participatory cultures handbook* (pp. 120–129). New York, NY: Routledge.

Chesbrough, H. (2003). The era of open innovation. *MIT Sloan Management Review*, *44*(3), 35–41.

Crook, J. (2012). Shutterstock CEO jon oringer on ipo success, The future of video. *TechCrunch*. Retrieved from http://techcrunch.com/2012/10/17/shutterstock-ceo-jon-oringer-on-ipo-success-the-future-of-video/. Accessed on February 24, 2013.

Deterding, S., Dixon, D., Khaled, R., & Nacke, L. (2011). From game design elements to gamefulness: Defining gamification. *Proceedings of the 15th international academic mindtrek conference: Envisioning future media environments* (pp. 9–15). ACM.

Ebner, W., Leimeister, J., & Krcmar, H. (2009). Community engineering for innovations: The ideas competition as a method to nurture a virtual community for innovations. *R&D Management*, *39*(4), 342–356.

Eisenhardt, K. M. (1989). Building theories from case study research. *Academy of Management Review*, *14*(4), 532–550.

Eisenhardt, K. M., & Graebner, M. E. (2007). Theory building from cases: Opportunities and challenges. *Academy of Management Review*, *50*(1), 25–32.

Elliot, S. (2013). Ford turns to the "Crowd" for new fiesta ads. *New York Times*. Retrieved from   http://mediadecoder.blogs.nytimes.com/2013/02/19/ford-turns-to-the-crowd-for-new-fiesta-ads/. Accessed on February 23, 2013.

Felin, T. (2012). Cosmologies of Capability, Markets and Wisdom of Crowds: Introduction and Comparative Agenda. *Managerial and Decision Economics*, *33*, 283–294.

Franke, N., & Shah, S. (2003). How communities support innovative activities: An exploration of assistance and sharing among end-users. *Research Policy*, *32*(1), 157–178.

Frey, B. S., & Jegen, R. (2001). Motivation crowding theory. *Journal of Economic Surveys*, *15*(5), 589–611.

Füller, J. (2010). Refining virtual co-creation from a consumer perspective. *California Management Review*, *52*(2), 98–122.

Glaser, B. G., & Strauss, A. L. (1967). *The discovery of grounded theory: strategies for qualitative research* (p. 262). Hawthorne: Aldine Publishiong Company.

Howe, J. (2006). The rise of crowdsourcing. *Wired Magazine*, *14*, 1–5.

Howe, J. (2008). *Crowdsourcing: Why the Power of the Crowd Is Driving the Future of Business*. New York, NY: Crown Publishing Group. (p. 311).

Howe, J. (2012). Retrieved from www.crowdsourcing.com. Accessed on August 17, 2012.

Jeppesen, L. B., & Lakhani, K. R. (2010). Marginality and problem-solving effectiveness in broadcast search. *Organization Science*, *21*(5), 1016–1033.

Kaufmann, N., Schulze, T., & Veit, D. (2011). More than fun and money. Worker motivation in crowdsourcing – A study on mechanical turk. *Proceedings of the 17th Americas conference on information systems* (pp. 1–11). Detroit, Michigan.

Kietzmann, J. H., Hermkens, K., McCarthy, I. P., & Silvestre, B. S. (2011). Social media? Get serious! Understanding the functional building blocks of social media. *Business Horizons*, *54*(3), 241–251.

Kim, W. C., & Mauborgne, R. (2005). *Blue ocean strategy*. Boston, MA: Harvard Business School Press.

Kozinets, R. V. (2010). *Netnography: Doing ethnographic research online*. London: Sage. (p. 232).

Lakhani, K. R., & Kanji, Z. (2008). *Threadless: The business of community*. Cambridge, MA: Harvard Business School Case.

Lakhani, K. R, & Von Hippel, E. (2003). How open source software works: "Free" user-to-user assistance. *Research Policy*, *32*, 923–943. (July 2002).

Lakhani, K., & Wolf, R. G. (2005). Why hackers do what they do: Understanding motivation and effort in free/open source software projects. In J. Feller, B. Fitzgerald, S. A. Hissam & K. R. Lakhani (Eds.), *Perspectives on free and open source software* (pp. 3–22). Cambridge: MIT Press.

Malone, T., Laubacher, R., & Dellarocas, C. (2010). The collective intelligence genome. *MIT Sloan Management Review*, *51*(3), 21–31.

Marjanovic, S., Fry, C., & Chataway, J. (2012). Crowdsourcing based business models: In search of evidence for innovation 2.0. *Science and Public Policy*, *39*(3), 318–332.

Pignal, S. (2012). KKR to take 50% stake in Fotolia-FT.com. *Financial Times*. Retrieved from http://www.ft.com/intl/cms/s/0/b8f30ddc-9eb0-11e1-9cc8-00144feabdc0.html#axzz2 LqbokXGn. Accessed on February 24, 2013.

Preece, J. (2000). *Online communities: Designing usability, supporting sociability*. Chichester, UK: Wiley.

Ren, Y., Kraut, R., & Kiesler, S. (2007). Applying common identity and bond theory to design of online communities. *Organization Studies*, *28*(3), 377–408.

Ryan, R. M., & Deci, E. L. (2000). Self-determination theory and the facilitation of intrinsic motivation, social development, and well-being. *The American Psychologist*, *55*(1), 68–78.

SEC. (2012). Shutterstock Inc. Form S-1 Registration Statement. Retrieved from http://www.sec.gov/Archives/edgar/data/1549346/000104746912005905/a2209364zs-1.htm. Accessed on February 24, 2013.

Surowiecki, J. (2004). *The wisdom of crowds*. New York, NY: Knopf Doubleday Publishing Group. (p. 336).

Von Hippel, E. (2005). *Democratizing innovation*. Cambridge, MA: The MIT Press. (p. 216).

Wasko, M. M., & Faraj, S. (2000). "It is what one does": Why people participate and help others in electronic communities of practice. *Journal of Strategic Information Systems*, *9*, 155–173.

Wooten, J., & Ulrich, K. (2012). *Idea generation and the role of feedback: Evidence from field experiments with innovation tournaments*. Retrieved from http://papers.ssrn.com/sol3/papers.cfm?abstract_id = 1838733

Yin, R. K. (1994). *Case study research: Design and methods*. Thousand Oaks, CA: Sage.